From the Critics . . .

Charming. Above all, charming. I never thought I would write those words about a member of the Communist Party of China who, in the CPC's traumatic early years when he was not yet twenty, associated with Mao Zedong, Zhou Enlai, Madame Sun Yatsen, Zhu De, and other historic leaders. Set during 1926-1927, this is Zhu Qihua's diary of his time as a mid-level Party propaganda official. The Party was about to lose its links with Chiang Kai-shek's Guomindang (GMD). After a brief honeymoon period with Chiang, when the senior Party leaders imagined they would march north to rid Peking of its warlord rulers and bring all of China under revolutionary rule, the Communists were forced to flee from the GMD. Mao escaped into the mountains and eventually onto the Long March; others, including Zhou Enlai—and Zhu Qihua—made a headlong flight on foot from bandits and Chiang's soldiers, during which many of them were killed. Zhu, wounded and helpless, and robbed of a small fortune in Party funds by some gangsterly opponents, managed to get to Hong Kong and then safety in Shanghai. It is sad to read that in 1945 he was executed in one of China's mindless bloody episodes.

China 1927 is elegantly translated by the incomparable Zhu (no relation) Hong. What makes it memorable is Zhu Qihua himself. Although very young, he has important responsibilities in many of the events he records: writing propaganda leaflets, haranguing large audiences and sometimes bemused peasants, and eventually caring for the wounded as the victorious march north turns into a flight under fire. He is usually armed, and every now and again feels like shooting some cowardly or corrupt colleague, but I don't think he ever fires a shot in these pages, confining himself to the occasional insult . . .

There are scenes worthy of an old-fashioned black-and-white movie. A pretty young comrade—one of the many in this account who defy their traditional families to join the revolution—is shot dead during the retreat, Zhu gathers her in his arms, and carries her to a house where he leaves her with a note entreating anyone who finds her body to give her a good burial. One day, as he sits penniless in a Shanghai park, a married woman he slightly knows spots him. He is eighteen, she somewhat older. She leans against him. They go to an expensive restaurant, where he eats one of those meals he loves, and after a night of passion—his very first, I believe—she departs, leaving him with a generous tip.

I felt sad when Zhu ended this memoir on his twentieth birthday with these words: "Twenty years of my life have passed, and what achievements do I have to show for those years? I am buried in shame." [p. 304] Well, well. On that same day he sends a poem to the mysterious "young lady in Canton." It ends with "I am ready to meet you with my valor intact."[p. 304]

I loved this book and I congratulate all those at MerwinAsia, the publisher; thanks for helping bring it to life.

Jonathan Mirsky
Human Rights in China

The year 1927 was a tumultuous one in the political history of modern China. It saw the last phase of the Nationalist Northern Expedition, the open split between the Kuomintang left and right, the collapse of the KMT–CCP united front, the purge of the Communists, the establishment of the Chiang Kai-shek regime in Nanjing, the Nanchang August uprising and the Guangzhou December uprising. The year ended in a debacle for the Communists and the complete eclipse of the CCP.

China 1927 is the memoir of a 20-year-old hot-headed revolutionary's involvement in the events of 1926–27. Coming from a working-class background and apparently a member of the CCP and a Trotskyite, Zhu Qihua had taken part in the Shanghai workers' movement before leaving for Guangzhou in September 1925 to become head of a propaganda team in the Allied Revolutionary Government's General Political Department. In December 1926, he followed the Revolutionary Government's move to Wuhan, the center of Wang Jingwei's leftist regime, via Nanchang. From Wuhan the revolutionary leadership launched the Henan campaign. Later developments forced them to return to Wuhan, and later to Nanchang, where the August 1927 uprising was to take place. They then marched south, fighting local warlords and other enemy forces on their way, culminating in the disastrous Guangzhou uprising. After the debacle, Zhu became a fugitive in Hong Kong, before making his way back to Shanghai . . .

Political memoirs are more often than not self-serving, but not this one. Zhu hardly took credit for what he may have done for the revolution. His honesty is extraordinary. He confesses to having bourgeois taste and sentiments. He castigates himself for lacking a truly revolutionary spirit, blaming it on his youthfulness and natural instincts. He fails to kill the Nezhdanov beneath his revolutionary exterior. Open about his sexual desires and love for beautiful girls, he enjoyed reading Zhang Jingsheng's book on the history of sexuality and often talked about it heatedly. He was infatuated with "the young lady from Canton". He tried to take advantage of a pretty young lady on the street where he was hiding as a fugitive in Hong Kong (until he discovered that she was the daughter of a detective with the Guangdong Provincial Security Bureau). He had an affair with an old acquaintance in Shanghai, the beautiful second wife of a Mr X, taking her to a hotel, where they had sex, and accepting 80 yuan from her before they parted. He confessed to being "completely shameless" (p. 298).

Indeed, one of the merits of the memoir lies in the humanizing of the revolutionary movement. The revolution is not glorified. Instead, the memoir lays bare the natural tendencies, if not moral weaknesses, of many of those involved. They would indulge in drinking, gambling and playing mahjong when they got bored; they would sometimes look down upon the rural folks for whose cause they were supposed to be fighting; they would become part of the ruling class in the townships occupied by the revolutionary forces; and they would enjoy fine foods and good wines and the occasional privileges of "revolutionary aristocrats" (p. 34), while urging others to go down to the masses. Zhu used to imagine occupying the mansions of the rich capitalists with their mistresses after the revolution was won. He felt ashamed of himself, thinking that he and other revolutionaries were "a bad lot" sometimes (p. 170). In short, *China 1927* makes compelling reading. It is fascinating and riveting—there is not a dull moment in the story. Besides being a personal record, it is a rare source of information for scholarly research on the period. It has also benefited from the superb translation and annotation by Zhu Hong . . . It deserves to be widely read by students of the Chinese revolution of the 1920s.

Edmund S. K. Fung
The China Journal

Few historical memoirs of the Nationalist Revolution of the 1920s were written at the time of the events they record. Zhu Qihua's eyewitness account of the military and political fortunes of Communist and Nationalist forces on the Northern Expedition, first drafted in 1928, appeared in Shanghai in 1933 under the title Memoir of 1927 (Yijiuerqinian huiyi). It reads with the ease and freshness of a contemporary record written by a guileless young man.

Zhu was certainly young. He joined the Communist Party in Shanghai in its inaugural year, 1921, as a fourteen-year-old typesetter. At seventeen he was dispatched to the revolutionary base in Guangdong to join the political section of the Whampoa Academy, and within a year was directing the Propaganda Section of the Guomindang Military Affairs Department in Guangzhou. At eighteen he was appointed head of propaganda for the Nationalist Fourth Army's Politbureau on the Northern Expedition. The following year, 1927, Zhou Enlai invited him to direct propaganda operations and, in time, Party Organization for the General Political Department in the wake of the left's break with Chiang Kai-shek during the later stages of the Northern Expedition. The General Political Department was a peak agency, within the left-wing rump of the Nationalist/Communist Alliance, that was headed by Guo Moruo.

Zhu Qihua was appointed Director of Propaganda and Organization to help manage the aftermath of the Nanchang Uprising of August 1, 1927, a date subsequently commemorated as marking the birth of the People's Liberation Army (PLA). A handful of military and revolutionary leaders who styled themselves the Wuhan Revolutionary Government—including He Long, Ye Ting, Zhu De, Zhang Guotao, Li Lisan, Liu Bocheng, Zhou Enlai, and others-had escaped to Nanchang from Wuhan a few days earlier and were pondering their next move when commander Zhang Fakui ordered them to proceed to Jiujiang. Sensing a trap, Zhu informs us, the leaders staged a military coup, disarmed soldiers loyal to Zhang Fakui, and reconstituted themselves as the Revolutionary Committee. It was all over in half an hour. "There were no mass rallies, no spark of revolutionary fervour in the air. . . . Rather than having gone through a revolutionary coup, Nanchang looked as if it had suffered a bandit rampage" (p. 218). It was then that Zhou Enlai, Guo Moruo's superior, tasked Zhu with penning the "Outline for the Declaration of the August First Uprising." By this account, one of the documents underlying the founding myth of the PLA rests on a few bold statements by Zhou Enlai elaborated by a peripatetic nineteen-year-old who had slept through the half-hour coup.

The memoir offers a lively account of the political intrigues, military battles, occasional coups, forced marches, and desperate hunger that accompanied one wing of the Northern Expeditionary forces as they traipsed from Guangdong north through Jiangxi to Hubei and on to Henan, then back south through now-desolate landscapes in Henan and deserted villages in Jiangxi to Fujian, and finally to Guangdong, from the latter half of 1926 through to the end of 1927.

Along the way, Zhu offers memorable pen-portraits of his fellow journeymen and women, lending interest and coherence to the story. We meet chubby and overfed Sun Fo, happy-go-lucky Peng Pai, useless and philandering Guo Moruo, self-aggrandizing Tan Pingshan, treacherous Wang Jingwei, strutting "toady" Li Lisan, the forceful Song Qingling, classes of women comrades from revolutionary academies in Guangzhou and Wuhan, and the slippery if serene figure of Zhou Enlai, whom Zhu depicts as a poor judge of character but a sincere and hard-working "quack." Some years later, Zhu Qihua was branded a Trotskyist. Although little in his political reflections bears out this claim, the accusation could well be justified by the harsh judgments he casts on his Leninist comrades.

While closely following the route of the Fourth Army, the narrative arc of the memoir traces the revolutionary armies' rise and fall from a band of heroic conquerors, driven by revolutionary zeal, to a starving and thieving rabble. Still, the story is not without its romance and romantic moments. The odyssey is peppered with snippets of classical poetry and historical references to sites through which the revolutionaries passed, where heroes of the Warring States and the Romance of the Three Kingdoms had left their mark many years before. Readers are also invited to share Zhu's reflections on the amorous passions and dalliances that distracted his comrades, and from time to time Zhu himself, from their commitment to the revolution. Two of his comrades found the loves of their lives among the girl students of Baoling Girls School in Nanchang.

The memoir ends with an account of a meeting in Shanghai with veteran Nationalist propagandist Shao Lizi, editor of the Party's Shanghai Republican Daily, during the closing weeks of 1927. Shao had recently turned down an offer to serve as director of the General Political Department under Chiang Kai-shek in Nanjing, explaining to Zhu that he felt caught between old friends in the Nationalist Party and sympathy for new friends in the Communist Party. But he cautioned Zhu against the Communist Party itself. The leadership is "excessively demanding," Shao said, with the result that would exaggerate figures in reports to the district level, which would further multiply figures in reports to county level, and so on up the chain of command, so that the central leadership was invariably dealing with figures way out of touch with reality. "This goes on in a vicious cycle level after level, inevitably leading to catastrophe," Shao cautioned (pp. 303-4).

Zhu did not live to see Shao Lizi's warnings borne out in the People's Republic. He was executed by the Nationalists in 1945.

John Fitzgerald
The Journal of Asian Studies

China 1927

memoir of a debacle

Zhu Qihua

China 1927

memoir of a debacle

Zhu Qihua

Translated by Zhu Hong

Foreword by John T. Ma

Edited with an Introduction

by Doug Merwin

Portland, Maine

59 West St., Unit 3W,
Portland, ME 04102
USA

Distributed by the University of Hawai'i Press

Library of Congress Control Number: 2011939896

978-1-937385-14-9 (Paperback)
978-1-937385-15-6 (Hardcover)

Printed in the United States of America

The paper used in this publication meets the minimum requirements of the American National Standard for Information Services—Permanence of Paper for Printed Library Materials, ANSI/NISO Z39/48-1992

Contents

FOREWORD

I was once a student of Zhu Qihua's. But that was at no ordinary school, and he was no ordinary teacher. And what he taught was also not ordinary.

During the War of Resistance against the Japanese invasion of 1937–1945, together with a group of college students from Peking, Qinghua, and Nankai universities, I joined the War Area Service Corps of the First Army in Xi'an, then under the command of Nationalist General Hu Zongnan. We were assigned to do mobilization, educational, and social work in Fengxiang District, Shaanxi Province. Since three members of our corps were medical doctors, we also did some public health work and treated some patients. Our services were deeply appreciated by the local people but at the same time they made some old political officers in the army jealous of us. So some of them falsely accused us of being Communists and reported this to General Hu.

Although during the War of Resistance being a Communist was not a crime, it was not appropriate for a Nationalist commander to hire Communists to do political work, especially for someone like General Hu, whose main responsibility was to control Chinese Communists. In order to protect himself as well as us, General Hu decided to establish a special class in the Fourth Wartime Political Officers Training Institute of which he was the dean. All students of this special class were we members of the First Army War Area Service Corps. He told us that once we had graduated from that class we became his students and nobody would dare to accuse us of being Communists.

Some members of our corps had been members of the front organization of the Chinese Communist Party (CCP), the Youth Vanguards of the National Liberation (Minzu jiefang xianfeng dui, abbreviated *Minxian*) when they were college students. Although they did not admit that they were members of the CCP , they had to some extent become indoctrinated with communism. Using the old Chinese strategy of combating poison with poison, General Hu appointed two ex-Communists to be our instructors. One of the two was Zhu Qihua.

Zhu Qihua's lectures were unique. He did not discuss the theories of communism or anti-communism. Nor did he comment on the political or military situation in China in the manner most political officers of that time did. He talked mainly about himself—his personal background and experiences. He took great pride in being a true member of the proletariat for whose liberation the communist movement was established. When he was a teenager, he worked as a typesetter at a Chinese newspaper in Shanghai. He was the very rare, if not the only, industrial worker among the early members of the CCP, who were mostly bourgeois intellectuals, landowners, and capitalists. Although he had received no formal education, he was a successful self-made man. His economic and sociological writings were scholarly. He was a prolific writer and used many pen names. It would be very difficult to compile his complete works.

Zhu Qihua was proud of his position as head of both the Propaganda and the Organization departments after the Nanchang/August First Uprising of the pro-CCP troops in 1927. Under the command of Zhou Enlai, the pro-CCP troops moved south toward Guangdong Province, and were defeated by the Nationalists in eastern Guangdong and disbanded. As head of the Propaganda Department, Zhu wrote some important documents and declarations for the CCP. This book, his memoir of the year 1927, is an important source of information for the history of the Chinese Communist Party during that period.

Zhu was an interesting lecturer and a capable teacher. He never hesitated to speak his mind or to express his opinion on controversial matters. I'll always remember Zhu Qihua fondly. When the CCP was gaining the upper hand during the civil war after the Japanese surrender, I was very sorry to learn from my brother, who was General Hu's aide-de-camp, that Zhu had been secretly executed in 1945 when General Hu found out that he was trying to re-establish his connection with the CCP. I lost a favorite teacher. And the CCP lost a very talented proletarian and industrial worker.

John T. Ma
Alameda, CA
May 25, 2012

ACKNOWLEDGMENTS

I wish to thank Zhu Hong for her excellent translation, her careful annotation, and her thorough research to get names, places, and dates right. The project would not have happened if Zhu Hong had not committed herself to it with great enthusiasm and cheerful optimism.

I am grateful to the Zhu family in Shanghai and Chongqing and the Chu family in the United States for their encouragement.

I thank Professors Joseph Fewsmith and Steven I. Levine for their helpful comments on the manuscript, Nancy Hearst for her efforts to locate the manuscript, Professor Roderick MacFarquhar for his encouragement in the early stages of this project, and Professor Chi Wang for his calligraphy and his friendship.

I also thank John T. Ma, a former student of Zhu Qihua's at the Fourth Wartime Political Officers Training Institute in Xi'an, for bringing Zhu's book to my attention in the first place and for encouraging me to have it translated. The entry on Zhu (under Chu Ch'i-hua) in Howard I. Boorman and Richard C. Howard's *Biographical Dictionary of Republican China,* Vol. I (New York and London: Columbia University Press, 1967, pp. 435-437) only strengthened my resolve to see it published in English one day.

Doug Merwin

INTRODUCTION

Zhu Qihua's memoir of the year 1927 actually begins with his departure from Shanghai in the fall of 1925 to join the GMD (Guomindang/Nationalist Party)-CCP (Chinese Communist Party) Allied Revolutionary Government in Canton, and ends with the ousting of the CCP from the Alliance and the debacle of their march south, intended to take Canton, at the end of 1927. Thus Zhu actually narrates his experience in the Revolution during the 1925–1927 period.

The years 1925–1927 are a critical period in modern Chinese history when the National Revolutionary Army carried out the Northern Expedition to wipe out the rampant warlordism that was dividing up the country. Owing to deletions in the original publication, the narrative passes over the first year of Zhu's work at the Whampoa Military Academy when the Northern Expedition had successfully taken a large part of south-central China. Zhu's memoir, as published, starts with the Revolutionary Government's move from Canton to the south-central tri-city of Wuhan at the end of 1926. He vividly describes the dilapidated and sorry state of rural China as he and his comrades pass through parts of Guangdong and Jiangxi provinces on their boat trip northward, rebutting claims about the advance of capitalism in China.

Because of strife within the Alliance, the Revolutionary Government was delayed in Nanchang for two months before moving to Wuhan to set up a new capital. An energetic political worker, Zhu used this interval to study the situation in Nanchang, leaving an unusual record of the malaise that infected the revolutionary movement from within.

In Wuhan, Zhu was elated by the prevailing revolutionary fervor. Once he had settled in, the leadership launched a second Northern Expedition into Henan Province to clean up warlord rule in east-central China, planning ultimately to take Nanjing, Shanghai, Baoding, and Peking. Against the larger background of the successful military campaign, "The Henan Campaign" chapters narrate in great detail Zhu and his propaganda team vigorously preparing the ground for imminent war and mobilizing the masses in the rear.

Meanwhile, in Wuhan, the CCP Left of the allied Revolutionary Army found itself in hostile political surroundings. Confronted by the GMD with proof of a conspiracy, the Communists were forced out of Wuhan back to Nanchang. There, Zhu was witness to the historic August First Uprising of 1927, now commemorated as the birth of the People's Liberation Army (PLA). The forces of the uprising, comprising an army of about thirty thousand men under the CCP, marched southward to establish a new base in Canton. Zhu's description of this march highlights many figures, some of whom—Zhou Enlai, He Long, Guo Moruo, Ye Ting, among others—would eventually become national leaders of the People's Republic of China (PRC). Hemmed in by the enemy, plagued by hunger and exhaustion, this ragtag CCP-led army melted away before they could reach Canton.

Zhu himself ended up penniless in Shanghai, where he passed his twentieth birthday, and decided to write an account of what he had just lived through, as recorded in *China 1927: Memoir of a Debacle* (original title *Yi-jiu er-qi nian huiyi*), which was eventually published in 1933 in Shanghai by Shanghai Xinxing chubanshe.

Zhu's memoir portrays a spirited, idealistic and hardworking young man playing a personal, albeit minor, role in critical turning points of twentieth-century Chinese history. Zhu wrote down the Manifesto of the August First Uprising as dictated by Zhou Enlai; called on General

Galen, the famous Russian adviser, on a mission of condolence on behalf of the CCP; gave speeches at mass rallies as a representative of the GMD; and was a guest at a dinner given by Chiang Kai-shek. Zhu worked under Zhou Enlai, hobnobbed with Mao Zedong, quarreled with Li Lisan, made sarcastic remarks about Guo Moruo, and criticized Wang Jingwei and others. In clear and direct prose, he gives us eyewitness descriptions of important turning points of this period: the Second Northern Expedition, the August First Uprising, the GMD-CCP Alliance and its final rupture, and intimate details of the CCP's failed march south to take Canton, perhaps its last attempt at *urban* revolution. The significance of this failure cannot be overstated—since following on the debacle of the march and the bloody suppression of the short-lived coup in Canton which followed, Mao Zedong set up *rural* bases in Jiangxi, and from there launched the Long March northwestward in 1934, leading ultimately to the establishment of the People's Republic of China in October 1949.

A young man in search of revolution, Zhu Qihua is self-educated and well read, despite having little formal education and working in a printshop starting at age thirteen (in other words, he was a worker). He is sincere and outspoken, sometimes naïve in avowing his personal beliefs, often acute in his analysis of the situation, and always endearing in his honesty about himself, such as his "confessions" of romantic attachments and his lack of diligence despite his resolution to read more. A colorful figure often driven by emotion (the death of one friend had led him to leave Shanghai, while thoughts of the comrades who had fallen in the march south had led him to exclaim: "Revolution, revolution, is this your bequest?"

Just as Zhu himself had once confessed, he had never managed to kill the Nezhdanov in himself. At the end of his memoir, he was back to his Nezhdanov self.[1]

The brief sketch emerging from this memoir does not cover the complete life and career of Zhu Qihua. According to other sources,

1. Nezhdanov, protagonist in the novel *Virgin Soil* by Ivan Turgenev. A revolutionary idealist who tried go down among the common people, he was rejected and ultimately committed suicide.

Zhu joined the CCP in his early youth and was active in leftist politics for many years. Zhu's involvement with the Revolution did not end with his escape to Shanghai: he later became an instructor in a military officers training institute in Xi'an, and was active during the War of Resistance against Japan, editing the journal *The War of Resistance and Culture* (Kang-Ri yu wenhua). Zhu Qihua died at the hands of the enemies of the Revolution in 1945, reportedly ordered shot or burned to death as a communist spy by Hu Zongnan, one of Chiang Kai-shek's most trusted generals.[2] In retrospect, one can say that Zhu Qihua was a significant figure in early Republican history. Recent interest in him as such has surfaced in mainland academic circles, with scholary articles about him beginning to appear in academic journals. He published a number of books, perhaps the best known of which is *Hongse wutai* (Red stage), which Benjamin Schwartz frequently cites in his *Chinese Communism and the Rise of Mao* (Cambridge, MA: Harvard University Press, 1951) under the pseudonym Li Ang, one of eleven names Zhu used in his short lifetime. Copies of the book were located in several libraries around the world—the one used for this translation was found and copied in the Shanghai Library.

It is important to note in closing that a significant feature of this memoir is that it provides a detailed description of the first time that political work was introduced into the military—in other words, soldiers finally understood what they were fighting for.

D.M.

2. Hu Zongnan, 1896–1962, native of Zhejiang and Guomindang military commander.

China 1927

memoir of a debacle

Zhu Qihua

Map: Routes Taken by Zhu Qihua

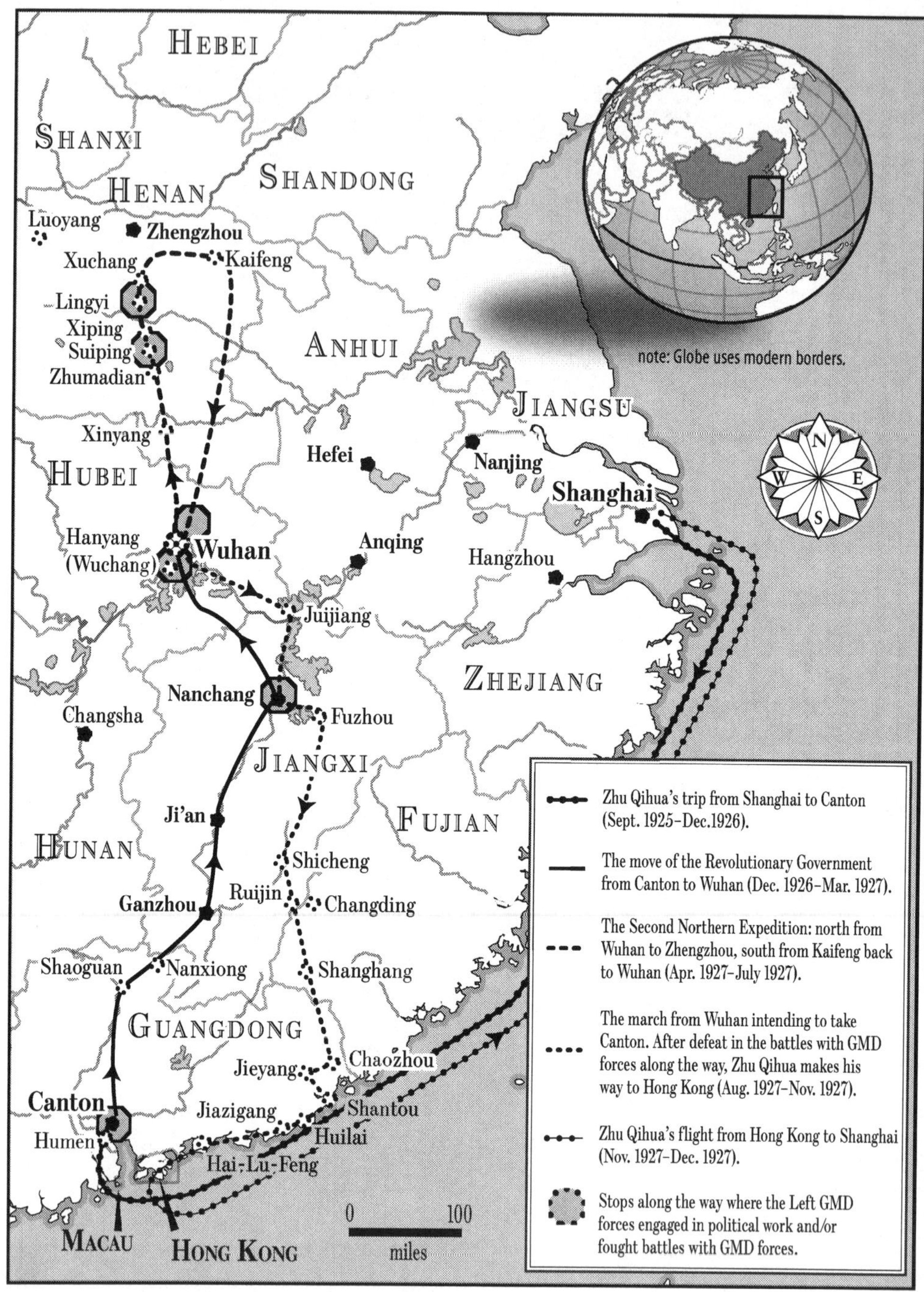

PREFACE

It has been six years now since I gave up politics. The events of six years ago have rarely been revisited, and the memories are beginning to fade. Last November in Macao I recovered several boxes of books that I had left with a friend for safekeeping. As I opened one of the boxes, the manuscript of "1927: A Memoir" turned up among a medley of papers. I felt transported into another world, another time. At the moment of writing, I had no thoughts of publication. Later, at the urging of friends, not to mention the pressure of my own strapped circumstances, I was led to seek publication. And now the book is actually going into print.

The original manuscript consisted of 460,000 characters in thirteen chapters, written in four different localities, under vastly different circumstances. The earlier chapters were written in Shanghai in the winter of 1927. The rest were completed in the following year—several chapters in Canton[1] and Hong Kong in February, others in Nanchang in June, while the last two chapters were finished in Qingdao in August of 1928.

1. Canton, capital city of Guangdong Province. It is called Guangzhou according to the phonetic system, pinyin, now in common use in China.

Before submitting the manuscript, I did have thoughts of revising it. But then, I wanted to preserve a truthful recording of the past as it was taken down at the time. Add to that a looming deadline, all I could do was to cut. Of the original thirteen chapters, nine now remain, some 240,000 characters out of the original 460,000. Made up of chapters thrown together, the book is bound to be a slapdash affair.

What you are about to read is an account of what I personally lived through. But surely, dear reader, you can see at a glance that what is presented here is more than a mere personal record.

The cut-and-paste earlier chapters may seem somewhat jerky. However, the chapters "Eve of the Split," "Jiujiang and Nanchang," "On the March South," and "Notes on a Retreat" did not undergo excessive cutting and may read more smoothly. Shao Lizi[2] and Zhou Fohai[3] have written forewords, for which I am deeply grateful, but owing to the publisher's deadline, they could not be used for this edition. If and when there is a reprint, the forewords of both these elders will certainly be included.

May 5, 1933
On the Lower Reaches of the Yangtze River

2. Shao Lizi (1882–1967) was an educator, politician, and member of the progressive Tongmeng Alliance. Shao, jointly with Liu Yazi, had established the Nanshe Club to promote modern literature. He joined the Communist Party in 1921, left in 1926, but continued to support GMD-CCP cooperation. Shao held many honorary positions on the mainland after 1949.

3. Zhou Fohai (1897–1948), one of the founders and an early leader of the CCP, was a delegate to the First CCP Congress. Zhou had studied in Japan. He left the CCP to become a prominent member of the GMD government, and later cooperated with the Japanese occupation.

CHAPTER ONE

From Canton to Nanchang

I

On the night of December 6, 1926, I was at a rowdy send-off party hosted by the locals. I had been drinking steadily, untouched by the gaiety around me. Quite the contrary, these official formalities and the well-meant but vacuous flattery were depressing. Glumly I downed one glass after another of the sparkling red wine. The party broke up at nine. Guests and hosts made off each their separate way.

Bored and dulled by wine, I walked listlessly along the embankment of the Pearl River. The chilly wind on my burning cheeks was energizing. I hopped into a rickshaw, got off at Pearl River Park, hired a boat, and rowed myself down the river. It was close to ten o'clock, but traffic was still busy along the embankment, pulsating with the vibrancy of the city. The river itself was crowded with rowboats occupied by officers in uniform like myself. But they were invariably accompanied by female companions, while I was alone. We were scheduled to leave by five the next morning. I had barely seven hours left to dally in lovely Canton, cradle of the Revolution. Though I was not leaving a lover behind, the petty bourgeois in me took over and I was inexplicably saddened at the thought of leaving the city where I had been living in for over a year. "Drifting on the Whampoa River," a poem about parting written by my friend Gao Yuhan came to my mind.

> Reading the Lamentations[1] and listening to the plaintive reed pipe,[2]
> Gazing at the ripples entangled like silver snakes,
> I have lived here through three moons,
> And now a strip of water cuts me off, exiling me to the ends of the earth.

I am not a poet, nor ever intended to be, but at the moment I was downcast with a poetic sense of loss. The imminent parting conjured up memories of the trials, some of them comic, that I had gone through as I made my way from Shanghai to Canton more than a year before. I had left Shanghai for Canton on September 1, 1925.

In Shanghai I had taken part in the workers' movement, which ended in what was later known as the May Thirtieth Incident,[3] and I had seen my friend He Bingyi lying bleeding on Nanjing Road. At the time, Shanghai, too, had been suffused with revolutionary fervor. For personal reasons, I had planned to leave in July with Peking as my destination of choice. But circumstances made me change my mind. I reached Canton by boat nine days later, on September 10, 1925. It was during the sixteen-month-long strike in Hong Kong against the British that foreign vessels sailing between Shanghai and Canton had stopped running, never mind that the foreign-run mail boats only served Hong Kong and never stopped in Canton anyway. As for the two Chinese boats owned by the Mercantile Bank, one was undergoing repairs while the other had been conscripted by the [warlord] Chen Jiongming. The few private boats running surreptitiously had stopped operations for fear of suffering the same fate. Thus, when I started on my trip from

---

1. *Li Sao* (Lamentations), a long poem by Qu Yuan (340–277 BCE), minister of the state of Qu and one of China's earliest poets.
2. A hidden reference to the long poem *Hu jia shiba pai* by Cai Wenji (177 ? – ? CE), a woman poet of the Eastern Han dynasty.
3. May Thirtieth Incident. On May 30, 1925, British-led police fired on unarmed student and worker demonstrators in Shanghai, sparking off a wave of demonstrations and strikes across the country.

Shanghai to Canton, there was no transportation by sea available.

I kept searching the docks, and one week later, on the afternoon of August 28, I found the *Fukang*, an old ship not exceeding 2,000 tons. I boarded on August 29, but we didn't set sail until the afternoon of September 1. As far as I could tell, the boat must have been at least forty years old, and like all such obsolete vessels, it was very slow. As a rule, it takes fifty hours for a mail boat to cover the distance from Shanghai to Canton, and only forty-five hours to reach Hong Kong. Even on small privately owned boats the trip would not take more than four days, but because of the strike, we had to make a detour through Macao[4], which we reached after a full seven days. Without a radio, we could not notify Macao of our precise time of arrival. Thus the Macao pilot was not ready to take us in when we arrived, and we had to cast anchor and wait.

We had run out of water the day before. The boat's owner had expected us to reach Canton within five days, so the overloaded boat had stored water for only six days. It was early September, but on the boat it felt like mid-summer. By day seven, water had become a serious problem. At dinner, we detected a strange smell in the rice. The captain, when confronted, drew a long face and said: "Sorry, we have run out of water and had to use seawater to rinse the rice." How could one eat rice rinsed in seawater! But what was one to do? There was a commotion. The owner announced that we would arrive in Macao the next morning, and that quieted everybody down. But being out of drinking water was a problem. A peddler of soda drinks on the boat began to do a booming business. The last couple of days, his substandard soda had not been selling well at twenty *fen* a bottle, and he still had nine bottles left. But now there was a rush, and he raised the price to two *yuan* each. Luckily I grabbed two bottles for four *yuan*.

That same night a passenger from Sichuan died. A dead man in that sweltering heat! And in the cabin right next to mine, too! The minute we heard the news, we all rushed up on deck. According to accepted

4. Macao is a port city in south China, fifty miles southwest of Hong Kong; it came under Portuguese territorial rule in 1557 and was returned to China in 1999.

practice, a dead body on a boat would immediately be lowered into the sea for the safety of all the other passengers. But in China, you can never take anything for granted. The unfortunate dead man was traveling in the company of five other men, two of whom were going to Canton to enroll in the Whampoa Military Academy, the other three to look for jobs. Among them, one was the dead man's brother. The dead man, a nobody himself, was a relative of Chen Zhaoying, commander of the Humen Fort.[5] When the shipowner announced that the dead man was to be lowered into the sea, the five men acompanying him rose as one in protest. The dead man's brother declared that if they did that Commander Chen Zhaoying of the Humen Fort would confiscate the boat, take the captain into custody, and make him do hard labor in the Fort. The captain, scared stiff, talked the shipowner into giving up the idea. This was a Chinese boat, but the owner was a White Russian with no legal status, so he had no choice but to give in. The corpse was wrapped and placed in the dining area of the boat. No one dared go near the place; we all squeezed in on deck for the night.

This episode aboard the boat left a very bad taste in my mouth. Isn't the Humen Fort under the jurisdiction of the Revolutionary Government in Canton? How dare Chen Zhaoying threaten to confiscate privately owned boats and take people into custody? And for no reason, except to do his relative a favor! On the other hand, how dare this group flaunt the rules for disposing of dead bodies at sea and risk the health of over a hundred people just because they had a relative who was a commander! It was infuriating, this privilege of the gun-toting class!

We got up the next morning and washed ourselves in seawater. We needed to drink some fresh water, but where could we get any? Our ship was sailing on a blue sea which merged into a blue sky with nothing in between—not the flight of a seagull, not even the shadow of a cloud, only the blazing sun hanging implacably over us as our little ship pursued its lonely course.

"When [do we get to] Macao?" The passengers were becoming

5. Humen, port city of Guangdong Province, with military fortifications.

restless, and the sailors looked worried. Suddenly there was a stampede. The corpse was beginning to stink, and some of the passengers demanded it be thrown into the sea. But the captain, obviously intimidated after living under the heel of warlords, feared the threat of conscription by the commander, and would not take that drastic step.

Just then a man among the group of Ningpo passengers stood up and claimed to be a relative of Chiang Kai-shek,[6] commandant of the Whampoa Military Academy, a much more powerful connection than that with Commander Chen Zhaoying! "Deal with the corpse this minute! Who is this piddling Chen Zhaoying! How dare he throw his weight around right under the flag of the Revolution! If he confiscates the boat, I'll report him to the Commandant himself [Chiang was often referred to as "the Commandant"—*xiaozhang*], and he'll be taken out and shot!" Saying which, this powerful Ningpo relative assured the captain of his support. Whereupon the Chen Zhaoying "faction" wilted and agreed to dispose of the corpse.

Fortunately, at that very moment, a group of islets was spotted in the distance, and the dead man's friends begged the captain to stop there so that they could at least bury the poor man. The captain agreed, and three sailors set out in a sailboat with the dead man's brother, taking away the corpse. The islets were just bare hillocks with nothing growing—no trees, not even a blade of grass—just mounds of burning red earth lapped by blue water. The view was stunning. If I were an artist, I would have tried to catch it on canvas. Or probably I would have done nothing even if I were an artist, for I was parched with thirst and dying for a drink of fresh water.

From the islets it was a short distance to Macao, but we had to wait a full twelve hours for the pilot before we were allowed to pass through. From Macao, we soon arrived at Humen, and in the distance

---

6. Chiang Kai-shek (1888–1975), military and political leader of the GMD after the death of Sun Yat-sen, commandant of the Whampoa Military Academy, leader of the Northern Expedition. Chiang broke from the GMD-CCP alliance and set up a Nationalist government in Nanjing in 1928. He fought against warlords, Japanese invaders, and the Chinese Communists until his defeat in the civil war and retreat to Taiwan in 1949.

I saw the flag of the Republic flying over a boat. "Blue sky, white sun, red earth"[7]—how that flag buoyed up my spirits! Being so used to the sight of the hated five-barred flag [of the old Republic, at the time flaunted by warlords in parts of China], the sight of the blue-white-red flag made me feel that we had emerged from darkness into bright light. Although I knew from hindsight that I would be disappointed in what the flag was supposed to stand for, at the moment, that flag flying over Humen was a thrilling sight. I thought to myself that under the Qing dynasty, the revolutionaries had hated the sight of the imperial yellow dragon flag and must have been thrilled by the sight of the five-barred flag, as I was now thrilled to see our blue-white-red! Who could have foreseen that in a short time this tri-colored emblem of brightness and glory would turn into a symbol of murderous darkness and terror! To think of the changes wrought by Time!

We finally arrived in Canton. For me, having lived under warlord rule for so long, Canton was a breath of fresh air. I don't mean to say that everything was ideal, but I must say that this new revolutionary capital did not disappoint me.

It had been over a year now since my arrival in Canton, and I had hardly left the city during that period. Canton is so lovely. Over the last couple of years I have breezed through more than a dozen cities but have never come across any that was the equal of Canton. It is not Utopia, certainly, but when a wide expanse of the country was under warlord rule and Canton the only spot where freedom reigned, how could we idealistic young people not look up to Canton as a beacon of hope?

But back to reality: I was about to leave Canton in a couple of hours, not knowing when I would be back. How could I not be downcast! Lost in thought, I let my rowboat drift in the middle of the river. What a lovely place is Canton!

II

I love Canton not only as the capital of the Revolution, but for many

7. The blue-white-red flag was formally adopted as the national flag on April 18, 1927, when Chiang Kai-shek set up his government in Nanjing.

reasons which have nothing to do with politics—there goes my petty bourgeois sentiment!

I love the climate of Canton. I can't speak for the world, but as far as China is concerned, no other place can boast of Canton's congenial weather. I abhor the extremes of heat and cold. True, I have never roasted in the South Pacific Islands, nor have I been frozen in icy Siberia. But I have been to Manchuria and still shiver at the recollection of winter nights on the banks of the Yalu River. On the other hand, our family had spent seventeen months in a little town near Lhasa in Tibet. I was a baby suckling at my mother's breast, but family stories of the heat in Tibet still give me nightmares. The cold of Peking, on the one hand, and the heat of Shanghai, Nanjing, Wuhan and Hangzhou, on the other, are all very intimidating. Take the cold for instance: in Nanjing the winter cold can drop below zero, while fifteen degrees centigrade would be considered normal. As for heat, the Shanghai summer heat can hit thirty-seven degrees, to be capped by Nanjing at forty degrees! But not so in Canton. Here, the coldest winter weather never drops below freezing. With the sea breeze to moderate the temperature, it is spring all year round and one can get by very comfortably in light clothes. What attracts me particularly to Canton, however, is the temperament of the people, so different from that of my native Zhejiang near the West Lake area, usually referred to as the land of "delicate mountains and sparkling waters." At the risk of offending my fellow Zhejiangers, I must say that I have no feeling for the place and totally dislike the people—hypocritical, mean, crafty, and cruel. But here in Canton, the people are open and direct, brave and honest. For instance, in the hotels of Nanjing, Shanghai, and other cities close to Zhejiang, the fawning airs of the bellboys are truly repulsive. Expecting tips, they will squeeze you to the limit given half a chance. Not the bellboys in Canton. If you tip them they will not refuse, but they do not expect it. Their job is to serve the guest—their behavior professional, their personal dignity intact. To members of the ruling class who expect bowing and scraping from service people, the Canton bellboys may seem offensive, but I consider their behavior an admirable display of national character. The average educational level in Canton is higher than in any other city. For example, few if any Shanghai rickshaw pullers can read, while almost all rickshaw pullers in Canton are literate. If you have problems ordering a rickshaw because of the local dialect, all you need to do is to write down the address, and presto, the problem is solved. Women, too, in Canton tend to be more literate than those in other parts of the country, and this includes domestic servants as well. In Shanghai, you would hardly find one maid in a thousand who could read her own name, whereas in Canton, most of them can read a little. So far in my year's stay in this city, I had hired three domestic maids in succession, and they were all literate.

Apart from Peking, no other city can compare with Canton in the combination of material comforts and natural beauty. Shanghai is well suited to satisfy one's material needs, but it is barren of rural scenes. Hangzhou has beautiful West Lake to enliven one's spirits, true, while Nanjing is replete with mountains, lakes, temples and gardens to fill our leisure hours. But they are both abysmally undeveloped, with no running water, no electric lighting, no decent transportation, and with narrow and bumpy roads. Canton stands alone among provincial capitals in south China for modern development matched with rural delights, as witness the wide and smooth paved roads and the profusion of parks big and small.

Among the parks in major cities of China, Canton's rank first in number and variety. Central Park, the largest, is not remarkable. Pearl Garden, though small, is an islet set in the Pearl River, only reached by ferry, though now a pontoon bridge has been built. Yuexiu Garden is situated atop the famous Guanyin Hill, while Aihui Park was originally part of the old French Consulate. The last, though small in scale, is designed like a winding grove, lined on either side by tall trees locked in an embrace at the top, blocking out the sun and thereby creating the illusion of a walk in the woods. Dongshan Park, one of the smallest of Canton's parks, has a charm all its own, and there are other parks still being designed. All these parks, some set on hills, some on islands, and some like forest groves, are full of delights, but Dongshan is the most endearing to me. Dongshan Park dazzled me with its tropical flora and fauna, most of which I could not identify, except for the common coconut tree. I had lived in the Dongshan area and often went for walks in the park, especially at dusk. Sitting on a bench surrounded by tropical foliage, I would forget where I was and feel myself being wafted to an exotic Pacific island. In a word, the loveliness of Canton lies in its combination of modern civilization and Nature's untamed beauty. As for the proliferation of historic sites and scenic spots, only Peking can hold a candle to Canton. To my acute embarrassment, I must own up to the fact that while in Canton I lived in Dongshan, the so-called upper-class district, where all the bigwigs of the city reside. Many overseas Chinese own villas there too. Green foliage embracing red bricks, gorgeous flowers setting off green tiles, or whitewashed walls highlighted by stained glass—every street in Dongshan is decked out with houses displayed like a row of beautiful maidens. Thanks to these buildings, Dongshan has been turned into a veritable gem of a place. Neatly kept avenues flanked by Western-style buildings set off by spacious lawns are a common sight in the French Concession in Shanghai, but they cannot compare with my favorite Dongshan in Canton. Here are no wide avenues, only pretty streets and sand paved alleys, which exude a special charm. I lived at No. 3 Guiyang Street, which was actually a short, dead-end alley, but I loved it. Every evening after dinner, I would take a walk in Dongshan Park and sit for a while on one of the benches, often to watch groups of sprightly young men and pretty young women get off the buses. After a while I would get up and take a walk along the streets and alleys of the Dongshan residential district. Whichever way I went, I would invariably come across bevies of students from a girls' school nearby. Gazing at their elegant postures and winsome ways, I was often gripped by an urge to grasp one of them and hold her to my bosom. The urge was so overwhelming it made me forget the Revolution and the suffering of the oppressed masses. I would scold myself for giving in to my petty bourgeois failings.

But after each self-castigation, I would defend myself, saying that for a young man like me about to turn twenty and still ignorant of the other sex, isn't it natural to be inflamed by a glance or a smile? Who, being a man, would not be tempted? Of course, that kind of self-justification is totally unacceptable. Once you are conscious of guilt, you should stop at once. To be conscious of guilt and still persist down the sinful path is downright perdition! But at the time, that was exactly the predicament that I was caught in. It is a long story. The fact is I became enamored of a young girl whose name I did not even know. I was completely smitten. This infatuation had been fired by something else more offensive, I would even call it pernicious. It all began in September of 1926.

At the time I was sharing a little Western-style building with Zhu Zhixin, a member of the Central Executive Committee (CEC) of the Guomindang. Mr. Zhu, being sickly and mostly bedridden, took the second floor of the building, while I took the third floor. A certain Miss Fan, said to be Mr. Zhu's student, shared the same floor with him. I was broadminded as far as these relationships were concerned. What riled me was a sense of injustice—if this Zhu, in his late forties and sickly to boot, needed female companionship, would I not need it more? Actually Mr. Zhu and Miss Fan had separate rooms. But I suspected that Miss Fan did not spend the night in her own room. Lying alone in bed, sometimes I couldn't sleep and would sneak downstairs. I wasn't trying to catch them in the act, why would I bother? I actually wanted them to be together, so that I could hear the sounds so thrillingly described in Zhang Jingsheng's book on *The History of Sexuality*.[8] Truthfully speaking, in my almost twenty years of life, I had never had any such experience, never knew what it was like—thus my curiosity. Actually it was silly of me to go eavesdropping. Separated by a thick wall and a firmly closed door, how could I have heard anything, whatever it was they were doing! It was precisely during this period that I became addicted to masturbation. But back to my story—it was under the circumstances described above when I was longing for companionship that I met the young lady in my daily walks in Dongshan and became infatuated. To this day I do not know her name, but I was head over heels in love. We ran into each other every

---

8. Zhang Jingsheng (1888–1970), a prominent scholar of the early Republican period. Educated in France, he taught at Peking University and promoted modern ideas of marriage, sexuality, and women's rights.

evening around seven o'clock, as if by appointment. Although we never spoke, I knew that she was also interested in me. But she always showed up in the company of her peers, so I never had the courage to go up and speak to her. Actually, even if she were alone I would not have dared to approach her. Every day before our meeting, I would be in a fever of excitement, planning to go up to her, or at least find out her name and address. But when the moment arrived, I would blush scarlet and my courage would fail me. This went on for a month. Whenever our paths crossed, I would experience a pleasurable sensation never felt before. Every evening, anticipating that thrill, I would hastily eat my supper and rush to Dongshan Park to await the appearance of this unnamed young lady. Sometimes important meetings were scheduled for this hour, but I would always find an excuse to absent myself. Now this was not only wrong, it was downright criminal! For my behavior, I was often chided by my superiors and admonished by my friends. But I was lost in the anticipation of that mysterious sensation and could not rid myself of it, wretch that I was. This continued until November of the same year when the young lady stopped coming.

And now I was about to leave Canton, not knowing when I would ever return to Dongshan for my evening walks. Dear young lady with no name, I wish you happiness to the end of time![9]

III

The Central Executive Committee of the Guomindang (GMD CEC) and the Revolutionary Government were about to leave Canton and move to the tri-city of Wuhan—[comprising Wuchang, Hankou, Hanyang], capital of Hubei Province in south-central China. It had been decided on as early as the past October [1926].

At the time, Jiangxi Province, lying in the path of the projected move, had not yet been taken [by the Revolutionary Army on its Northern Expedition], while Wuchang, one of the tri-cities of Wuhan, had just barely been taken, on October 10 [1926]. The situation being what it was, no specific plans had yet been made regarding the move.

9. See Translator's Note at the end of the book.

Sun Fo

By the end of October, however, the CEC had dispatched Party elders Sun Fo,[10] Madame Soong Qingling,[11] Chen Youren,[12] and others, including Borodin,[13] the Soviet adviser, to Wuhan as well as to Jiangxi

10. Sun Fo (1891–1973), son of Sun Yat-sen. He was a member of the GMD CEC and mayor of Canton for several terms in the 1920s; he was a member of Chiang Kai-shek's government in Nanjing from the 1930s through to the late 1940s, when he retired and left China to live abroad.
11. Soong Qingling (1893–1981) was married to Sun Yat-sen in 1914. After the death of Sun, she supported the GMD-CCP alliance, remained in China after 1949, and was named to nominal positions, including vice-chairman of the PRC.
12. Chen Youren, Eugene Chen (1875–1944), was a Trinidad-born national and a supporter of Sun Yat-sen; he served Sun as adviser on foreign affairs and as his English secretary. Foreign minister in the Revolutionary Government in 1926, Chen successfully negotiated the release of the British concessions in Hankou and Jiujiang.
13. Mikhail Borodin (1884–1951) was born to a Russian-Jewish family, grew up in Latvia, spent time in the United States as a teacher of English to immigrants, returned to Russia after October 1917, and undertook secret assignments for the Comintern in Europe. Borodin reached Canton on October 6, 1923, engineered the GMD-CCP alliance, was named special adviser by Sun Yat-sen and advised the Revolutionary Government under the GMD-CCP alliance. Borodin had to leave China after the break-up of the alliance. Implicated in an American spy case, he was arrested and died in a Siberian labor camp but was later rehabilitated by the Soviet government.

Province, to make on-the-spot feasibility assessments. The decision was handed down on November 20, 1926: we were to leave Canton on December 7, take the train north, passing through the towns of Shaoguan and Nanxiong [moving through Jiangxi Province], to ultimately enter Wuhan.

The decision to move was not without controversy. Arguments in support ran as follows:

First. Now that the provinces of Hubei, Hunan, and Jiangxi have been taken, the arm of the Revolution has extended from the Pearl River delta up to the Yangtze River basin, and will continue to move northward to the Yellow River area. Thus, Hubei Province, located in South-Central China, would be an important base out of reach of the Revolutionary Government situated [to the south] in Canton. Therein lies the need to move northward to Wuhan, in response to the fast developing situation.

Second. The workers' and peasants' movements of Hunan and Hubei provinces have been gaining momentum. Likewise, the peasants in Jiangxi are being mobilized. They need a central authority to provide on-the-ground leadership and direction.

Third. Although the laboring masses in Hunan, Hubei, and Jiangxi are being mobilized, the general population, especially in Wuhan, is still living in fear and uncertainty. Rumors abound of the northern warlord Wu Peifu[14] making a comeback in Hubei and the warlord Sun Chuangfang's[15] occupation of Changsha [capital city of Hunan]. There are even rumors that Sun's men have broken Chiang Kai-shek's leg, all indicators that the Revolutionary Government should be on site in Wuhan to control the situation.

Fourth. The popular revolutionary movement has struck deep roots

14. Wu Peifu (1874–1939), a powerful warlord in Hubei and Hunan during the 1920s, was notorious for the suppression of the Peking-Wuhan railway workers' strike in February 1923.

15. Sun Chuanfang (1885–1935) rose swiftly in the ranks by serving Wu Peifu's Northern faction, and by 1925 he had managed to gain control of the five provinces of Zhejiang, Jiangsu, Anhui, Jiangxi, and Fujian. Sun designated himself commander-in-chief of the Five Allied Armies but was ultimately put down by the GMD-CCP Allied Northern Expeditionary Army.

in Canton, so the move of the Revolutionary Government north to Wuhan will not adversely affect the security of the base in Canton. Arguments against the move:

Wu Peifu

First. Precisely because Wuhan has only recently been taken, the situation is still volatile and the city therefore unsuitable to serve as a revolutionary capital.

Second. Wuhan, given its location, could easily be surrounded by the enemy. Worse, it is vulnerable to economic boycott, which could have disastrous consequences.

Third. The revolutionary base in Canton is not rock solid. Once the Party and government move up north, the situation at the rear is not to be counted on.

Fourth. One argument in favor of moving is that we could always move again if Wuhan proves uncongenial. But such precipitant reversals would surely affect the authority and prestige of the Party and the Revolutionary Government—even a tofu store will pick an auspicious day to make a permanent move.

Both the "pro" party and the "con" party elements had arguments to back up their positions. But the "pros" were in the majority, counting among their supporters such heavyweights as Chiang Kai-shek, Sun

Fo, Deng Yanda,[16] Tang Shengzhi,[17] Zhang Fakui and others, while the "con" party was made up of a handful of nobodies. Now I must say something about myself. At the time, I was just a lowly member of the office staff and often treated as a child on account of my youth. But I do have views and opinions of my own.

Tang Shengzhi

I was against the move, not because of my love for Canton, but for the sake of the Revolution. The highest leading organ of the Revolution should not move hither and thither like a field headquarters and thus be

16. Deng Yanda (1895–1931) started military training at an early age and joined Sun Yat-sen's army. After Sun's death and the assassination of Liao Zhongkai, Deng become the pillar of the GMD Left, leading the Northern Expedition as general political director. He joined Madame Soong Qingling, He Xiangning, and others in obstructing Chiang Kai-shek's attempts to seize power, and was assassinated, possibly on Chiang's orders.
17. Tang Shengzhi (1889–1970) had pursued a military career since his youth and eventually became one of the military strongmen in his native Hunan. In 1926 Tang worked with the GMD-CCP allied government in Wuhan and led the Northern Expedition into Henan. Throughout the 1930s and 1940s, he had complicated relations with the Chiang Kai-shek government in Nanjing. In 1949, Tang, working with other military leaders, staged a coup which enabled the peaceful takeover of Hunan by the CCP. He held honorary positions in the PRC until his death in 1970.

dependent on the moves of the army. The reasons for our revolutionary center to stay put in Canton were as sound as those for moving north. The goal of the Revolution is not to stake out territory, it is to liberate the masses. The question is how. The answer is to set up revolutionary state power and consolidate a revolutionary base. And where was our base? In Canton, of course! And was our base consolidated? Certainly not! The revolutionary base in Canton was made up of the seventy-to-eighty thousand striking workers of Canton and Hong Kong. Next, there were 800,000 organized peasants, whose organizations were loose and scattered compared to the striking workers. At the same time there were thirty million *unorganized* peasants in the province of Guangdong alone, of which the 800,000 organized peasants constituted a mere two percent!

We must remember that the landlord classes in Guangdong Province held sway in the vast countryside, and thus the peasants had not been able to set up any power structures of their own. The Guangdong provincial government itself was in the hands of the landowning classes despite the National Revolutionary Government's presence in Canton. The head of the Guangdong provincial government was the notorious Gu Yingfeng—and all the magistrates of the various counties were in his pocket. This bunch had completely disregarded the GMD program to "support workers and peasants." It is owing to the physical presence of the Party Central Executive Committee and the Revolutionary Government in Canton, *which at the moment was controlled by the Left Wing*, that the local despots had not yet closed down all the peasants' organizations and publicly executed their leaders—though in some places they had already done so—according to reports coming in daily from Zhongshan, Kuangning, Huaxian, Puning and other counties.

The army left behind in Guangdong Province would be in the hands of Li Fulin of the Fifth Army and Li Jishen[18] of the Fourth, all

18. Li Jishen (1885–1959) was a high-ranking GMD military leader and at one time vice-commandant of the Whampoa Military Academy. Li survived an off-and-on relationship with Chiang Kai-sek until 1949, when he founded the GMD Revolutionary Committee and cooperated with the CCP, holding the position of vice-chairman of the People's Republic of China.

defenders of landlord interests. The latter actually took upon himself the powers of a commander-in-chief, overriding the Revolutionary Government. For instance, the government would now and then send out a "resolution," a "manifesto," or a cable in support of workers and peasants, but Li would put down all popular movements in the name of "security at the rear." Meanwhile, Li's own hysterical proclamations would be posted from Canton all the way to the outlying counties, even down to the villages. Such proclamations invariably prohibited workers' strikes and peasants' demands to lower rents and taxes, all in the name of consolidating "security at the rear." But thanks to the presence of the Party CEC and the Revolutionary Government in Canton, Li Fulin, Li Jishen, and company had so far not dared to execute worker and peasant leaders in the public square as "bandits." In a word, our revolutionary base in Canton was being threatened by crises on all sides. Therefore I felt that our top priority was to consolidate our revolutionary base by hitting back at the reactionary forces within the province, especially the landlord classes. If we moved precipitately to Wuhan, we would leave Canton exposed to the vengeance of all the reactionaries, while at the same time we would be confronted by hostile forces ahead. Under such circumstances, even if we succeeded in setting up a new base in Wuhan, it would be at the price of losing Canton. The above were my arguments against leaving Canton.

Furthermore, there were equally strong reasons against setting up our revolutionary capital in Wuhan. Canton is a seaport city; if the British imposed an economic blockade, there are other ports in Guangdong. But we cannot say the same for Wuhan. Wuhan is an inland city. Its economic lifeline is the Yangtze River, linking it southward to Shanghai by river and northward to Peking by the Peking-Wuhan railway. Blockading the river (which would have been relatively easy to effect) and cutting off the railway line (which was often plagued by stoppages already) would effectively shut down the city. Wuhan consumes forty to fifty tons of coal monthly, eight-five percent of which comes by river from Shanghai, the rest from Peking by rail transport. Once out of coal, the Hanyang Arsenal as well as other industrial plants would shut down. Meanwhile, the urban population would be out of coal, kerosene and rice, the last two being exclusively transported by the river route. In a word, the consequences would be disastrous beyond imagination. Besides, Wuhan is closely tied to the Shanghai financial markets. If the river route were blockaded, the products of the interior regions, which rely on Wuhan for transshipment, would be choked off, causing financial loss to Wuhan. Once we were stuck in Wuhan, our enemies would not need to attack us from all sides—economic blockade alone would paralyze us.

Thus we should not set up a new revolutionary capital in Wuhan. To meet the needs of the growing revolutionary movement, we could set up a high-level command center in Wuhan. Why rush to move the Party CEC and the Revolutionary Government? The above were my reasons against moving to Wuhan. But having no say in the matter, I kept my opinions to myself.

IV

The decision for the move to Wuhan was made. Well, so be it. At least we young fellows would get a change of scene. It was decided that all Party CEC and government personnel should be prepaid one month's salary, a 100-*yuan* allowance for a new outfit, and a transportation allowance of 100 *yuan* for travel by rail and seventy *yuan* by boat. Meanwhile, Party CEC personnel were to head for Wuhan by railway, cutting through Jiangxi Province. That was lucky for me, getting the bigger stipend. Actually, I had hoped to go by boat and make a stop in Shanghai to see old friends. But it was not to be. I was not afraid of the warlord Sun Chuanfang's hooligans on the Bund. No, I could not travel by boat because I was strapped with a new job. I was appointed head of the Propaganda Section of the Military Affairs Department of the GMD CEC. It had happened on the spur of the moment.

The fact was, moving the Party CEC and the seat of government to set up a new capital was a major event and should be heralded with a lot of publicity and propaganda. But there we were up against a problem. It's a long story.

At the time, the head of the Party CEC Propaganda Department was the notorious *Mr. Slack.*

Wang Jingwei[19] had been head of the Propaganda Department. But after the Zhongshan Gunboat Incident,[20] Wang had to keep a low profile and so left for France; Mao Zedong was deputized to take his place. Then followed the May Fifteenth Decision,[21] which decided that comrades with GMD and CCP dual membership should not hold GMD positions. Thus Mao was disqualified and *Mr. Slack* appointed in his place.

On taking office *Mr. Slack* removed all current personnel and filled the vacancies with his own men. This may be the practice in Peking, but it did not sit well with us here. And there had been some unpleasantness. Not to mention the fact that *Mr. Slack's* sycophants did not do a bit of work, apart from the feat of getting themselves cozily installed. To complicate matters, none of the other departments in the Party CEC or the Revolutionary Government had been staffed with propaganda personnel to do the work of *Mr. Slack,* now that propaganda work was called for.

To get around the problem, the CEC Military Affairs Department, where I was serving at the time, decided to set up a Propaganda Section of its own, and I was appointed head of this newly created section. A propaganda team was also created to conduct propaganda work en

19. Wang Jingwei (1883–1944), an early associate of Sun Yat-sen, had held top positions in the GMD during the GMD-CCP alliance, representing the GMD Left from 1923 to 1927. He then broke with the CCP and joined Chiang Kai-shek's government in Nanjing (1928–1937). In 1940, Wang became titular head of the Japanese puppet regime in Nanjing, while Chiang's GMD government retreated to Chongqing in southwest China.
20. On March 20, 1926, the gunboat *Zhongshan,* commanded by a CCP captain, appeared near Whampoa Island. Chiang Kai-shek used the incident to proclaim martial law in Canton, and thereby dealt a blow to the CCP forces within the GMD-CCP alliance.
21. Known as "The Purge" of May 1926. At a meeting of the GMD Central Executive Committee on May 15, it was decided that no CCP member should be chairman of the CEC or head of any GMD department, and that a list of CCP members with dual GMD-CCP membership should be submitted to the GMD.

route as the Party and the Revolutionary Government made their way northward. Try as I would, I could not get out of the appointment, and thus were dashed my hopes of sailing by the Shanghai route. We had spent five days making preparations and were expected to leave by five in the morning on December 7. This was to be my last night in Canton. I was dead tired after five days' packing and dealing with the inevitable courtesies and formalities of parting. Yet after that noisy send-off party, I was not ready for sleep, and had dallied in a rowboat on the Pearl River until midnight. When I finally returned to the office after midnight, I found that many of our people had taken away their belongings, getting ready to leave. So I returned to my lodgings and brought out my things too.

At daybreak, we started off for the harbor, where the steamboats of the Great Southern Pacific Co. were chartered to take us to the Yellow Sand Railway Station on the other side of the city. It was still early, and Mr. Mao and I stood on the wharf idly looking around. Groups of well-wishers carrying banners flocked to the station to say goodbye.

A group of young ladies from the Women's Movement Training Institute stood out conspicuously, waving a sign bidding farewell to their director, Madame He Xiangning.[22] In a playful mood, I called out to them: "Hey, how come you only give send-off wishes to your director and not to the rest of us? That's not fair!" They tittered without answering me. In fact, I had just given a talk at their Institute a couple of days before, the only time I had been in their classrooms. The minute I walked in, they had started giggling. Their Institute was situated within the office compound of the Party CEC; I used to run into them during office hours and had even been an invited guest at the inauguration of their Institute. Even so, every time we met, they would "blush and lower their gaze," like the maiden in *Romance of the*

22. He Xiangning (1879–1972) was among the first generation of Chinese women to receive a higher education. She was a revolutionary, an artist, and the wife of Liao Zhongkai. She worked ceaselessly to help uphold Sun Yat-sen's legacy on many fronts, remained on the mainland after 1949, and held honorary positions, as well as leaving a rich heritage of paintings.

Western Bower.[23] These young ladies and young matrons, presumably the liberal-minded vanguard among women, had been selected from the grass roots for study at the Institute. Yet they always acted shy when they ran into me. I wondered if they did the same with other young men. It is so hard to break down the sex barrier, and this is only *one* of the problems facing the Revolution. Anyway, we all got on board, and set sail to the strains of a marching band. The Yellow Sand Railway Station, where we arrived shortly, was also swirling with people waiting to give us a send-off. Two carriages were designated for our use, and we all scrambled on board. I had to make an appearance at the reception area within the station itself, to meet with representatives of the locals who had come to see us off. Finally our train chugged away to the strain of martial music and the popping of firecrackers. Once out of the noisy little railway station, our train picked up speed, leaving Canton and all its memories behind. Softly, again, I repeated to myself Gao Yuhan's poem "Drifting in on the Whampoa River":

> Reading the Lamentations and listening to the plaintive reed pipe,
> Gazing at the ripples entangled like silver snakes,
> I have lived here through three moons,
> And now a strip of water cuts me off, exiling me to the ends of
> the earth.

Although I was on a train on solid ground, not on a boat on a river, I was deeply moved by this poem on the pain of parting from a beloved place.

V

Through a combination of circumstances, this was actually the *second* time that I was taking the train from Canton to Shaoguan. The little towns en route—Yuantang, Yingde, Liling, and others—all looked familiar.

The fact was, I had made a brief trip to Shaoguan the previous July when someone had recommended me for a position at the Political

---

23. *Romance of the Western Bower* (Xixiang ji) is a famous play with a romantic theme written by Wang Shifu (1250–1337?) of the Yuan dynasty.

Department of Cheng Qian's Sixth Army, which was about to move to Shaoguan. But it had not worked out. At the time, I had immediately reported to Lin Zuhan, director of the Political Department of the Sixth Army. Lin and I had known each other from the old days, so I was shocked by his attitude at that meeting. Without any preliminaries, he demanded to know why I always locked horns with Mao Zedong! He proceeded to lecture me on the correct way to handle relationships, deploring my hotheadedness, and suggesting that I improve my social manners. Then he ordered me to pack up and leave for Shaoguan with the Sixth Army. I value admonition from my elders, but that harangue was completely unjustified and humiliating as well. However, I still packed and left in the retinue of the Sixth Army. On arrival in Shaoguan, I was further shocked at the insufferable airs of a certain Secretary Li. Enough was enough, I decided. I turned around and headed back to Canton. That was the long and short of my previous trip to and from Shaoguan on the north-south railway.

Politically as well as economically speaking, Shaoguan, on the North River, is an important route northward in Guangdong Province. Goods from central Hunan as well as from south-central Jiangxi pass through Shaoguan to reach the seaport at Canton. Likewise, imported goods [from Canton] must go through Shaoguan before they can be distributed to their destinations in Hunan and Jiangxi. Shaoguan's economy should be highly developed; in fact it does not compare to a third-rate town in my native Zhejiang. There is no modern industry, and obsolete handicrafts dominate. Imported products do have a limited market, but people still depend on local handmade goods for the daily necessities of life. Though considered strategically invulnerable, Shaoguan itself is a poky little town; its lanes laid with stone slabs can hardly accommodate a horse-drawn carriage. Water is drawn from the North River in buckets and carried into town by an unending line of shoulder-pole carriers. The dark, narrow streets are wet and slippery all year round from those sloshing buckets. Electricity is out of the question. By eight in the evening, the whole town shuts down with no signs of life.

Nowadays, certain individuals go around saying that capitalism is highly developed in China and that feudalism is fading away. But as demonstrated in Shaoguan, agriculture and handicrafts dominate the local economy. There is not much evidence of capitalism. And why is Shaoguan's economy so backward? The answer lies in feudal exploitation. The feudal form of exploitation is twofold: on the one hand the tenant farmer has to give up fifty percent of his crops to the landlord, while on the other hand warlords and local despots further tax them mercilessly. They hand down quotas for the purchase of bonds, for example. Township and county officials then clap these quotas onto additional mandatory quotas, and more on top of that, onto the shoulders of the peasants. The local people barely manage to keep body and soul together and can hardly spare a copper for a box of matches. And thus the economy atrophies. In contrast to the economy, however, the scenery in Shaoguan is entrancing. The North River flows outside the city gates. Once you get off the train, you must cross the river to get into town. The best spot for a panoramic view is at the foot of the city wall hard by the river. The North River is wide, flanked on both sides by embankments of sand flecked with lovely multicolored pebbles. From the vantage point of the town wall, the scenes across the river spread out like a watercolor painting. On the right is a hill, with a battered temple clinging to its side and a crumbling pagoda perched on top. If you stay on the other side of the river, near the railway station, you face the ramparts of the ancient town wall, with pennants flapping in the wind, conjuring up the image of an "ancient town, a deserted battlefield," as commonly described in classical poetry. A flight of seagulls soaring from the ancient wall to the hilltop, from the hilltop to the temple, and from the temple to the pagoda draw a line in the air to form a picture. I love the quiet beauty of the scene, more attractive than the lush beauty of West Lake in my native parts. When I first arrived in Shaoguan on that unfortunate job assignment the previous July, there had been a full moon, and I had caroused with friends on the sandy beach under the moonlight before heading back to Canton. This time there was no moon. During this layover in Shaoguan, Mr. Mao Zedong and I spent a day together enjoying the sights and sounds of the town. At the time Mao was the head of the Organization Section of the Military Affairs Department [while I was the newly appointed head of the Propaganda Section]. We had been colleagues for the last few months and got along very well. He carried a camera so we took many pictures.

When our group first started off from Canton, we thought that we would have to walk the rest of the way after Shaoguan. So we were all in uniform, shod in straw sandals, and only carrying small items on our persons, leaving our luggage at the army depot. But by the evening of the second day of our arrival, we were told that we would set sail for Jiangxi Province on the ninth, two days after our departure from Canton on December 7, 1926.

VI

It had been five or six years since I had traveled aboard a sampan, so this trip by boat to Jiangxi was something of a novelty. Each boat accommodated twenty to thirty people, making for quite a squeeze. But we officers had our privileges. Six or seven of us spread out our bedrolls side by side to make a big communal bed, taking up all the available space. Our orderlies, however, had a hard time of it. They had no fixed spot for rest, barely enough for standing room. Even so, they had to serve us hand and foot. When provoked, we officers would lash out at them, sometimes even using our fists. Officers' monthly salaries ranged from eighty *yuan* upward and could run into the hundreds, while orderlies were paid seven or eight *yuan*, never exceeding twelve. According to the theory, all men are equal—but officers and orderlies actually live worlds apart. We chant revolutionary slogans, we write revolutionary essays, we claim to work for the masses, to lift them out of oppression. Now aren't those orderlies members of the oppressed masses? How do we explain our behavior toward them?

Our boat gliding along the North River was quite a treat, really, though the lack of speed was annoying. My thoughts wandered from sailboats to steamboats to motorcars, and then flew off on a tangent to Tagore,[24] the old man [from India] who was opposed to all material

24. Rabindranath Tagore, Nobel Prize winning Indian poet who visited China in 1923 and lectured on nonviolence and self-sufficient rural communities, among other topics.

wealth. Nowadays, a number of Tagore's disciples have cropped up in China, promoting so-called Oriental civilization and culture, opposing all forms of materialism. A bunch of blockheads who know nothing about the enjoyment of life!

Motorcars are certainly superior to Zhuge Liang's[25] wooden four-wheeled cart, modern houses certainly more comfortable than thatched-roof huts. Why should we give up modern houses for huts? Why should we give up motorcars for wooden four-wheeled carts? We are against the capitalist system, not against the material wealth produced under that system. We are against the capitalist system under which material wealth is exclusively enjoyed by the ruling class. We propose that this wealth be enjoyed by the whole society. It was never the goal of the Revolution to oppose, much less destroy, material wealth; on the contrary, our goal is to raise the level of productivity of material wealth for the enjoyment of the whole society. After the victory of the Revolution, we should work harder than ever to build material wealth. We know perfectly well that modern houses are more comfortable than thatched-roof huts, that electric lighting is stronger than candlelight; we know that in the heat of summer it is not the "cultural civilization" that will cool us down, but the fan and the man-made air-conditioner will. When the temperature drops to twenty below zero centigrade, the so-called "cultural civilization" will not keep us warm, but the electric stove and thick walls will. "Cultural civilization" cannot connect us to our friends from afar, but the radio links up London and Shanghai in a couple of seconds. Material wealth is not the enemy: it is the goal of the Revolution that all men enjoy the fruits of material wealth. We want all men to live in comfortable modern houses, we want every one living in the country to have electric lighting, to enjoy the comforts of the city, perhaps even to attain a state when men and women can live forever, like the gods. It is not an empty dream, but it can only be realized in a highly developed society which can put into practice the

25. Zhuge Liang, or Kong-Ming, one of the main characters in the classic Chinese historical novel *Romance of the Three Kingdoms* (San guo yanyi), in which Zhuge Liang was military adviser to Liu Bei, and later prime minister of the kingdom of Chu.

principle *"from each according to his ability, to each according to his needs."* People usually think of the Revolution in terms of destruction; it just goes to show that they do not understand the Revolution.

Accustomed to the mild weather of Canton, I was dreading the cold up north. Shaoguan, our first stop, had already given me a taste of the northern chill, and now that we were heading farther north, the cold was making me shiver. Being on a boat made matters worse, as the wind off the river felt like daggers on our cheeks. It made me miss Canton and the amenities of a modern city all the more keenly.

Among personnel from the various departments of the GMD CEC traveling in our group was the acting president of the Revolutionary Government himself—Tan Yankai![26] This explains the high level of security, which consisted of the Presidential Guards of the Revolutionary Government, two platoons from the Canton Military Police, as well as a secret service detail dispatched by Chen Jiayou, commander of the division now stationed in Shaoguan. At first we felt that being on our own territory this excessive security was just a show in keeping with the move of the seat of government. Little did we know that such a show of force was hardly enough when we really needed protection. On the afternoon of the third day since setting sail from Shaoguan, all the boats suddenly stopped at the foot of a hill. It was barely three in the afternoon. We felt that something must be wrong. It turned out that a dozen or so *li*[27] farther upstream was a bandit holdout. Sailing past it by night, not to mention mooring nearby, was out of the question. Thus, we had to wait for morning in order to proceed. We were shocked that bandits on the North River could operate so freely in Nationalist territory. Since it was mid-afternoon, we clambered ashore and enjoyed ourselves scrambling up and down the hills nearby. Female comrades

26. Tan Yankai (1880–1930), a native of Hunan Province, Tan navigated his way through the power struggle of local politics in his native Hunan before he joined the GMD and achieved a position in the Revolutionary Government and the army. In 1927, during the breakup of the GMD-CCP alliance, Tan went over to Chiang Kai-shek and held military and administrative positions, including head of the Administrative Yuan and acting president.

27. One *li*, Chinese traditional measurement of length, equal to one-half kilometer (1.609 kilometers=one mile).

from the Department of Women joined us, hopping nimbly from rock to rock in their straw sandals.

Speaking of female comrades, I must own up to the fact that throughout the entire duration of this boat trip they had consumed our minds and had been our main topic of conversation.

What intrigued us first and foremost were their sleeping arrangements. After thrashing out all sides of the question, we still could not figure out how they arranged their bedding at night. The problem was that in addition to these four young women, there were several young men from the Peasants' Department and the Secretariat on their boat. Did they spread their bedrolls side by side as we did, forming a big communal bed? To get to the bottom of this question, we dispatched a "spy" from our boat to uncover the mystery. Our "spy" returned from his mission and duly made his report: men and women spread their bedrolls side by side and slept side by side, exactly as we did. Not only that, but one female comrade, a secretary, actually shared a blanket with a male officer. It was already midnight, but we sat up and listened rapt with attention. We wondered if those men and women lying side by side had "slept" in the way so graphically described by Zhang Jingsheng. I had brought the book with me, and it turned out that six among the eleven of us on that boat had brought the same book! But digging further into the question depressed us, as we became keenly aware that that such sexual felicity was beyond our reach. What intrigued us next was the question of how these women relieved themselves. There were no buckets or any other kind of accommodation for the purpose. To move your bowels, you must go to the edge of the plank, turn your trousers all the way down, squat on the edge of the plank and empty your bowels directly into the river. Your frontal private parts may be hidden, yet you could hardly avoid exposing your cleft bottom to public view. I myself would always wait until no one was around to open my fly to piss into the river. If I, a young man, found it so embarrassing, then how did those young women cope?

Apart from the problems of sleeping and shitting, tales of the romantic escapades of some of the young women made the rounds among the boats. It was said that a female secretary at the CEC had a lover who was also a secretary, but in the Revolutionary Government. A few days before we were due to start on our trip, a local Canton paper had broken a story under the screaming headline: "A Disgrace for Party and for Government." According to the report, the female secretary in our group and her lover had been caught in the act by the man's wife, in broad daylight no less, and that there had been a scene. But the female secretary's romance did not stop there. The story goes that apart from the government secretary, this lady had two other lovers, and the three took turns sleeping with her, each given his own time slot. The first, by virtue of his office as secretary, had first right to her favors in the daytime. By night he needed to fulfill his conjugal duties. The second lover was a clerk at the CEC; his time slot was from eight in the evening to midnight. His wife, being a countrywoman, was not in a position to complain. The third lover was a proofreader in the newspaper office. His designated time slot was from midnight to six o'clock in the morning. He had no wife, but proofreading kept him busy until midnight. So he would arrive after midnight, when the female secretary had taken a break after her second bout with the clerk. Thus the story ran that our female comrade would wrestle with the secretary, the clerk, and the proofreader in a nightly merry-go-round. It was indeed as the saying goes: "*From each according to his/her ability: the more capable, the more you perform.*" I report this not to disparage the female secretary or to pursue a steamy story. According to my view, she was not a disgrace but a glory to the government and the Party. We should be proud of these heroines that surpass Pan Jinlian[28] and Pan Qiaoyun[29] of legendary fame. It means that some of us have overcome the bounds of feudal ideology. Others—the ideologically backward—might consider sexual relations as something unmentionable, but it is actually a glorious act. I hold that the more lovers a woman enjoys, the

28. Pan Jinlian, a character in the classic historical novel *Heroes of the Marsh* (Shuihu zhuan). The adulterous Pan poisons her husband and is later killed by Wu Song, her husband's younger brother.

29. Pan Qiaoyun, another character in *Heroes of the Marsh*, wherein the adulterous Pan Qiaoyun sowed discord between her husband and his friend and was killed by her husband.

more glory to her. As to wrestling day and night with members of the opposite sex without fear of public opprobrium, as in the case of the female secretary, I consider her nothing less than a heroine. I support free and open relationships between the sexes. I say this not to shock, but because I believe that only open and free sex is in keeping with the very nature of human beings. For humanity to be truly liberated, sex among humans should be as free and open as between all other creatures of Nature. Sex-related crimes such as rape and murder, or ill-health induced by over-indulgence in sex, can all be traced back to the bigoted attitude toward sex, which is especially solidified in the concept of virginity. If man could satisfy his sexual appetite any time anywhere, then there would be no need to overindulge when sex is available. All the above problems are the result of the mystification of sex. Another reason for promoting free and open sex is to use it as a weapon to demolish feudal ideology, make a clean sweep of feudal concepts, and strike down all archaic moral standards and outdated rules of behavior.

VII

On the morning of December 15, after seven days' sailing, we arrived at Nanxiong, a major town on the bank of the North River, next only to Shaoguan in size and consequence. On the border of Guangdong Province, Nanxiong is close to Jiangxi and an outlet into Guangdong for such local Jiangxi products as medicinal herbs, china, rice paper, grass cloth, and other products, to be marketed locally or for export. Such was the importance of Nanxiong for the local economy. We wandered around town and came upon the local attraction—a stone slab carved with six calligraphic characters:

Foremost City South of Ling Mountain

But Nanxiong itself was disappointing. The streets were even narrower than those of Shaoguan, and sloppy from the previous day's rain. Being the key transportation link between the two provinces of Guangdong and Jiangxi, the town was replete with small inns, but you could hardly find a place to sit down to a decent meal. Transportation was arduous: the trip from Shaoguan, which we had just left, to Nanxiong was only doable by old-style sailboats, as we knew from our own experience. Farther on, the 120-odd *li from* Nanxiong to Nan'an, our next stop, was blocked by the Dayu Mountain range. Transportation of goods relied exclusively on manpower—the shoulder pole. There were at least ten thousand men working as carriers between the two towns, further living proof that industrial manufactoring was nonexistent, and transportation miserably backward. The economy is made up of small-scale handicraftsmen—shoemakers, ironmongers, carpenters, bamboo craftsmen, tailors, barbers and such, surviving as they had done for thousands of years. Yet Nanxiong, as well as Shaoguan, were considered major towns—one can imagine what the surrounding rural areas were like.

En route from Shaoguan to Nanxiong, we conducted some social investigation. We found that:

One, most of the peasant population were tenants;

Two, tenants must surrender to landlords sixty to seventy-five percent of their crops;

Three, most tenants pay rent in grain—very few pay in cash;

Four, apart from rent in the form of grain, tenants have to offer gifts of chickens or ducks to landlords during the traditional festivals and do unpaid labor during assigned periods;

Five, landlords dominate in the countryside, and peasants' associations are suppressed and have no say in local affairs;

Six, peasants live at subsistence level.

The above observations apply to the countryside of all three counties we had passed through. It is obvious that conditions have remained unchanged for hundreds if not thousands of years. Some people claim that capitalism is making headway in China. Our investigation has totally disproved this view. Apart from what we have already seen, it must be added that all agriculture in the above three counties is still part of a natural economy that relies on manual labor.

The GMD Nanxiong branch Congress took place on the day of our arrival, and I attended and gave a speech in my capacity as a representative of the Party CEC. I was favorably impressed by what

I saw. Attendance was of course dominated by the educated classes, but workingmen in their coarse working clothes were conspicuously represented and lent a special luster to the gathering. Only in Canton had I ever seen such a sizable representation of the working class, and even that was only at peasants' or workers' own associations, never at a Party Congress. I was deeply moved by the sight.

That same evening, I attended a party held in conjunction with the Congress and was given a warm welcome. At the party, I came across a lovely young female comrade. She had lived for four years in Peking as well as six months in Nanjing, and she spoke perfect Mandarin. We were in earnest conversation for the best part of the evening. Then the party ended and we parted, never to meet again. We stayed another day in Nanxiong. I gave a speech at the No. 6 Middle School. Attendance was sparse; I did not feel inspired, nor was I inspiring. We went to see the town, but there was not much to see. There was a little garden called Sun Yat-sen Park perched on top of the city ramparts. A statue of Buddha greeted us at the entrance to an open pavilion surrounded by little flowerbeds. It was nothing extraordinary but quite impressive for such a small town. On the morning of December 17, we left Nanxiong for the Dayu Mountain Range. That was our last day on Guangdong soil. Once over the mountains, we would be in Jiangxi Province. Dayu Mountain (also known as Plum Rose Mountain) is a famous scenic spot, best known for the beauty of the plum rose. Spring arrives earlier than elsewhere for the plum blossoms on Dayu Mountain. It was December, the tenth month of the lunar calendar, but we were told that the plum blossoms were already in bloom. We were very excited and eager to ascend the mountain.

From where we were in Nanxiong to the foot of the Dayu Mountain was a distance of 100 *li*. Once over the mountain, there would be another ten *li* to reach the town of Nan'an. Taking into account the trek up the mountain—an extra ten *li*—the whole distance from Nanxiong to Nan'an would be roughly a 120 *li*. There was no waterway. The locals had already prepared sedan chairs to carry us over the mountain. But having been confined to the boats for so long, we decided to use our own two legs to scale the mountain and reach Nan'an on the other side.

The road across the plain was smooth, with not a village in sight, except for little clusters of dilapidated hovels. After walking a few hours, we came across a village where we were able to buy wine and some rice, but no proper dishes. We had to make do with peanuts, cabbage, and tofu to go down with the wine. Other things that the locals rounded up were inedible. I was ashamed of myself. Here we were, shouting slogans, urging others to go down to the masses, but in truth we were but revolutionary aristocrats. Compared to the vast majority of the Chinese people, most of whom were living at subsistence level, the likes of us deserve to be taken down a peg or two. By late afternoon, we arrived at a village a mere twenty *li* from the foot of the mountain. In the village there was a Peasants' Association and an elementary school named the Lenin Elementary School. Interesting. We made for the office of the Peasants' Association. On the wall of the office as we entered we saw an unusual painting which was obviously meant to be satirical. On one side of the wide canvas was the drawing of a park, captioned "World Revolutionary Park," and within the blank space in the park were drawn two figures set on supporting stands, one figure captioned "Marx," the other captioned "Lenin." Beside those two figures, there was an empty stand, unoccupied by any figure. Opposite the "World Revolutionary Park" in the picture was a drawing of a Confucian temple. In the middle of the canvas, between the World Revolutionary Park and the Confucian Temple stood a man in a Sun Yat-sen suit, carrying a statue of Sun Yat-sen on his back and walking toward the Confucian Temple. Under this figure was a caption: "Sun Yat-sen belongs to the World Revolutionary Park, but Dai[30] is forcibly taking him to the Confucian Temple."

Strictly speaking, the message of the painting was untenable. The question of which historical figure belongs where should only be decided by the actions of the said person and not be determined by

30. The translator conjectures that this refers to Dai Jitao (1891–1949), an early theorist of the GMD and highly regarded by Sun Yat-sen. He was elected to the GMD CEC in 1924 and served as head of Propaganda. After the death of Sun Yat-sen, Dai joined the conservative Western Hills group and later served as adviser to Chiang Kai-shek. He committed suicide in February of 1949.

anyone else. Even so, it was an interesting picture. By evening we had arrived at the foot of Dayu Mountain. After a hasty meal at a little eatery, we started climbing. The path to the summit was cut out of the slope, smooth and wide, flanked by tall trees on either side. Night had descended and the moon cast a distant light upon the scene. Singing and shouting, we were elated beyond words. Halfway up the mountain, the breeze wafted the scent of plum roses toward us and, lo and behold, the apparition of red and white plum roses appeared, taking my breath away. We had arrived at the famous "Plum Rose Pass"—a tablet engraved with the three calligraphic characters shimmered in the moonlight. There were more plum roses farther up the Pass, beautiful white plum roses. As we went through the Pass, we saw another larger stone tablet carved with four characters:

Plum Rose Country Revisited

We could not make out the smaller characters carved at the edge, however. Within the Pass was an open pavilion where we stopped to catch our breath. The top of the Pass is where the two provinces of Guangdong and Jiangxi meet. I placed my two feet firmly on the spot and looked around. It was a high point of my life. Here was I, my left foot planted on Guangdong soil, my right foot treading Jiangxi territory. Further ahead lay the province of Hunan, while not far back in the distance was the province of Fujian. There was I, overlooking four provinces of our country. As I cast my eyes over the undulating mountain range, for a moment I felt myself lord of all I surveyed. Here was I, high in a mountain pass, surrounded by white plum roses, under a shimmering moon. What a scene, what a moment! I could not help incanting in a loud voice:

> A once-in-a-lifetime moment, which is not to last,
> Where will I see this moon again next year?

It was getting late, but none of us could bear to leave. There was still a last stretch of about ten *li* before we would reach Nan'an, north of the mountain. Regretfully we made our way down. We reached the town of Nan'an by midnight and immediately boarded the waiting boats, setting off early the next morning along the Gan River, having seen nothing of the town of Nan'an.

VIII

On December 18, 1926, our boat set sail for Ganzhou; we were now in Jiangxi territory. Perhaps it was just my imagination, but I was deeply struck by the difference between the two provinces in everything I laid eyes on: the sights and sounds of the town, the locals, even the scenery drove home the difference and made me miss Canton. It was twelve days since we had left that city. As long as we were still in Guangdong Province, I did not miss Canton so much, but now that we were in Jiangxi Province, moving farther and farther away with each passing day, I looked backward and felt keenly that one strip of water cutting me off from Canton.

The scenery on either side of the Gan River was lovely, somewhat similar to my own native region south of the Yangtze River. Unfortunately, by now we were short of time and had to keep moving. We hastened past villages, townships, and towns unseen and unremembered.

Now let me go back a little and talk about our work. I was head of the Propaganda Section and had a budget of several thousand *yuan* for propaganda purposes. We had printed magazines, posters, pamphlets, sheets, and declarations for distribution, and had laid out elaborate plans for propaganda work en route to Wuhan. But I am ashamed to admit that apart from distributing the printed material at every stop, all we did was mouth a few speeches by rote. As for these mechanically repeated speeches, it was questionable whether our audience ever understood a word. The situation got worse after we had crossed the mountain, when we became even more dilatory. As work slackened, we threw ourselves into gambling: poker, dice, varieties of Chinese games, excepting mahjong, which was too unwieldy to handle in the crowded boat.

Gambling and the female sex: those were our two consuming interests. Stuck on the boat, we gambled day and night. For the gambling addict, winning was not the point. I had long since lost all sense of private property; money meant nothing to me. I just enjoyed the game, especially on that boring boat ride. At first we played poker, then quickly turned to Chinese games of dice in pursuit of more excitement. Our gambling would reach a feverish pitch as the night progressed. Such goings-on were not limited to our group, but we seemed to have been the most abandoned in our gaming. It was unforgivable, of course, but considering the circumstances, understandable. We were young, we needed action, but we were stuck on the boat day and night with hardly any space to move. Moreover, it was very cold. In the first leg of our boat ride, from Shaoguan to Nanxiong, our only relaxation had been reading Zhang Jingsheng's book on sexuality and talking about sex. Our sexual urge having no outlet in the environs of the boat, inevitably we resorted to unnatural satisfaction. Rampant masturbation led to an unnatural expenditure of energy that weakened our bodies. Therefore, on the day we reached Nanxiong, we made a collective decision to throw all our copies of Zhang Jingsheng's book into the water and never talk about sex again. Not reading Zhang's book, and not talking about sex made life more boring still and thus we bought more gambling paraphernalia in Nanxiong as soon as we had gotten rid of the books. But back to the account of our trip. On the evening of December 21 we set sail and arrived in Ganzhou after four days. It was night, and raining, but we were so desperate for a change of scene that we went ashore anyway. There was not much to see. Ganzhou was the most important and economically developed city in south Jiangxi, but we roamed the streets without finding a decent place for a sit down meal. Finally we were shown up to a dirty room above a small eatery. The dishes, however, were tasty, and we ate and drank to our hearts' content before heading back to our boat.

The next morning, we went ashore again, this time to conduct social work among the masses. One of our teams had already done some preliminary investigation, so we knew that the town boasted four high schools and four newspapers. We headed straight for No. 4 High School. Unfortunately, classes were in recess. We then tried the South Jiangxi High School and the other schools, but they were all closed. We had better luck at a girls' elementary school, where I gave a little speech. Although an elementary school, many of the students were already young ladies, some of whom were probably engaged to be married.

In the afternoon, after a meal, we looked up the offices of the local newspapers, beginning with the *South Jiangxi Daily*. The editor requested a calligraphic inscription to commemorate the occasion of our visit, and I gladly obliged. We were happily surprised by the elevated state of culture and education in this small inland town with four middle schools and four newspapers. It was outstanding, considering the general backwardness. The Commercial Press and the Zhonghua Book Company, both nationally known names in publishing, had branches here. There were also two other bookstores, which carried periodicals old and new. I was surprised that *Weekly Guide*[31] and *China Youth*[32] were both available. In answer to our inquiries, the clerk answered that the *Weekly Guide* sold seventy to eighty copies regularly while *China Youth* sold fifty to sixty copies. He added that in the past they had been mailed directly from Shanghai but since the resumption of war they had to be mailed from Canton. Apart from the above, some exclusively pro-GMD periodicals also had a following here, we were told. Jiangxi Province was culturally developed but economically very backward. There was no industry to speak of, much less modern industry. There were only two streets in Ganzhou worthy of the name. A few shops sold imported Western goods or local delicacies of dried fruit. And there were a few Chinese herbal medicine pharmacies. That was it.

One striking aspect of Ganzhou was the organization of craftsmen. We visited the headquarters of the Provisional Committee of the Ganzhou Workers' Union and were met by a robust looking middle-aged man, Mr. Xiao, a member of the Standing Committee. Mr. Xiao, a carpenter by trade, was well informed, levelheaded, and talked like a seasoned politician. The workers of Ganzhou were lucky to have such a leader. Mr. Xiao gave us a detailed account of the state of the workers' movement and their plans for the future. So far, the existing union was a combination of the builders' union (including plasterers and carpenters),

31. *Weekly Guide* was the journal of the CCP, at one time edited by Mao Zedong.

32. *China Youth/La Juenesse* (Zhongguo qingnian), a weekly journal of the Communist Youth, launched in Shanghai in 1923, and later moved to Canton, then Wuhan. Altogether thirty-three issues were published—not to be confused with *New Youth* (Xin qingnian), a leftist magazine founded by Chen Duxiu (1879–1942) in Shanghai in 1915, moved to Peking in 1917, and suspended in 1922.

the barbers' union, the water-carriers' union, the teahouse and restaurant workers' union, the blacksmiths' union, and several apprentices' unions. Xiao told us that had he known that Party Central and the Revolutionary Government would be passing through he would have organized a big welcome rally. A few days before, he [added], he had staged a rally when Commander Yan Zhong, leading the Supplementary Division, had passed through. Mr. Xiao pelted me with questions about theory that made me ashamed of how I had underestimated craftsmen. Here was Mr. Xiao standing in front of me, a man writ large. I could hardly answer his questions—such as, what is the difference between Communism and Sun Yat-sen's[33] "Three Principles of the People" and can the cooperation of the GMD and the CCP last.

Sun Yat-sen

33. Sun Yat-sen (1866–1925), revolutionary leader and founder of the Guomindang, led the movement which paved the way for the overthrow of the Manchu Empire in 1911. Sun served briefly as China's first president before yielding power to Yuan Shikai. In 1923 Sun forged an alliance with the CCP, backed by the Comintern. In seeking to wipe out warlordism, rein in the Western powers, and unite the country under a republican government, Sun formed the " three alliances"—with the Soviet Union, with the Communist Party, and in support of the workers and peasants. Sun also formulated the "Three principles of the People"—namely nationalism, democracy, and people's livelihood—as the ideology of the GMD. In 1940, the then Republican government passed a resolution to confer on Sun Yat-sen the title "Father of the Republic."

Once out of the office of the Provisional Committee of the Ganzhou Workers' Union, we could tell ourselves that our job was done, and now it was time for fun. The best-known scenic spot in Ganzhou is the Eight-View Platform, where we were taken by comrades from the local Party. It is actually just an ordinary building higher than the surrounding buildings, standing beside the city wall. From the top of the building, the view extends beyond the city wall to take in the placid waters of the Gan River embracing both sides of this ancient town, while hills roll away into the distance, forming a majestic panorama. Born and bred on the flatlands and having gotten used to city life in the last few years, I was filled with joy at the loveliness of the mountains and hills. But I love water, too, having grown up near the Fuchun River, still a vivid memory for me. Now atop the Eight-View Platform looking at the Gan River flowing quietly among the rolling hills, dotted with white sails and seagulls flitting hither and thither, it was pure enchantment. I thought to myself that if I could build a house nearby and enjoy the view every day, the Revolution would lose most of its attraction for me—there go my petty bourgeois sentiments again! Our plan had been to stay another day in Ganzhou, but then orders came down to arrive in Nanchang before the end of the year. To meet this deadline, we had no choice but to set sail on the morning of December 23, 1926, heading first for Ji'an, and from there to Nanchang, capital of Jiangxi Province.

IX

We arrived in the town of Ji'an by the afternoon of December 25. Ji'an, situated in a prosperous part of south-central Jiangxi Province, had been a prefecture in dynastic times but was relegated to the status of a county seat after the founding of the Republican government. Judging by its neatly kept streets and pretty shops, Ji'an was decidedly a cut above Ganzhou, which we had just left. Culturally, however, it could not compare with Ganzhou. Here Christianity had a strong hold. The day we arrived happened to be Christmas Day, and the whole town was in a frenzy of celebration. Luckily we had some anti-Christian pamphlets with us, so our propaganda team spilled out into town in full force for a vigorous anti-Christian campaign. The Supplementary Division, which had preceded us to Nanxiong, was still in Ji'an. They were holding a rally in solidarity with the masses, and I rushed over to make an appearance. At the rally I met Kuang Yong, a colleague from the days when we had both worked at the Political Department of the Whampoa Military Academy.[34] He was currently head of Propaganda for the Political Department of the Supplementary Division. After the mass rally, we went to the local GMD Party headquarters. Their housing was spacious and the set up quite up to par. We visited the various departments and sat down to tea with some of the staff. Also present along with staff members were representatives from the Women's Federation. Altogether there were thirty-eight people, six of them women. The discussion lasted until six, when we broke up. Just as I was about to leave, three young women from the local Women's Federation came up to me and invited me to a gathering that same night. It was being held in honor of Madame He Xiangning, director of the Women's Movement Training Institute, who was passing through, and also to demonstrate against Christianity. Happily surprised, I immediately accepted. That same night, some fifty or sixty women showed up, some of them as lovely as the women of my native Zhejiang. We chatted the evening away. For me, that was the high point of this whole twenty-two day trip. We left the next morning, the twenty-sixth of December. We were supposed to board steamboats, but the water being too shallow—we were back to sailboats.

The evening of the twenty-seventh, we arrived at the bustling little town of Zhongshan. Regrettably, it was getting dark. We dug into a satisfying meal and headed for Nanchang [the provincial capital], where we arrived the next day. According to plan, we were supposed to move on to Wuhan, capital of Hubei Province. But on our arrival in Nanchang, word came down that owing to the current situation,

34. For Zhu Qihua's position at the Whampoa Military Academy, see *Historical Documents of the Whampoa Military Academy 1924–1927*, compiled by the Guangdong Museum of Revolutionary History, published by the Guangdong People's Publishing House, 1982. On page 510, the author is listed as "Zhu Yaling (朱雅零 one of the author's many pseudonyms), staff of the Propaganda Department," among a list of staff members for the third year of the Academy.

we would not be moving immediately to Wuhan. We were to stay put in Nanchang for the time being, thus ending the first stage of our journey. We had started out from Canton on December 7, 1926, and arrived in Nanchang on December 28, spending a total of twenty-two days on the trip.

For the first leg of the journey from Canton to Shaoguan we had been on a train and could not stop to see anything along the way. Other than that, we had traveled by boat and had never missed a chance to take in the sights and sounds of the places we passed through, from Shaoguan to Nanxiong [in Guangdong Province], and from Nan'an to Nanchang [in Jiangxi Province]. As for the little townships and villages along the way, they are too many to recount. From this very cursory view of the territory that we passed through, I came to the following conclusions:

One: China's economy is very backward; there is no budding industry in the interior, as claimed by some. Commerce is wobbly at best, and generally in a shambles.

Two: Transportation, in keeping with the state of the economy, is underdeveloped. The thousand-*li* distance between Shaoguan and Nanchang, for instance, intersecting with important urban centers, has no transportation other than old-style sailboats, unchanged for the last thousand years, and thus it took us twenty-one days to complete our journey. And this is traveling between two big towns. One can imagine what it must be like in the countryside.

Three: The state of agriculture has not changed much down through the centuries. Irrigation relies on manual labor—agricultural machines, totally unheard of.

Four: Owing to the state of the economy, culture and education are lagging far behind, and feudal ideology holds sway.

Five: Owing to the primitive condition of agriculture and commerce, exploitation by the landlord and comprador classes is destroying the livelihood of the people, driving them to the path of revolution.

The above sums up my personal observations during this trip from Canton to Nanchang, lasting from December 7 to December 28, 1926.

CHAPTER TWO

Days in Nanchang

I

Throughout the boat trip, we had cherished visions of the wonderful city of Nanchang, immortalized through the famous descriptions in the "Tengwang Pavilion" by Wang Bo.[1] When we first started out from Canton, I had brought with me a copy of the anthology *Guwen guanzhi*[2] and had read this famous work of prose in one sitting. I was totally enraptured by such lines as: "sunset clouds tangling with wild ducks in flight, autumn waters merging with the disappearing horizon . . ." and had looked forward to seeing the city. But now that we were actually in Nanchang, all our illusions were shattered by harsh reality. We were brutally disappointed.

Our little sailboat was moored beside the Zhang River Gate; we went ashore and moved into a small hotel for the time being. The service staff explained that all the bigger hotels had been fully booked. Actually, there were no hotels worthy of the name. The Jiangxi Hotel,

1. Wang Bo (650–676), Tang dynasty prose writer. His essay in praise of the Tengwang Pavilion is generally considered a masterpiece of classical prose.
2. *Guwen guanzhi* (Anthology of classical prose).

supposedly the best in town, would be no better than a third rate hostel in Shanghai.

The little hotel where we were staying had its advantages though: the upper floor offered a view of the river. True, we had been sailing for a full week. Even so, I always enjoy a river view. But as far as the city itself was concerned, all my illusions were shattered. Here was no brightness, only darkness.

Take the hotel service, for example. Seeing us all in uniform, the bellboys would address us as "Your Excellency," as if we were warlords. Whenever we happened to call for some small service, they would rush over, bowing obsequiously.

"Get a pot of tea." "Yes, Your Excellency, immediately."

"Sweep the floor, don't you see how dirty it is!" "Immediately, Your Excellency. Beg your pardon, Your Excellency."

I could not stand this craven attitude, and said: "We are not Excellencies. Stop addressing us like that. Just call us Sir if you must." Actually, even "Sir" was stretching it a bit, but the man said: "How dare I, Your Excellency!"

After we were settled, a Cantonese comrade from the Secretariat popped over and suggested we take a stroll. Strolling was a popular activity in Canton, I myself have always enjoyed strolling. When in Shanghai, I usually walked to the newspaper office where I worked. I could have caught the No. 1 or the No. 2 Route trolley and gotten off near Nanjing Road, which was close to my office. But I always chose to walk whenever time permitted. Not that I couldn't spare the few cents for the fare—though sometimes I was completely broke. The fact was, I loved strolling the streets of Shanghai, especially the section between the famous Jing'an Temple Road and North Sichuan Road.

Gazing at those imposing buildings, spacious gardens, and the sleek motor cars gliding by, I would imagine the young ladies, beautiful mistresses, and big fat capitalists living in those houses or sitting in those cars, and my imagination would run wild, thinking of all the ways of dealing with those houses and gardens and cars after the victory of the Revolution. Thanks to the economic might of capitalism, the revolution will be left with a rich legacy. I would get completely carried away, as if those houses and cars were already in our possession. Then I would look severely at those capitalists and their daughters and mistresses [as they sped by in their motor cars] and wonder how we were going to deal with them, those hateful but at the same time, pitiful prisoners of the Revolution. Thinking thus, I would forget the fatigue of walking. I would stride past hotels and department stores and sail into my office.

But "strolling" in Nanchang was a totally different matter: the streets were dirty, dark, wet, uneven, and jammed—strolling in Nanchang was downright punishing.

Our little group passed through the Zhang River Gate and wandered around, ending up in the most prosperous part of town, where we ran into the bookstores of the Zhonghua Book Company and the Commercial Press, where I picked up a few books.

We wondered, is this all there is to Nanchang? After roaming the streets without coming across anything interesting, somebody thought of the Tengwang Pavilion. It was said to be by the river, not far from the hotel. We headed toward the spot, only to be disappointed.

The Pavilion had been ravaged just recently when Nanchang was taken by the Revolutionary Army during this current Northern Expedition, and all that was left of the Pavilion was crumbling ruins. I thought of the last two lines of Wang Bo's essay: "Where are the princes of the Pavilion? Beyond the balustrades, quietly the river flows."

Mao suggested that since we were there, we might as well look for something to take back as a souvenir. Yang added that the Pavilion was built during the Tang dynasty, so we might find some Tang bricks and tiles. We all agreed, and set to work digging through the rubble.

"Oho, a Tang tile!" Zeng, the first to score, shouted happily. We all went to take a look. Zeng's find was a large piece of brown tile, exuding an air of antiquity. This whipped up our enthusiasm and we dug on eagerly, although it was getting dark. Mao found one piece of tile, following which, I myself found two.

We went back to the hotel with our precious finds, carried proudly like trophies of war, and stored them carefully in our suitcases.

Later, we left the hotel and moved into new accommodations in nearby Xinyuan University. During the move, Mao's orderly dropped his precious tile, and it was smashed to smithereens. Mao flew into a rage and lashed out at the fellow. But what's done could not be undone; firing the wretch was pointless. Fortunately, I had two tiles, so I gave one to Mao, and that was the end of the matter.

Mao Zedong

A couple of days later, Mao's orderly rushed in breathlessly while we were chatting in our new quarters.

"Director Mao, there are lots of tiles over there!"

"Where?"

"The roof of the public toilet!"

"Nonsense! How could there be Tang tiles over the public toilet?!"

"It's true! I saw them myself!"

We decided to check it out. The orderly went and took a piece of tile from the roof and compared it to ours. Indeed, the tile from the roof of the public toilet was identical to ours. We realized that our precious souvenirs could not possibly be Tang tiles, else how could they be used as roofing for a public toilet? That would be a golden toilet indeed!

At our request, the orderly went and brought back a janitor who worked at the University, an honest looking old man. He listened respectfully to our questions and told us that those tiles were not Tang dynasty tiles, but a local product, selling for pennies apiece, slightly more expensive than ordinary tiles.

What a joke! We made haste to throw our tiles into the garbage, after having hoarded them for many days.

II

Commander-in-chief Chiang Kai-shek extended a dinner invitation for the evening of January 3, so we dutifully showed up at Headquarters at seven sharp.

Headquarters was situated in the residence of the former military supervisor [of the old regime]. It had been occupied by the various warlords who had held sway in the area: Deng Ruzhuo, Fang Benren, and Cai Chengxun. In those days, the mansion was off limits to the likes of us, but now we were entering as honored guests. I couldn't help thinking: "We are in revolutionary times indeed!"

Staff greeted us on arrival and showed us into the West Parlor, saying that the commander-in-chief was still in conference with Generals Tang Shengzhi, Li Zongren,[3] and others. We looked around and saw many notices and orders posted on the wall of the little reception area connected to the West Parlor where we were asked to wait. I saw that such orders always began with "By order of His Excellency the Commander-in-chief . . ."—not a bit less intimidating than the wording used by the erstwhile warlords. *We are here today due to the fact that we have become part of the ruling class,* I thought to myself. As far as ordinary folks were concerned, these quarters were just as closed to them as ever.

Finally, staff led us into the dining room. Checking right and left, I found my designated seat near the high table reserved for the commander-in-chief.

---

3. Li Zongren (1891–1969) was a GMD general, the founder of the Nanning (Guangxi) campus of the Whampoa Military Academy, one of the military leaders of the War of Resistance against Japanese Aggression, one-time vice-president of the Republic of China in Nanjing. In 1965, at age seventy-four, Li returned to China from the United States and died in Peking in 1969.

Chiang Kai-shek

The connecting door to the meeting room was open, and we could see the meeting still in session.

"That is Tang Shengzhi."

"The other is Li Zongren"

"And that one is General Galen."

"Look, there's Cheng Qian"

We were whispering, trying to identify the VIPs at the meeting.

Finally, the meeting was over; we saw the VIPs rise and chant slogans:

"Down with Sun Chuanfang!"

"Long live the National Revolution!"

"Long live Commander-in-chief Chiang!"

After the slogans, Commander-in-chief Chiang led the way into the dining room, followed by General Galen, Tan Yankai, Li Zongren, Cheng Qian, He Xiangning and others, all seated at the high table. And then began that expensive but tasteless Western-style banquet. The drinks— brandy and red wine — were not bad, though.

Commander-in-chief Chiang Kai-shek then gave a welcome address in his heavy native Zhejiang accent, ending on a high note: "Comrades," he said, "Let me be the first to give you the good news that came in early this morning: the revolutionary masses in Hankou have taken matters into their own hands and have reclaimed the British Concession! This was the latest telegram to arrive at General Headquarters . . ."

Good news indeed: the masses rising spontaneously to reclaim the British Concession. Wonderful!

Amid the cheers of his audience, the commander-in-chief continued, "For the Revolution to succeed, we must bring down imperialism! Reclaiming the concessions is but the first step. Let me say in all seriousness, we will bring down imperialism in a thousand days (meaning within three years). If we do not accomplish this in a thousand days, you, comrades, may cut off my head!"

It was wonderful that the commander-in-chief promised to accomplish the revolution in a thousand days. However, his words became something of a joke. A revolution is not fortune-telling. Supposing imperialism is not brought down in a thousand days, would anyone really go and cut off the commander-in-chief's head? Even if someone volunteered for the job, would the commander-in-chief volunteer his head? This made me think back to his speeches at the Whampoa Military Academy. If we may say that Liu Bei[4] had wept his way to the kingship of Chu, we might just as well say that the commander-in-chief had sworn himself all the way to the top. At the Whampoa Academy, he used to end his speeches to the students by saying: "If I your commandant turn counterrevolutionary one day, you my students may kill me," or, "If future events prove that I have turned counterevolutionary and you students do not get rid of me, I will commit suicide in front of you!" I cannot begin to count the number of times the commander-in-chief had sworn such vows.

The day after the dinner, another comrade and I called on General Galen[5] at his residence. General Galen shook our hands and made us welcome. He talked to us about the Chinese Revolution, the Bolshevik Revolution, and the future of the world revolution. The general spoke English, and we conversed with him through an interpreter.

---

4. Liu Bei, one of the three contenders for supremacy described in *Chronicle of the Three Kingdoms,* (San guo zhi) and in the novel *Romance of the Three Kingdoms* (San guo yanyi). Advised by Zhuge Liang, Liu Bei secured the riverlands in China's west and founded the short-lived kingdom of Shu.
5. Vasily Blyukher, alias "General Galen," was the head of the Soviet advisory mission to China during the Northern Expedition.

There were stories floating around about the general, the best known being that he was not Russian but Austrian, that he had been a staffer in World War I, that he had been caught by the Russians, and that he had taken part in the October Revolution and had ultimately acquired a high position in the Red Army.

To our question about his nationality, General Galen said "I am Russian, a down-to-earth Russian, and I was never a staffer in the German army. I was a factory worker. Don't you believe me, Comrades? What does it matter if I am Austrian? So long as one works for the Revolution, it makes no difference whether one is Austrian, Polish, American, Indian, or Japanese . . . we are all comrades. On the other hand, if someone were counterrevolutionary, wouldn't we want to strike him down, even if he were Russian? Wouldn't we, as in the case of Smirnov or Meliukhov? . . ."

As we were in animated conversation with the general, a staffer brought in a plate of oranges. General Galen personally peeled them for us, saying: "These oranges are good, try some. They are from Russia, but we Russians don't eat them ourselves, we pack them and send them to America or Europe. Our countrymen are patriotic. They know that our country is being encircled by imperialism and struggling to survive. They choose to sell the oranges for money to help their country's economic construction. They cannot bear to eat these oranges."

Listening to him, we felt ashamed of ourselves. Our country, too, is poor, but we were eating these imported oranges.

III

The Nanchang office of the General Political Department was situated near East Lake, one of the scenic spots of the city. The day after our arrival, I made a call. At the time, the Nanchang office was headed by the poet Guo Moruo.[6] This poet/politician was not in his office when I arrived. I met his secretary, Li Minzhi, and the head of the Social

6. Guo Moruo (1892–1978), scholar, poet, historian, archaeologist. After 1949, Guo held official and honorary posts on the mainland, including president of the Chinese Academy of Sciences and the Chinese Academy of Social Sciences in Peking and other honorary titles.

Affairs section, Yuan Wenbin, whom I had previously met in Canton. Mr. Li was a new face. The office was lavishly furnished, and a charcoal fire blazed away in the corner.

At the General Political Department, I also ran into Zhu De,[7] the political commissioner for the Twentieth Army from Sichuan (commanded by Yang Sen). I did not know Zhu De personally but had heard that he was quite senior, having served as chief of police in Yunnan during the early days of the Republic, and having served under Cai Songpo.[8] It was said that Zhu had spent many years in Germany and was very knowledgeable in military science. But I personally never thought much of the veterans of the pre-Revolutionary days who had crossed over. What had struck me were his looks—he bore a striking resemblance to the writer Lu Xun.

Back in Canton, I had heard of the vigorous work at the front conducted by the General Political Department, but seeing is believing. These reports were overblown. Actually, the atmosphere at the Nanchang branch was very depressing. Those officers, more like spoiled offspring of the rich, were just chatting comfortably around the fire as if [contrary to Dr. Sun Yat-sen's dying behest] the revolution was *accomplished,* and *we need not exert ourselves* anymore.

Later it dawned on me that not only the local branch of the General Political Department but also the whole of Nanchang was enveloped in an atmosphere of gloom and doom.

Leaving the Nanchang branch of the General Political Department, I went to call on Li Fuchun, director of the Political Department of the Second Army, and Zhu Kejing, who held the same position as Li in the Third Army. Both Li and Zhu carried themselves with pompous official airs, especially Zhu, a man who left a bad taste in one's mouth. Later, in Li's residence, I met the confidential secretary

---

7. Zhu De (1889–1976), Mao Zedong's chief military associate from the days of the Jiangxi Soviet. Zhu was commander-in-chief of the People's Liberation Army and a member of the Standing Committee of the CCP Political Bureau.
8. Cai E (1882–1916), also known as Cai Songpo, native of Hunan, military commander, remembered in Chinese history for efforts to save the old Republic against Yuan Shikai's imperial ambitions.

at Headquarters, a certain Jiang, who showed up wrapped in rich furs, like a bandit in a mountain redoubt.

After visiting the Nanchang office of the General Political Department and calling on the two political directors of the Second and Third Armies, respectively, my general impression could be summed up in one word: stagnation.

Is this what the Revolution was supposed to bring to Nanchang? If my friend Zhao Xingnong could see this from where he was in the other world, how he would weep!

Zhao Xingnong, alias Zhao Gan, and I had met each other in Shanghai in 1925 during the height of the strikes and demonstrations [which had ended in the bloody suppression of May Thirtieth]. We had met in the home of a mutual friend and took to each other immediately. Soon after that meeting, Zhao left for Nanchang. At the time, he had held the dual position of head of the Organization Department of the GMD Jiangxi branch, as well as being a prestigious leader of the workers and peasants' movement in Jiangxi. When the Revolutionary Army of the Northern Expedition was about to take Nanchang in the summer of 1926, Zhao was executed by the warlord Deng Ruzhuo outside the city gate.

The day after my depressing visits, Mao and I called on Lin Zuhan, director of the Political Department of the Sixth Army. I still remember his uncivil treatment of me when we met the previous year over my prospective job with the Sixth Army. It had left me with a very dim view of this white-haired old gentleman. But during this meeting, he was very genial and expressed himself bluntly regarding the current situation. "When we first started out from Canton on the Northern Expedition, there had been only eight Armies, and now we have almost forty Armies," Lin said, and added, "The army is growing in size, but those newly incorporated . . ." Lin shook his head and didn't finish the sentence.

I visited the headquarters of the Workers' Union, which was situated right next to the General Political Department. The director, Xiao Nufeng, gave me an animated description of the workers' movement of Jiangxi Province. According to his narrative, the situation was quite satisfactory.

The Peasants' Association of Jiangxi Province was situated in the Hundred Flowers Retreat, the best scenic spot in Nanchang, better than the riverside venue of the General Political Department. We met a member of the Standing Committee of the Peasants' Association, Fang Zhimin,[9] a hollow-eyed young man who seemed to be suffering from consumption. Fang was in high spirits, however, and gave us a detailed overview of the peasants' movement in Jiangxi. He was optimistic. He explained that there was no industrial proletariat in Jiangxi; the so-called workers' movement, he said, was limited to craftsmen, and was understandably dragging its feet. As for the peasants' movement, Fang went on, it was a different story: the peasants of Jiangxi were extremely poor; they yearned for revolution and could be properly organized so long as there was competent leadership. According to Fang, the most urgent problem in the Jiangxi peasant movement was the lack of cadres.

Actually, as I saw it, this lack of competent cadres was not limited to the Jiangxi Peasants' Association—it was widespread: the lack of capable people anywhere, the presence of useless people everywhere.

I then called at the Students' Union. A heavyset young man by the name of Zou Nu greeted me. By the way he spoke, one could tell that he was very capable. In our conversation, we were both indignant and deplored the prevailing air of stagnation.

Finally I went to the GMD Provincial Party Headquarters but could not find anyone in charge. To judge by appearances, it was pretty chaotic down there.

IV

Nanchang may be depressing in general, but not so the sight of pretty young women, which always sent us into a flutter of excitement.

Several of us[10] went to the Baoling Girls' School outside Desheng

---

9. Fang Zhimin (1899–1935), one of the early members of both the Communist Youth League and the Communist Party, was a leader of the CCP Soviet base area in Jiangxi Province in the late 1920s and early 1930s.
10. Due to cuts, the comrades are not specified by name. They could be Zheng Junsheng and Mao Du, since later both "had found their mates among the students of the Baoling Girls'School." (See Chapter 9.)

Gate for the purpose of holding a speech rally; it was to be our first encounter with young women since arriving in Nanchang.

The buildings and facilities at the Baoling Girls' School were superb, considering its location in China's interior. We looked for the student union but were told that the union was yet to be formed. We tried to talk to some students, but they were scared stiff and did not want to have anything to do with us. In these reactionary missionary schools, we realized, the principal held absolute authority and could expel students at will. We had to talk directly to the principal to get what we wanted.

We found the principal, a woman in her thirties. Her ugliness was absolutely staggering. Obviously living in the illusion of her own beauty, this principal covered her face with powder as a plasterer paints a wall. She said she was from Hubei and that she had been to the United States twice. No one had asked, but she volunteered the information as if having been to the United States had put a halo around her head. Such a shameless woman was beyond our contempt. She was so carried away by the narrative of her trip to the United States that we had to stop her to put in our request to hold a speech rally. She refused outright. Her first excuse was that the school was founded by foreigners and had never hosted speech rallies for outsiders. This odious woman actually tried to put us down by holding up her foreign masters. I was furious and interrupted her rudely: "Precisely because your school is founded by foreigners, we find it imperative to hold a rally. Those northern bumpkins may be scared of foreigners, and you too may worship foreigners like your own ancestors. But not us. We are out to overthrow imperialism."

The principal retorted that as far as she was concerned, we could overthrow imperialism all we wanted, but there would be no speechifying in her school, since it was against missionary school rules. Seeing that imperialism did not scare us, the principal now shifted her position to put us down with the Church. To squash her high-handed manner, I countered: "Whatever you say, we are determined to hold a speech rally here. The purpose of our talk is to mobilize your students to rise up in revolution, to overthrow imperialism, and to throw out their running dogs—the Christians. Whoever opposes us, we will treat as counterrevolutionaries. We will take them to the garrison for questioning. And if that doesn't work," I added, "we have guns in our hands."

We were hotheaded youths, after all, and may have gone too far. But it worked with that odious woman. She said lamely: "Well if you must, you must." And off she went in a huff.

And so we set about rallying students and giving speeches. The students, rich young ladies to judge by their clothes, expressed interest in our activities and did not seem to mind that we had insulted their dreaded principal.

Leaving Baoling Girls' School, we went across the street to the Yuzhang School, a missionary school for boys. The principal there was an American who spoke fluent Chinese. Missionary schools always separate male and female students. If a female student were caught corresponding with a male student, she would not only be expelled but blacklisted as well, so that no other missionary school would accept her. This sharp separation between the sexes—wasn't it all for show? Wasn't their own Jesus Christ born out of wedlock? Not to mention the fact that many leaders of the church were themselves sexually depraved.

Over the next couple of days I gave many talks. Apart from missionary schools, I also talked at the Provincial Girls' High School and the Professional Training School for Women.

When we first set out from Canton, our destination had been Wuhan. Nanchang was to be just one stop. Actually it would have been easier to reach Wuhan via the Hunan route [and avoiding Nanchang altogether]. On arrival in Nanchang, we assumed that it would be a short stay of a couple of days. Who would have thought that we were there to stay, with no prospect of going to Wuhan in the near future!

It goes without saying that the Party Central Executive Committee and the Revolutionary Government represented s*upreme authority*. But now, being stuck in Nanchang, the *supreme authority* found itself at the bidding of the commander-in-chief [Chiang Kai-shek], who had set up shop in Nanchang. Unfortunately, what I had foreseen before setting out from Canton had now materialized. In the debate previous to the move, the commander-in-chief was all for moving to Wuhan, but now that we were in Nanchang, halfway to Wuhan, he changed his tune and maintained that Wuhan was not suitable for setting up the Revolutionary Government, and that we should wait in Nanchang until *Nanjing* was taken and then set up the government in *Nanjing*. Stuck in Nanchang, the Revolutionary Government and the Party CEC had no choice but to defer to the commander-in-chief and take their orders from *him*.

At the time of our arrival in Nanchang, several senior members of the Party CEC were already settled in Wuhan. They now wired their opposition to the Revolutionary Government's delay in Nanchang and urged the move to Wuhan as planned. Headlines in the foreign press claimed that Commander-in-chief Chiang Kai-shek had hijacked the Revolutionary Government. A situation arose that seemingly pitted Wuhan and Nanchang against each other. To dispel the rampant rumors, the commander-in-chief sent a telegraph to Wuhan, assuring them that the Revolutionary Government was making a temporary stop in Nanchang and that if it did not move to Nanjing, it would certainly move to Wuhan. At the time, Nanjing was in the hands of the warlord Sun Chuanfang—moving there was out of the question.

Since the move to Wuhan was still under wraps, we had to make long-term arrangements for accommodations. We staff at the Party CEC left the little hotel and moved to Xinyuan University, as mentioned above. It goes without saying that Xinyuan University was the highest seat of learning in Jiangxi Province; but as far as learning was concerned, it was a sham. The school was closed for the holidays when we moved in, so we did not meet any students. The president, Xiong Yuxi, was a wizened little man whom the locals nicknamed Monkey Xiong on account of his monkey-like looks. Xiong's son served as dean, so people referred to the institution as Father-Son University. The rooms were small, but better than the hotel, and good enough for the time being.

After a short stay at the University, regular housing was found for us in the residence of a certain individual by the name of Bao, who had previously been head of the Bank of Jiangxi and a supporter of the warlord Sun Chuanfang. Understandably, Bao had fled at our approach, and all his property was confiscated. We needed permanent housing because by now Commander-in-chief Chiang Kai-shek had decided that the Party CEC and the government should remain *permanently* in Nanchang. Mao and I and a couple of other colleagues went to take a look inside the Bao residence. The architecture was uniformly traditional, with very little lighting, the ceilings were so low that they reminded me of the garrets in Shanghai. Rooms were already allocated to the various departments, though they had not yet been cleaned up and were still very cluttered, witness to the precipitate nature of the owner's flight.

Just as we had rummaged among the debris of the Tengwang Pavilion, we now looked around for something to keep as a souvenir. There were a lot of letters addressed to "His Excellency," testifying to Bao's supremacy in his heyday. There were also photographs of Bao taken with notables of his time. More interesting were the many pairs of embroidered shoes and women's fripperies, all witness to a young lady's presence.

Since the Party CEC offices were to be quartered in the former Bao residence, we staff members were faced with a problem: we most definitely did not want to be squeezed into those low-ceilinged rooms for living quarters. Mao and I looked around. Rented rooms were easily available, but landlords would always inquire if we had family. It finally dawned on us that they refused to rent otherwise. Mao said dejectedly: "What shall we do?" We finally found satisfactory rooms right behind the Bao residence and promptly said "Yes!" when asked if we had family. After we had moved in and were asked again about our families, I immediately replied, "They are still in Shanghai and will be here shortly," and that was the end of the matter. But the rooms were still unsatisfactory. Later I found new quarters in the upper story of a house near the East Lake area, sharing with Zhang, Tian, Cai, and other colleagues.

The Party Central Executive Committee was not yet opened for work, and we staff idled the days away. As the saying goes, the devil finds work for idle hands. Most of my colleagues spent their days in town chasing skirts. I was otherwise occupied—I had started a correspondence with a young lady in Canton, sending her love letters regularly.

Guo Moruo

The atmosphere in Nanchang was depressing. In Canton, mass rallies of a hundred thousand or even two hundred thousand people were an everyday occurrence, demonstrating the might of the masses. But here in Nanchang it was another story. Take January 21 for instance, the third anniversary of the death of Lenin. If we were in Canton, we would be holding big rallies, but here in Nanchang, the commemorative event hardly made a ripple. The meeting was held in the public stadium and I attended, sitting with Guo Moruo on the platform among the guests of honor. I was not acquainted with poet Guo; we were introduced to each other at the event by one of his staff, and I was favorably impressed by his scholarly air. He did not appear to be an officious humbug, which seemed to be the public perception. Or perhaps he had dropped his officious airs for me.

At the end of the rally, about a dozen young ladies went up on stage to sing "The Internationale": "Arise, you prisoners of starvation! Arise, you wretched of the earth . . ." Those sonorous words sounded quaint mouthed by these young ladies. I personally prefer the "The Internationale" sung by rough workers and peasants. These young misses would be better off singing: "Pitter patter goes the rain," or "Shiny sunshine in the sky . . ."

V

[not included in the original Chinese edition]

VI

We stayed on in Nanchang through the New Year, and then through the Spring Festival [entering the year 1927].

On the eve of the Spring Festival, we four roommates roamed the streets looking for a good restaurant, but most restaurants were closed. It seemed that they would rather lose business than miss the Spring Festival family get-together. Ultimately we found one, a Tianjin restaurant.

As we were enjoying the food, the sound of shots pierced the air.

"Listen, gunshots!"

"Firecrackers. Have you forgotten this is New Year's Eve?"

"No, it doesn't sound like firecrackers," I countered, "Listen again."

"Don't overreact. Of course it's firecrackers. Gunshots? Nonsense." Tian and Cai concurred with Zhang. The waiter also said that it was firecrackers, so we continued eating and discussed where to have some fun after dinner.

As we walked around after dinner, the streets seemed strangely quiet and deserted; all the shops were shuttered, and there was not a rickshaw in sight. We were just starting to wonder what was up when suddenly there was a commotion, and we saw groups of soldiers coming our way. A couple of them shouldered machine guns.

Now what was this all about? The shock shook us out of our wooziness after all that drinking. Fortunately, we were in plain clothes because one of the soldiers approached us.

"Don't be afraid, we do not hurt civilians. We are going to the commander-in-chief for our pay. Damn it! The officers are enjoying themselves while we haven't been paid for the last three months!" As one group of soldiers went off, another group approached.

We decided to play it safe and sought shelter in a tobacco shop. We knocked and the owner opened up and kindly took us in. We learned from him that soldiers from the Third Army had mutinied. Indeed, we had heard vague rumors that soldiers of the Third Army were complaining about not getting paid, and now they were really taking action: carrying machine guns to the commander-in-chief, demanding pay. I shuddered to think how all this would end.

Zhu Peide

Fortunately, the unrest was quickly quelled: Zhu Peide, head of the Third Army, promised to shell out a month's pay—the soldiers went home, and we returned to our rooms.

The next morning, however, as we went to our offices in the Bao residence, the corpses of two local people lay on the street, victims of the crossfire of the night before. Comrade Jiang of the Military Affairs Department had been walking along the street in his uniform when he was seized and beaten by soldiers. Now if we had been in uniform last night, we would not have gotten off so easily.

This incident made us realize that our Revolutionary Army was becoming demoralized. True, the government budget was tight, but not so tight as not to issue the soldiers' pay. Why did the Third Army hold back three months' pay? And why was it that the minute the soldiers mutinied, those big shots coughed up one month's pay? Later it was said that Headquarters' method of handling of the riot was to shoot a few of the ringleaders.

After this incident, the atmosphere in Nanchang sank to a new low. The local population began to lose confidence in the Revolutionary

Army. News leaked out that the newly incorporated First Division had shot union leaders in Ganzhou. The Ganzhou Worker's Union and locals sent three representatives over to Nanchang to petition for justice. The Provincial Party leadership sent the three men to the Party Central Executive Committee. The CEC, seeing that the case involved the army, sent the three men to Headquarters. The three representatives went to Headquarters every day to plead their case, making more than ten visits, with no results whatever. They returned to Ganzhou, having accomplished nothing but a tour of Nanchang.

And thus the situation in Nanchang deteriorated day by day. I was losing patience and had decided to leave, but just then word came down that the commander-in-chief had suddenly given permission for the Revolutionary Government and the Party CEC to move up north to Wuhan, while he himself would head east for Anhui Province.

VII

It was a morning in February when we started out from the former Bao residence, heading for the Buffalo Market Train Station. We had to cross the Zhang River, as the station was on the other side. We had dragged through two months in Nanchang, but now that we were ready to leave, I myself was inexplicably dejected. The shifting morning light reflected in the river seemed like the lingering gaze of a woman. Too late it dawned on me that Nanchang was a lovable place.

The train stood waiting at the platform; we quickly boarded, and the train left. It was a dismal departure. I still remember the send-off in Canton, overflowing with good will and affection. But now, not a single person turned up to see us off. We were like a criminal gang being shipped off under the cover of darkness. Our train made two brief stops [on its way northward] and dropped us off in Jiujiang at about three o'clock in the afternoon.

Once in Jiujiang, Mao, Zhang, Tian, and I left our luggage with orderlies and went to town. We installed ourselves in a little hotel, where invariably we were addressed as "Your Excellency." The Party CEC had requisitioned a steamboat to transport personnel and documents straight to Wuhan, but the four of us were most unwilling to be squeezed into a little steamboat all the way from Jiujiang to Wuhan. We made our own arrangements to board a commercial boat. It had the added advantage of giving us an extra day in Jiujiang.

Jiujiang was pitifully small, but because of the presence of a foreign concession, this small town boasted a paved road, and had a more modern look than Nanchang. We four shared a meal in a restaurant, one of the most expensive meals I have ever had. We had merely ordered four ordinary dishes, a soup and a popular alcoholic drink—a meal that would have cost five or six *yuan* in Shanghai—but here we were handed a staggering bill of over eighteen *yuan*. Everything is expensive in Jiujiang; the shopkeepers here are a vicious lot!

The next morning we four friends visited South Gate Lake, the local attraction. The lake was much smaller than East Lake, and the water was turbid. But with Lushan[11] as a backdrop, it had a special attraction.

In the middle of the lake was the Misty Water Pavilion, and it is said that General Zhou Yu[12] of the Three Kingdoms period had been quartered there. A little courtyard within the pavilion offered a quiet retreat, an ideal spot for reading on a summer's day. After spending some time in the pavilion, we returned to shore and spent some more time enjoying the lake and the view of Lushan in the distance. The local architecture, too, was unique. These capitalists certainly knew how to enjoy life, and their homes were understandably superior. We looked in on the Jiujiang Business Association to find out something about the state of commerce, but all we got from the staff was some nonsensical jabber.

Christianity was a powerful influence in Jiujiang. Several schools such as the Juli Girls' School had been established. We had wanted to hold a speech rally there, but time was short, so we gave up on the idea. We also paid a visit to the Party branch in Jiujiang and met several very spirited young people.

---

11. Mt. Lu, known for it's scenic beauty, is located between Nanchang and Jiujiang in Northern Jiangsu Province. Lushan was designated a UNESCO World Heritage Site in 1996.

12. Zhou Yu, military chief under Sun Quan, lord of the southland—Sun Quan being one of the three contenders in the struggle for supremacy between Cao Cao (north), Liu Bei (west) and Sun Quan (south) during the Three Kingdoms period, as described in the classical novel *Romance of the Three Kingdoms* (San guo yanyi).

CHAPTER THREE

Impressions of Wuhan

I

At long last, the soft breezes of spring brought us into Wuhan.

For almost three months I had been confined to towns of the interior, with no paved roads, no imposing buildings. In fact I had not even seen a passing car. Now, in Wuhan, I was glad to be back among the signs of material progress. But what really cheered me up were the slogans hanging down at intersections, and the sight of fully armed blue-uniformed worker squadrons picketing in the streets. Some of the slogans such as "Down with Imperialism!" or "Down with Remnants of the Warlords!" were familiar. But more to the point were such slogans as "Down with One-Man Dictatorship!" "Down with Senility!" or "Down with Military Control of the Party!" which were distributed widely in Wuhan. After two suffocating months in Nanchang, this was indeed a breath of fresh air.

On arrival we found temporary accommodation at the People's Club. It was an amusement center somewhat like the Great World in Shanghai, the only difference being that this one was steeped in a revolutionary atmosphere. The Great World, for instance, was decorated with photographs of famous actors and actresses such as Mei Lanfang and Cheng Yanqiu,[1] while here the walls were covered with pictures of Marx and Lenin or photographs of vast rallies of thousands. Charts for the statistics and figures of the revolutionary movement in the province were on display. Slogans such as "Oppressed Slaves, Arise and Make a Last Stand!" hung down from the walls. A newcomer would have taken the place for a museum of world revolution. Technically this People's Club was still run as an amusement center; imagine what a *non*-amusement institution would be like!

Mao and I strolled into the Yangtze River Bookstore, which was the main outlet for revolutionary publications. The place was tightly packed, unlike some of the bookstores in Shanghai. We pushed our way inside, only to be told that the *Weekly Guide* had sold out. "A fifth printing will be available tomorrow morning." Saying which, the salesman turned to the next customer. "So this last number of the *Weekly Guide* is going through a fifth printing? Selling so well!" Mao was impressed.

We left the packed bookstore and continued our walk. Even a cursory look around was enough to infect us with a revolutionary spirit and make us forget our fatigue.

II

The Party Central Executive Committee had decided to set up temporary quarters at the [Hubei] Provincial Assembly situated in Wuchang, one of the tri-cities which made up Wuhan (Wuchang, Hankou, Hanyang). I found the narrow streets of Wuchang offensive, but then I remembered that we were not here to enjoy the view. Wuchang was fired with revolutionary zeal, and that was what counted. My colleagues and I left the People's Club where we had stayed one night. We crossed the river and wound our way through narrow alleys to the site of the Provincial Assembly. The leadership there, looking up to us as their superiors, had made special efforts to accommodate us. I was given a room with a view.

The Provincial Assembly building, enhanced by a view of Snake

1. Mei Lanfang and Cheng Yanqiu were world famous actors (female impersonators) of Chinese opera in modern China, Mei in Peking and Cheng in Shanghai.

Mountain in the background and a square in the foreground, stood out conspicuously among the drab buildings of Wuchang. After being cooped up in the cage-like rooms of Nanchang, my present accommodation was a welcome relief indeed.

The first thing we did after settling in was to call on the various departments of the Hubei Provincial Party organization. Many cadres, such as Secretary of the Agricultural Department Han Yangchu, or Secretary at the Women's Department Ge Jiying, were old friends from Canton. Others were new faces, but we were made welcome by all.

I was pleased to see that all the departments of the Hubei Party organization were functioning competently. I remember that back in Canton people would refer to provincial Party cadres as "Your Highness," but one could not say that about the Hubei office. The cadres here were young and energetic. When we called, we found them all busy at work. When we struck up a conversation, they talked about their work in detail, showing zeal and understanding. In some of those mega-bureaucracies, officials were just there for the 80 or 100 or 300 *yuan* monthly pay. But not the young people here at the Hubei Party offices: they were not there for the *yuan*, they were part of something greater. Seeing them at work, I felt that we staff at the Party CEC should be ashamed of ourselves!

III

After settling into Wuchang, my colleagues and I went to visit the Wuhan campus of the Central Military Political Academy. Here I came across more friends. Yun Daiying[2] was the General Political Director, and there were more familiar faces within the Political Department.

The most outstanding aspect of the Wuhan campus was its women's section. Back then in backward China, co-education was not unknown. But for a military institution to accept women was not only unknown in

2. Yun Daiying (1895–1931), one of the earliest leaders of the CCP youth movement, played an important role during the May Fourth Movement, joined the CCP in 1921, and founded *Zhongguo qingnian* (China Youth—not to be confused with the *Xin qingnian* [New Youth] later founded by Chen Duxiu) and other journals which were very influential at the time.

China, it was rare around the world. The fact that the Wuhan campus of the Military Political Academy accepted women students had sparked controversy from as far away as Canton. Deng Yanda, one of the Party elders, was a stout supporter, while others such as Gu Mengyu and Ding Weifeng were opposed. According to the latter, a line should be drawn between the sexes: women were fit only to do embroidery in the maiden's chamber; speaking in public was a breach of propriety and bad enough; but for a young woman to pick up a rifle and march in straw sandals was a perfect outrage, a loss of face for China. However, the tide was inexorable and here they were, young women on the Wuhan campus of the Central Military Political Academy.

Yun Daiying

Deng Yanda

We should have the deepest respect for these young women who had broken through the shackles of feudalism, left the maiden's chamber, and strode onto the battleground. Most came from good families and were well educated. To leave everything to join the military, one can imagine the struggles they must have gone through—all of which would be fit subject matter for song and story.

Take for instance Miss Liu. From a landlord family in Fengrun County in north China, she had been educated in Peking and was living the sheltered life of a rich young lady. But she rejected that parasitic life and wanted to dedicate herself to the oppressed masses. Obviously, her newfound allegiance was incompatible with her family background. Overruling her objections, Miss Liu's parents betrothed her to the only son of a landlord family; the wedding day was fixed, and fast approaching. What was the young woman to do? She had no choice but to leave. She had first wanted to go to Canton, but when she heard that the Revolutionary Government was moving to Wuhan, she headed for Wuhan. Unfortunately, Miss Liu lost all her money soon after leaving home, and as a fugitive, she could not approach relatives in Peking. She stole her way onto the Peking-Wuhan train, and was chased off halfway because she had no ticket. She walked a little way and then sneaked onto another Peking-Wuhan train, and managed to ride a little distance before she was chased off again. Thus between walking along the tracks and sneaking onto trains, Miss Liu managed to reach Wuhan after sixty-one days, a shadow of her former self. Shortly after her arrival in Wuhan, she joined the Military Political Academy.

Very touched by Miss Liu's story, I had a friend introduce us. Before our meeting, I had imagined her as being toughened by all she had gone through. Actually, when she did show up, she turned out to be a slender young woman. It seemed that Miss Liu was a combination of iron will and fragile constitution. She said that when at home she had been constantly ill, but not anymore. I asked her what she thought of the military training.

"I am very happy with my present life," she answered.

"Do you sometimes think of your parents in your native place?"

"Yes, I sometimes think of them."

"Does it give you pain to think of them?"

"No, none at all. It is natural for mother and daughter to think of each other; being separated is painful, of course. But I think of all the other mothers and daughters that are separated, and I feel their pain. And what is the use of being sorry? Sympathy alone will not solve anything. We must carry out the Revolution. To leave one's parents for the sake of the Revolution, to give up home and family, to give up one's life for the Revolution is not pain, it is happiness."

This female comrade had such a clear vision, such an iron will! I was thoroughly ashamed of myself.

There were many young women on the Wuhan campus with stories like Miss Liu's. Take for instance Miss Huang of Hunan Province, the treasured daughter of a rich family. She was a student at a high school in Changsha, the capital city, and was swept up in the wave of the revolutionary movement. The following story is a good example of her deep sympathy for the oppressed masses. It was the summer of 1926 when the army of the Northern Expedition was passing through Hunan Province, and some field hospitals were set up in the Changsha area. One day, Miss Huang and other comrades went to visit the sick and wounded. It was mealtime and she saw a wounded soldier grabbing cold rice out of a tin can. She saw maggots in the festering wound on his back. People passing by would hold their nose against the smell. But Miss Huang, full of sympathy, approached the man:

"Comrade, you have suffered; glory belongs to you. You have shed blood for the oppressed masses, for the Revolution. You are great," she said as she handed him an orange.

"Comrade, I am just doing my duty," said the wounded soldier. "Oh, what a wonderful orange! Thank you!"

"I'll come and see you again."

"Oh no, I am not worthy. Would you like to share a meal?" and he shook his tin can, which gave off a bad smell.

"Thank you, I have eaten."

"Oh no! My mistake, how can a young miss like yourself eat our food!" The soldier apologized. But to his surprise, she snatched the can out of his hands.

"Comrade, if this is what you think, then I'm determined to eat your food. I am not a young miss, I am your comrade, and I should share your food. To tell the truth, I've eaten already, but I will try your food," saying which she swallowed two mouthfuls of the rice from the can.

This Miss Huang had done a lot of work in Hunan before being accepted to the Wuhan campus of the Military Political Academy.

There was another young lady, a Miss Tan, whose father was a so-called respectable businessman in Southeast Asia. She had joined the

Revolution when attending school in Canton. The previous summer, some female students from Canton had grouped together to extend support to the striking workers of Hong Kong.[3] At the time, these striking workers were the pillars of the Revolutionary Government. But their lives were hard. They lived in unfurnished public housing and lay on cement floors, sometimes with two blankets drawn across five people. Some did not have decent clothes and had to cover themselves with gunnysacks. Many were sick. In the eyes of the businessman they were a pack of brutes and should be gunned down. Miss Huang, the "unfilial" daughter, proclaimed that those businessmen who refused to accept the striking workers' terms should be gunned down. Mr. Tan decided that his daughter should leave school in case she was corrupted by the "red government" in Canton. Miss Tan not only refused to leave Canton, she went one step further and joined a group to extend support to the striking workers. If it was just greeting the workers, it wouldn't have been so remarkable. The fact was this Miss Tan started kissing the workers. She was so touched by their pitiful situation, she could not help embracing and kissing them. But she did not stop there; she organized a kissing detachment of women, and appointed herself its leader. Her father disowned her right away. Finally Miss Tan found her way to the Academy.

There were many such women in the Military Political Academy whose stories were equally moving, truly worthy of our respect.

IV

The First Provincial Convention of the Hubei Peasants' Association was held at the Hubei Party Headquarters, just three days after our arrival. The place was buzzing with activity, as can be imagined.

Delegates to the Convention were dispatched from the various

3. See Jonathan D. Spence, *The Search for Modern China* (New York: W.W. Norton & Company, 1990), p. 340: "The tragedy of May Thirtieth (in Shanghai) was compounded by events in Canton the following month, when Communist and other labor leaders combined to protest against the Shanghai killings with the launching of a major strike in Hong Kong directed at the British . . ." The strike lasted sixteen months.

provinces, many of them showing up barefoot in short jackets. These people who had never been to the provincial capital before were now sitting down to hold a meeting. It struck me that times had indeed changed: the warlord Wu Peifu had been chased out of town, landlords had disappeared from the countryside, peasants had taken over the running of local affairs, and now they were convening in the provincial capital.

The various peasants' associations from the outlying counties of Wuhan jointly dispatched a three-thousand-strong Peasants' Self-Defense Force to serve as security for the Convention. They were an imposing presence, uniformly turned out in dark blue jackets and wide-rimmed bamboo hats, Mauser or spear in hand. No wonder the landlords have made themselves scarce.

The Convention opened on March 4, and I attended the opening ceremony as an invited guest. There were a 160 delegates, representing peasants' associations from thirty-six counties, as well as over thirty invited guests, among them Deng Yanda, director of the General Political Department; Zhang Fakui, second in command of the Fourth Army; and Sun Fo, member of the Party CEC. They all spoke at the Convention, Deng getting the most applause.

The Hubei Provincial GMD Party organization hosted a dinner in honor of the Convention, and I was a guest. At the dinner, many of the delegates freely expressed their views on various issues. The Convention represented the height of the peasant movement in Hubei Province.

The various organizations of the peasants' movement in Hubei were as follows:

One: the Peasant Affairs Department and the Peasants' Movement Committee of the CCP Central Committee, headed by Mao Zedong.

Two: the Peasant Affairs Department of the GMD CEC, headed by Deng Yanda.

Three: the GMD Peasants' Movement Training Institute, headed by Mao Zedong.

Four: the Provisional Committee of the All-China Peasants' Association.

Five: the Committee for the Study of the Peasant Problem under the GMD CEC General Political Department;

Six: the Peasants' Department of the GMD Hubei Provincial Committee.

Seven: the Hubei Provincial Peasants' Association.

Eight: the Wuchang County Peasants' Association.

Nine: the Peasants' Department of the GMD Hankou Special Branch.

Ten: the Hanyang County Peasants' Association.

Individual research projects on the peasant problem are too numerous to be listed. Moreover, there were also many Soviet specialists on the peasant problem being posted to Wuhan.

V

The Third Plenary Session of the Second GMD Central Executive Committee was convened in Wuhan in March 1927. This meeting has been considered an extreme show of force for the GMD Left. The most important decisions adopted at this meeting were the reorganization of the Revolutionary Government and the setting up of new departments of Labor Affairs, Peasant Affairs, Health and Hygiene, etc., with CCP members Su Zhaozheng heading the Department of Labor Affairs, and Tan Pingshan[4] heading the Department of Peasant Affairs.

At the meeting it was decided that the GMD CEC quarters would be situated in Hankou, initially on the former premises of the British-American Tobacco Corporation, and later to be moved to the site of the Chinese Businessmen's Association.

4. Tan Pingshan (1886–1956), an early follower of Sun Yat-sen, took an active part in the May Fourth Movement and founded the Guangdong branch of the CCP. Working with Zhou Enlai and Yun Daiying, Tan had taken part in the August First Uprising. In the vagaries of revolutionary politics, Tan had been expelled from both the GMD and the CCP. In 1937 Tan threw himself into the war effort to combat Japanese aggression. He took an active part in founding the GMD Revolutionary Committee and held many government positions in the People's Republic of China.

Tan Pingshan

But the Military Affairs Department [under which I had been serving as head of the Propaganda Section] was dismantled, the reason given was that it had been set up for the personal aggrandizement of XXX [Chiang Kai-shek]. After being dismantled, some of the staff went to join Commander-in-chief Chiang in Jiangxi and later followed him to Anhui. The rest of us were kept on in Wuhan: Mao and Luo at the Organization Department of the GMD CEC, Zhang at the General Political Department, Tian at the Wuhan campus of the Military-Political Academy, while I myself was moved to the Political Department of the Fourth Army.

I was happy to be assigned to the Fourth Army, because the Fourth Army had the reputation of being invincible and had distinguished itself in the Northern Expedition.

The Political Department and Fourth Army Headquarters were both located in a row of old buildings, which were part of the Public Stadium. I called on the director of the Political Department, Liao Qianwu, an elderly man from Shaanxi. He designated me as head of the Propaganda Section of the Political Department of the Fourth Army. I went and took my things from the Provincial Assembly and moved into housing in the Public Stadium. I suppose it was childish on my part, but leaving my former colleagues to work in a new place cast gloom over me, and I was dejected for the first few days.

It is a universal truth that hearsay is not to be trusted. Back in Canton, I remember hearing Zhou Enlai say that the Political Department of the Fourth Army was the best of all the political departments. But the reality was not at all as it had been touted. The Political Department needed restructuring and I, as head of the Propaganda Section, had my job cut out for me.

The day I reported for work at the Fourth Army's Political Department, news arrived that the Revolutionary Army had taken Shanghai. We were happy because it meant that finally all the land south of the Yangtze River had been cleared of warlords. But there was nothing like the celebratory mood that had prevailed back in Canton when Wuchang or Nanchang had been taken. By now we realized that after Shanghai and Nanjing have been taken, there would be more internal friction.

However, the same day that news of the victory in Shanghai reached Wuhan, Chiang's telegram to the Soviet adviser Borodin also arrived, asking him to leave. Moreover, supporters of Chiang had printed and distributed the talk that he had delivered on the eve of leaving Nanchang [for Nanjing]. In that talk, Chiang had attacked the GMD CEC's meeting of March [when the Left had gained ascendency]. People in X [Chiang]'s faction now left Wuhan and flocked east to join him in Nanjing. Senior officers of the Eleventh Army [commanded by Chen Mingshu] left en masse.

In Wuhan, the anti-X [Chiang] atmosphere from the Left intensified. The General Political Department had set up a plainclothes detachment. An Anti-X [Chiang] Committee was in the works. The *Republican Daily* [Mingguo ribao] was turning out pages and pages of "anti-X . . ." and "down with X . . ." articles, hinting that verbal opposition was not enough, that it was time to bring him down.

The Party Central's Political Conference in Wuhan passed a resolution to firmly oppose the new government that was being set up in Nanjing [by Chiang].

The Fourth Army was secretly mobilized to march east [to Nanjing], the Political Department had already prepared anti-X [Chiang] propaganda materials, and the army had begun to move down river toward Nanjing [for a punitive campaign again Chiang].

In early April, the Political Department received orders to move together with the army.

We got on steamboats at Xujiapeng, a suburb of Wuhan. The Seventy-fifth Regiment [of the Twenty-Fifth Division] filled one big steamboat. We at the Political Department occupied a smaller boat. I and my boss, director of the Political Department Liao Qianwu, and a few others sat very comfortably in the mess hall, discussing the work ahead.

Our first stop was supposed to be some place past Anqing. Going down the river, we did not expect resistance in Jiujiang or Anqing. Chiang's new base in Nanjing had some forces stationed at Wuhu in Anhui Province, so we expected some resistance there. Once Wuhu was taken, we figured, there would no problem taking Nanjing. That was because, first, a part of Nanjing's Sixth Army was sympathetic to us. Second, Nanjing did not have a big army, and what they had was mostly stationed to the south in the provinces of Zhejiang and Fujian. In the Shanghai/Nanjing area, there were just some forces of the warlord Bai Chongxi standing in our way. Thus taking Nanjing was not perceived to be a problem. We assumed that starting out from Wuhan, we would be able to [overcome resistance and] arrive in Nanjing in four or five days. Once we got a firm footing in Nanjing, taking Shanghai would not be a problem. And once Nanjing and Shanghai were taken, taking Hangzhou, my native place, would be a cup of tea. I might even pay my family a visit on my way back.

As to my native place, I really did not have any longing for it. It is a famous scenic spot, but full of darkness, overrun with corrupt officials and blood-sucking landlords. I never miss the place. I actually detest it. But to get back into the storm of the Revolution, that would make me happy. I wanted to bring light to the oppressed masses of my native place.

But man proposes and God disposes. Just as I was indulging in dreams of bringing the Revolution to my hometown, we received orders to cancel the expedition! We had stayed aboard the steamboat for two days and two nights and now were ordered to return to our quarters near the Public Stadium.

What had happened was that Wang Jingwei had shown up in Wuhan, and had revoked the order for the expedition [eastward against Chiang Kai-shek].[5]

Wang Jingwei had been my colleague in the old days in Canton, and at one time he had been president of the Revolutionary Government there. He had left for France after the fiasco of the Zhongshan Gunboat Incident. After that incident, Chen Duxiu[6] had praised him to the skies, and his followers had taken up the chorus, urging Wang to resume his former leading position, as if once Wang Jingwei was re-installed, China's revolution would be accomplished and the Chinese Communist Party would have fulfilled its mission and could be dissolved.

There was a virtual whirlwind of excitement when Wang Jingwei showed up in Wuhan, as if a holy prophet of the Revolution had descended upon us. Wang Jingwei carried himself with an air that suggested that he himself believed it too. The minute he arrived in Wuhan, he had thrown out the challenge: "Revolutionaries, stand to the left! Non-revolutionaries, back off!" Such slogans were wildly applauded. The tri-city of Wuhan decided to give Wang Jingwei a welcome rally, to be held in Wuchang.

Before arriving in Wuhan, Wang Jingwei had made a stop in Shanghai and published a joint declaration with Chen Duxiu—"Joint

---

5. Wang Jingwei, at the time a leading figure of the GMD Left, had been forced out of the country after the March 20 (1926) Zhongshan Gunboat Incident. Now, following the GMD's Third Plenum in March 1927, Leftist influence was clearly dominant: a GMD Political Council was established as the supreme organ of Party power in Wuhan, and steps were taken to subordinate the military to civilian control, steps obviously directed at Chiang Kai-shek and the GMD Right. Under these circumstances, Wang Jingwei was invited back from abroad in the hope of staying the revolutionary course and cementing the GMD-CCP alliance.
6. Chen Duxiu (1879–1943), founder of the journal *New Youth* (Xin qingnian, also known as *La Jeunesse*). Chen played an important role in the May Fourth Movement (1919). China's leading Marxist, he was one of the founders of the Chinese Communist Party in 1921, and headed the CCP from 1921 to 1927.

Declaration of the Leaders of the GMD and the CCP," promising longstanding cooperation between the two parties.

When he arrived in Wuhan, Wang had hoped that Nanjing [meaning Chiang Kai-shek] would make some concessions to Wuhan, but it was not to be. The April Twelfth Incident[7] took place in Shanghai, followed by the April Fifteenth Incident in Canton.

Furthermore, on April 18 [Chiang Kai-shek] set up his own government and his own Party Central in Nanjing and conducted a violent purge of the Party.

Thus the confrontation between Nanjing [represented by Chiang Kai-shek and the GMD Right] and Wuhan [represented by Wang Jingwei and the GMD Left, including the Communists] was out in the open.

VI

With the flare-up of open conflict between Nanjing and Wuhan, the atmosphere in Wuhan became extremely tense. Worker pickets, now fully armed, were functioning as military police and arresting counterrevolutionaries right and left. Plainclothes men from the Political Department were also out in full force, while an Anti-X [Chiang] Committee was formally established. Besides the above, many other organizations were set up, such as the Service Center for the Oppressed Comrades of Southeast China, the Service Center for Political Workers, the Office for Party Affairs of Jiangsu, Zhejiang, Anhui, and other similar organizations.

In this intense anti-X political atmosphere, I myself had actually been arrested as a counterrevolutionary. The whole thing was a downright farce. It was a Saturday evening and I had crossed the river into Hankou to attend a send-off party. At the time, I was supposed to depart with the Fourth Army [as previously described], so my friends took turns feting me. On that particular evening, Luo was throwing a party for me at the Apricot Village Restaurant, and there were about

7. The April Twelfth Incident in Shanghai. At 4:00 AM, heavily armed gangsters launched an attack against the headquarters of the city's unions, killing many union members and arresting hundreds more. At a protest rally the next day, protesters were fired on by GMD troops and almost one hundred were killed.

a dozen guests, all of them my former colleagues from the Party CEC. We ate and drank merrily and planned to wrap up the day with mahjong at the Whampoa Military Academy Alumni Club. Mao and Luo were both staying at the Club. After dinner, we broke up and I was the first to jump into a rickshaw. The rickshaw stopped at the entrance to the Alumni Club. I jumped out, paid, and was about to walk in when I saw that the entrance was filled with picketing workers in dark-blue uniforms. The situation was serious, but I never imagined that it would involve me. The minute I crossed the threshold, however, two workers pointed at me with their pistols while another two twisted my arms behind my back and tied them together.

"Hey, this is a mistake! How can you arrest me?"

"Shut up, you counterrevolutionary!" a young worker thumped me on the back.

"Counterrevolutionary my foot! I am propaganda chief of the Fourth Army's Political Department!" I protested, but to no avail.

"Who cares about your rank! We are now in revolutionary times. You counterrevolutionary, you are caught!"

Since explaining didn't work, I had no choice but to see this mix-up through to the end. By now, the workers had nabbed five "counterrevolutionaries." Of the other four people, I knew Xu, who had also been staff at the Political Affairs Department and was staying at the Alumni Club since the Department had been dismantled.

The five of us were all in uniform, our leather leg wrappings gleaming, our shoes tapping the pavement smartly. Unfortunately, our hands were tied behind our backs, and we were being frogmarched by a group of worker-militiamen in dark-blue uniforms. It was after dark, but still there were people around who stopped to gape.

"Oho, another batch!"

"Wow, all in uniform!"

"Goodness, five of them!"

I could hear what the people were saying, and I could imagine how those people were cursing and wanted to see us in jail. I was only conscious of the situation as being ridiculous, a stupid misunderstanding.

"Comrade, where are you taking me?" I asked in amusement.

The young fellow answered: "Who is your comrade? Your comrades are in Nanjing!"

His ferocity caught me by surprise, and I countered by saying, still joking: "Me, a counterrevolutionary! When I joined the Revolution, you were still in your mommy's tummy!" He had no answer to that, and soon we reached the General Workers' Union, and from there I was transferred to the police station.

At the police station, we were handed over to the crime investigation team. We gave our personal information and then an officer said: "Take them into the detention room!"

"Take it easy," I said, "I need to talk to your bureau chief. By what right are you detaining me?"

"By what right?! You are a spy from Nanjing. Talking to the bureau chief won't help you!"

"I am an old friend of your bureau chief. He knows who I am. Talk to your bureau chief before you lock me up, my friend!" I tried to persuade him.

Just as we were arguing, their captain appeared.

"Goodness! Zhu! Is it you? What are you doing here?" He was very surprised to see me as a detainee. I was also surprised. This Captain Chen was an old acquaintance. I had no idea that he had become head of investigation for the police. Actually I did not know their bureau chief—I had been bluffing. Their captain, an old acquaintance of mine, turned up in the nick of time.

"Chen, what is all this about, arresting me? I have done nothing!"

After some explaining, I was released, thus ending a three-hour farce.

VII

After having played out my role in this misunderstanding, I fully realized the strength of the workers of Wuhan. The next day, I went to call on the Hubei Workers' Union, this time not as a prisoner, but as an honored guest. We were a small group from the Political Department of the Fourth Army and our boss, Liao Qianwu, had written us a letter of introduction addressed to the head of the Union, Xiang Zhongfa.

The two men had worked together in the underground back in the old days and were good friends. Xiang personally showed us around the various departments, filling us in about their work.

Xiang, of working class background, was himself a native of Hubei. He had won the trust of the workers by dint of hard work and an indomitable spirit. Dressed in dark-blue pants and a short jacket like a worker, he had the emaciated look of an opium addict, though he was only in his forties. It must have been the result of long years of overwork. Xiang was a good speaker and very capable. Zhang Fakui, deputy commander of the Fourth Army, thought highly of him.

The National Convention of Workers was about to be convened in Wuhan, and the delegates were beginning to arrive, thus the extreme pressure of work on the Hubei Workers' Union. During the May Day celebration the previous year, when the Workers' National Convention was held in Canton, I had been a guest of honor at the opening ceremony. And now that the Convention was soon to be held in Wuhan, I was hoping to be invited again. But it was not to be, since soon after this visit I had set out with the Fourth Army on that aborted expedition against Nanjing.

As delegates to the National Convention were arriving, I met some old acquaintances. Zheng Futa, the delegate from Shanghai, was an old friend, and we were happy to meet again. Zheng had been a spirited union leader in Shanghai. Still in his early twenties, he had once been head of the Hubei Workers' Union, a member of the Executive Committee of the General Workers' Union, and a member of the Standing Committee. Later he returned to Shanghai and became head of the Shanghai Workers' Union. Looking at my friend and considering his accomplishments, I felt very ashamed of myself. Within the year or so since we parted, he had forged ahead, but what had I to show for it? Nothing—I was just my same old self.

Su Zhaozheng, head of Labor Affairs for the General Union, was also of working class background, like Xiang Zhongfa, but his accomplishments were even more spectacular than Xiang's. Su was the head of the Canton-Hong Kong Dock Workers' Strike Committee, in a word, the most important figure in that event. We met for the first time in the spring of 1926 at a huge rally held on the campus of Sun Yat-sen University. Short and thin, wearing the short jacket of a worker, he had shown up surrounded by seven or eight armed bodyguards, and for a moment I almost thought that those men were guarding a criminal. Then I was told that he was the nationally known leader of the Canton-Hong Kong striking workers Su Zhaozheng. I had disapproved of his retinue of bodyguards—*Why put on these official airs?* I thought. Then I learned that the Hong Kong authorities had put a 10,000 silver *yuan* price on his head! Right now Su Zhaozheng has become head of the [newly created] Department of Labor Affairs for the Party CEC. It was a specially designated position which carried a monthly salary of 120 *yuan*. I had imagined that he would have even more bodyguards, but this time when I met him at the General Union in Wuhan, he did not bring any.

He and I sat down for a long conversation; he was very bitter over the tragedy of the April Twelfth Incident in Shanghai and the April Fifteenth Incident in Canton.

The International Workers' Delegation arrived in Wuhan and was warmly welcomed. The head of the International Workers' Delegation was an Englishman, Tom Mann.[8] A vigorous old man of seventy-one, Tom was the head of the minority in the British labor movement [known as the leftist, or revolutionary, faction]. Apart from Tom Mann, there was the Frenchman Jacques Doriot,[9] and the American Earl Browder.[10] They were all from the leftist faction, opposed to the Amsterdam International (which was allied to the "yellow" union of the Second International). The delegation's itinerary had included a first stop in Canton. But the April Fifteenth Incident in Canton, following the April Twelfth Incident in Shanghai, had put an end to all their planned activities; in fact they had hardly any freedom of movement in Canton.

8. Tom Mann (1856–1941), British labor activist, Communist Party member, and president of the General Labourers' Union. Tom Mann had fought for the eight-hour day.

9. Jacques Doriot (1898–1945), French working-class leader, member of the French Communist Party.

10. Earl Browder (1891–1973), general secretary of the Communist Party of the United States from 1932 to 1945.

But now in Wuhan, they were happily surprised at the warmth of their welcome. The various mass organizations and institutions took turns throwing their own welcoming events. We staff at the Fourth Army all attended the one held by the Central Military Political Academy on its Wuhan campus. The rally was steeped in revolutionary fervor. Slogans in Chinese and English hung from every wall, indoors and outdoors. The meeting started shortly after the arrival of our group. Deng Yanda gave the opening welcome speech, followed by Tom Mann. This old gentleman was so full of vigor and enthusiasm, it really put us youngsters to shame. Tom began by describing his happy impressions on arriving in Wuhan.

"In the past," he began, "we Brits, with the exception of revolutionary workers, had only contempt for the Chinese people. Some actually think of the Chinese as pigs, to be slaughtered for dishes to go down with their drinks. But since the outbreak of the Great Revolution, their contempt has turned to fear. They do have something to fear. If Neville Chamberlain[11] and company and all the lackeys of the bourgeoisie could see the current great revolutionary upheaval, they would shake in their boots . . ." Then Tom went on to give a summary of the British working class movement. His speech was greeted with thunderous applause. At the end of his speech, Tom took out a big red kerchief and waved it vigorously, shouting "Long live! Long live!" in Chinese, while sending the audience into rapture.

As Tom left the stage amid another wave of applause, he seized a young female attendant nearby and gave her a kiss before descending the platform, making the poor girl blush scarlet like Tom's kerchief which he was still waving in the air. Spontaneous strains of the "The Internationale": "Arise, you prisoners of starvation! Arise you wretched of the earth! . . . Let us group together and tomorrow . . ." sounded from different corners of the hall, reverberating far and wide.

After Tom, it was the French delegate Jacques Doriot, then the American delegate Earl Browder, and then the representative of the Third International, the Indian M.N. Roy. After Roy, representatives

11. Neville Chamberlain (1869–1940), conservative British politician, prime minister of Great Britain from May 1937 to May 1940.

from Korea, Vietnam, South Africa and Taiwan all spoke, and Borodin gave the final speech.

The delegates had come from the four continents of Asia, Europe, America and Africa, from countries as far apart as Russia, Britain, America, France, India, Korea, Japan, Vietnam, Mongolia, South Africa, and elsewhere.

One can truthfully say that the meeting was a historically significant gathering of international revolutionaries.

VIII

By order of the Special Party Branch of the Fourth Army, I was sent on a mission to pay a visit to Borodin, whose wife had been arrested by the warlord Zhang Zongchang.

The Russian adviser's residence was in Wuchang, in a district known as Garden-by-the-River. I and a colleague from Fourth Army Headquarters arrived just after the paunchy adviser had returned from Hankou. He made us welcome, and was pleased by the formal letter [of condolence] from the Party CEC which we presented. He said, however, that he was not overly upset by his wife's arrest, explaining that arrest and imprisonment were part of the life of a revolutionary, and execution often the inevitable end. He then told us stories of the revolutionary activities that he and his wife had carried out in Russia, England, Turkey and other parts of the world, and that they had both been arrested in Russia and in England.

Borodin then changed the subject and talked about the tragic death of Li Dazhao[12] at the hands of the warlord Zhang Zuolin.[13] He praised Li as one of the most talented of China's revolutionary leaders and expressed sincere condolences for his loss. We had gone

12. Li Dazhao (1889–1927), early Marxist and important figure in the May Fourth Movement, one of the founders of the CCP. An influential leader during the GMD-CCP alliance, Li was captured and executed by the warlord Zhang Zuolin.

13. Zhang Zuolin (1875–1928), a warlord from Northeast China who controlled Manchuria, Eastern Mongolia, and finally Peking. He was defeated by Chiang Kai-shek's Northern Expeditionary army and killed by Japanese officers on his way back to the Northeast.

to console Borodin for his misfortune, but our visit had ended with Borodin consoling us. There was a string of people coming to offer him condolences, so we took our leave.

Li Dazhao

Zhang Zuolin

In the days back in Canton and in the Whampoa Military Academy, I had met Borodin on many occasions and had heard his speeches. At the time, his residence in Canton was on Dadong Street, across from the Party CEC headquarters. We met almost daily, and I enjoyed our conversations. He was a mine of information about the world revolution. Borodin's wife was plump, like her husband, and spoke English. Although a revolutionary, her attention to her personal appearance was nothing less than that of a bourgeois aesthete, and she also decorated their home most tastefully. In Canton, when she spoke at the Inauguration of the Women's Movement Training Institute, she pointed out that women should care for their personal appearance, though she did not elaborate on what constituted female beauty. I am not against the idea of female beauty, but more pertinent is that the relationship between the sexes should be free and casual as part of Nature, as I explained earlier. I believe that if we remove the mystery enveloping sex, a lot of evil could be avoided.

IX

One Sunday morning, a group of colleagues and I crossed the river to Hanyang. The streets of Hanyang were narrow and dirty, not to be compared to Wuchang. Our first destination on our arrival in Hanyang was the Arsenal. We approached Wang, a committee member of the Party branch at the Arsenal, and he gave us a tour. I did not understand the technicalities, so I found my way to the workers' club and night school, and struck up a conversation with two workers.

Leaving the Arsenal, we were intending to climb Tortoise Mountain, but on our way there, I met my old friend Yi, who was then heading the Peasants' Association in Hanyang, and he insisted that we all have a meal together. It then occurred to us that, indeed, we needed a meal as we had not eaten anything since that morning. So we retraced our steps into town, walked along a dirty street, and found a dirty restaurant.

We ordered several dishes and their best drinks. The place may have been small, but the dishes were up to standard. We ate and drank to our satisfaction and stayed until past two in the afternoon.

The owner of the restaurant was from Tianjin, a stout middle-aged man who told us that he had taken over the restaurant from his father, who had started the business, and that by now the restaurant was a fixture in town. We sat there the best part of the afternoon, ordering up wine and dishes one after another. It was a rare coup for the little restaurant, and the owner bent over backward to give us satisfaction. I asked him about business in Hanyang, and he shook his head dejectedly.

"Nowadays, it's really hard."

We asked why. At first he refused to talk, but after some coaxing he lowered his defenses and opened up.

"Revolution—we ordinary folks of course want revolution, but sometimes these workers go too far. There are six apprentices here in this little restaurant. After the Revolutionary Army took over, they set up a workers' union and all our apprentices joined. Since then, it has been endless: one day they want a raise, the next day they want better working conditions. One day a union official turns up, the next day, a union letter arrives. If I do not raise wages, they will take me to the police station. If everyone gets a raise, I will not be able to manage. I wanted to discharge two apprentices, but that is not allowed. The union accuses me of oppressing the workers and threatens to take me away as a counterrevolutionary. I want to close the shop and go back to my village, but that is not allowed either. I am accused of being an evil capitalist . . ."

The problem was not limited to Hanyang—the same situation prevailed everywhere in the tri-city of Wuhan. Nowadays the workers who had been oppressed were indeed lording it over the owners.

In Wuhan, the salesmen and apprentices' movement was moving ahead full speed. Combining forces with the students, they raised bold demands of owners. The unions had their own pickets and their own arms. They could detain non-cooperative owners, take them to the union, set up court, and put them on trial. The workers had become the masters now, and the former masters were trodden underfoot. Times had indeed changed.

If the owner was in custody and the problem could not be solved quickly, then the business would be run by the apprentices, or the enterprise would be turned over to the Workers' Union. I did not have time to find out how that would work out.

X

The foreign press has painted the situation in Wuhan as a reign of confusion and terror. But we in Wuhan saw the situation as a preview of the ideal future of humanity.

Wuhan was surging forward, full of vitality. People were trying to forge a new future for humanity. In this vast project, it was inevitable that sometimes things go wrong.

I did have a complaint, though. My complaint was against the official newspaper, the *Republican Daily* [Mingguo ribao].

The *Republican Daily* was the official voice of the GMD. It was operating under the direction of the CEC Propaganda Department; the head of the Department, Gu Mengyu, was concurrently editor-in-chief of the newspaper. This in itself was a clear indication of the importance of the paper. But to judge by the way the paper was run, the editor-in-chief seemed totally unaware of the importance of what he was doing.

The working editor was an obscure "scholar," Chen Qixiu. Scholarship apart, Chen's qualifications as an editor were dubious. His writing was unreadable, the uniformly stilted titles such as "The People of Jiangxi Have Risen Up," "The People of Southeast Asia Have Risen Up," and so on were enough to put readers off. The supplement page was edited by Sun Fuyuan, a typical petty bourgeois. One can imagine what kind of supplement he could turn out.

Other papers were spreading the rumor that Wuhan had destroyed education. Actually, schools from primary school to college were running normally, the only difference being that students were more active than before. They were not satisfied with merely sitting in classrooms, they were taking part in practical work. This was offensive in the eyes of those who wanted students to stick to their textbooks to the exclusion of everything else. But the question remains: how dare we keep students away from real life?

CHAPTER FOUR

The Henan Campaign

I

The drooping peach blossoms in Victoria Garden were a reminder that spring was coming to an end.

It had been over a month since we had reached Wuhan. We had been reveling in its intense revolutionary atmosphere and barely noticed that spring has come and would soon be gone. Shouldn't we try to grasp its last lingering charms? But I had lost myself in meetings and office affairs and had completely ignored spring. In fact I had never gone on an outing, never looked at a flower, until I found myself in Victoria Garden, where the peach blossoms were already drooping. Should I say that I have not done justice to the charms of spring? But we do not have any right to seek pleasure when so many people are struggling to keep body and soul together, much less do we have the right to luxuries. Should we envy those bourgeois lords and ladies whose lives are a round of pleasures—today on West Lake, tomorrow on Lake Tai? Is that the kind of life that we aspire to? Is that the lifestyle that we should emulate? Certainly not! Let us not forget that in the miserable factories, machines do not stop for the workers to catch a breath of spring. The workers are sweating in ragged winter clothes; their lighter clothes are still in the pawnshop and cannot be redeemed. Moreover, there are many more people who cannot even find a factory job. I am enjoying a much better life than the workers: how can I complain? Actually I should be ashamed of myself, I should strive harder. We have no time to spare for the beauties of spring. We must tie on our straw sandals, shoulder our bags of dried rice, strap on our revolvers, and march off on a new expedition.

Before this, we were supposed to go *east* to Nanjing [to take down Chiang Kai-shek]. That plan having been aborted, we were now starting out on another northern expedition, this time north toward Henan. What's more, we were to start off barely five days after getting our marching orders. These quick changes of plans are part and parcel of the military life, I suppose.

But the fact remains that when the [Chiang Kai-shek separatist] government in Nanjing had not yet been set up and the [bloody] April Twelfth Incident in Shanghai had not yet taken place, the Wuhan Revolutionary government had indeed made preparations for an *eastward* expedition [targeting Chiang]. Now that [Chiang] has set up a [separatist] government in Nanjing, pitting himself against the Revolutionary Government in Wuhan, we were not going east for a punishing expedition against him after all, but actually going north! It didn't make any sense to me.

Two days before setting out, Director Deng Yanda of the General Political Department got us officers together to brief us on the plan of action and the work ahead following the success of the expedition. I seized the chance to ask him why were we giving up the eastern campaign [to Nanjing] and going north to [Henan] instead.

According to Director Deng, there had been two opinions concerning the direction of the planned expedition. One group maintained that it would be easy to go east and nip the Nanjing government in the bud. A second maintained that the eastern expedition *might not necessarily succeed*, in which case the Northeastern warlords might seize the chance to descend southward along the Peking-Wuhan railway line and take Wuhan hands down. What this meant was that while we *might not be able to take Nanjing,* we will certainly *lose Wuhan.* According to this line of thinking, going east was decidedly risky.

This group advocated going *north,* claiming that the Nanjing government [to our east] was not strong enough to march against us, so we need not worry about our rear. Besides, the argument ran, in going north against the Northeastern warlords, we Wuhan forces had an obvious military advantage. An added argument in favor of going north was that we expected to combine forces with [the Christian warlord] Feng Yuxiang[1] in Henan. Feng Yuxiang was not only opposed to the Northeastern warlords, he had additionally denounced the Nanjing government as an "illegal organization" and had pointed out that XXX [Chiang Kai-shek,] was himself nothing less than a "warlord."

At the time, Tang Shengzhi and Zhang Fakui supported the eastern expedition to Nanjing, while Wang Jingwei and the Soviet adviser Borodin supported going north. The latter prevailed, so northward we were bound.

Tang Shengzhi's and Zhang Fakui's men constituted the main force of the expedition and were divided into three columns, with Tang Shengzhi as commander-in-chief.

The First Column, led by Zhang Fakui, was comprised of the Fourth Army and the Eleventh Army as well as the independent Fifth Division led by He Long. These forces constituted the *Right Wing.*

The Second Column, led by Liu Xing, was composed of the Thirty-fifth and the Thirty-sixth armies. Deployed along the Peking-Wuhan railway line, they constituted the *Front Line.*

The Third Column was composed of newly incorporated forces led by Tian Weiqin and Jin Yun'e, along with the Provisional Third Army of Liang Shoukai, the Provisional Fifth Army of Pang Bingxun, the newly incorporated Fourteenth Division of An Juncai, and the newly

1. Feng Yuxiang (1882–1948) began his military career under the old Republic in the early 1920s, visited the Soviet Union in 1926, and briefly joined the GMD during the Northern Expedition. Later, he joined up with the CCP in the War of Resistance against Japanese Aggression. After the war, Feng opposed Chiang Kai-shek's civil war and was instrumental in founding the GMD Revolutionary Committee.

incorporated Sixteenth Division of Zhang Wanxin. They made up the *Left Wing*. Generally speaking, these newly incorporated miscellaneous forces were weak.

The rear guard: the Twenty-fourth Division of Ye Ting's Eleventh Army would guard Wuhan while Ye Ting himself would lead the Wuchang garrison; Zhu Peide, commander of the Third Army and the Ninth Army, was to remain in Jiangxi Province to guard against possible attacks from Nanjing and Anhui Province. Part of the Thirty-fifth Army led by He Jian, part of the Second Army led by Lu Diping, and the Fourteenth Army led by Chen Jiayou were ordered to remain in Hunan Province to guard against possible attacks coming from Guangdong Province.

We at the Political Department started out from Wuchang on April 22, 1927, in the company of Division Headquarters. Our departure had been hasty. Before leaving, we had been caught up in the Party's internal problems in the so-called "Party Power movement," and in dealing with problems coming from Nanjing, and hardly had time to prepare for the expedition. Thus, we were still up to our eyes in work on the eve of departure. But thinking of the coming expedition and the prospect of destroying the Northeastern warlords north of the Yellow River, I was elated. The straw sandals on my feet, and the cotton leggings which had replaced the leather ones, all felt very comfortable.

We started off from the Public Stadium and made our way to Hanyang Gate to board the little steamboat which brought us to Xujiapeng, from where we had to cross the river to Jiang'an station to board the northbound train on the Peking-Wuhan line.

On a previous stop in Xujiapeng, it had rained through a whole day and night and we had not gone ashore to see the sights. But now that our train was late we had a chance to look around. Xujiapeng was a little township on the outskirts of Wuchang, where Nature offered a beautiful retreat from the city.

After stepping off the little steamboat that brought us to Xujiapeng, the first problem that confronted us was how to feed our bellies. The logistics people immediately ordered the cooks to go ashore to set up a kitchen. But being too hungry to wait, I dragged my colleagues from the Political Department—Zhang from the editorial section, Fan from the training section and Chen from Party Affairs, and the four of us went ashore and headed straight for a little restaurant, where the dishes clearly beat the big restaurants in Wuhan.

Speaking of restaurants, I could not help thinking of my depraved life in Wuhan during the past two months. Since arriving in Wuhan, although I had indulged in high-sounding rhetoric, the life I led had been thoroughly depraved, the first offense being my fixation on food. I had eaten my way through all the restaurants of the tri-city of Wuhan. In Wuchang, my favorite was a place near the Yuemachang, whose name now escapes me. There were also Tong Xing and One Glimpse of Heaven and countless other smaller ones which I patronized—too many to remember. In Wuhan, there had been Elegant Taste on Jiaotong Street, not to mention Apricot Village, Tong Hua House, Pu Hai House, and many more. Although my gourmet taste did not get in the way of work, when I think of the hungry masses, I feel ashamed of myself.

When we finished our meal—coming back to that day in Xujiapeng—we went to call on the local Party Special Branch, but did not find anyone there. The office was located on Wuchang Street near the Town Hall, a beautiful Western-style building with a garden. The sight reminded me of what the papers had been saying about the imminent bankruptcy of Xujiapeng Township. To judge by appearances, it seemed unlikely.

It was already close to three months since our arrival in Wuhan, and now we had finally discovered this wonderful retreat in Xujiapeng. Walking on the main road paved over with sand was such a good feeling, with willows lining the road to shade us from the sun. As evening closed gently around us, a soft breeze wafted down wisps of catkins, transporting us into a fairy scene. It made me think of Jia Zhi's[2] "Stirrings of Spring":

2. Jia Zhi (718–772), a Tang dynasty poet.

Green grass and willow's tender buds,
Peach trees and pear trees in bloom.
The east wind does not dispel sadness,
But prolongs the days of gloom.

That in turn reminded me of Wang Changling's[3] poem of a young woman's stirrings on a spring morning:

The young wife in her boudoir knows no care,
Richly decked out, she goes to the upper chamber.
Seeing the willows sprouting new leaves,
She regrets sending her man to seek imperial favors.

Thinking of the poem stirred up my own feelings of loss. Of course we ourselves were not young women confined to boudoirs, nor were there any young women pining for us in their boudoirs. But it was precisely this reality that cast gloom over me—that no one was missing me. Of course, if there had been a young woman waiting, things would have been more complicated; it would *have been* an added burden. For instance, if I were in a situation as described in the two famous lines

Pitiful bones lying by the Wuding River,
The man living in some young woman's dreams . . .[4]

it would have drained all my courage in the revolutionary struggle. In fact, I was often seized by these unhealthy daydreams. No, we must not let ourselves be overcome by poetic sentiments or philosophical musings. No! We must forge ahead in the revolutionary struggle!

II

We spent one whole day in Xujiapeng waiting for transportation, but at least it had been a pleasant day. The next morning, we were transported across the river to the opposite shore.

We got off the boat at a point close to the train station on the Peking-Wuhan line. What met us, however, was the news that our

3. Wang Changling (698–756), a Tang dynasty poet.
4. By Chen Tao (812–885?), a Tang dynasty poet.

designated train was still chugging along on its way from the Wusheng Pass and would not reach us before noon, and that it was problematic whether we could leave that same afternoon. Our luggage was sitting on the platform; it would be too much trouble to move it again. We decided to leave our luggage and find somewhere to stay in the little wooded area near the station—the minute our train arrived, we could take off immediately.

In the little grove near the station, we found ourselves surrounded by tall willows, enlivened by red flowers blossoming on unnamed bushes scattered here and there. The mild winds of late spring stole through the woods, lightly pelting us with snowy catkins. The air was buzzing with bees, and butterflies flitted around us airily. Overhead, the song of a thrush filled the air. It was incredible that I could find myself in such a charming spot while marching off to war.

The name of the station, the Jiang'an Railway Station, is a name revered in China's revolutionary history. This was the execution ground in the aftermath of the railway workers' strike of February 7, 1923. Lin Xiangqian, leader of the Jiang'an branch of the Peking-Wuhan Railway Workers Union, had been beheaded right here. Years have passed by as I write this; the bodies of Lin Xiangqian and other martyrs have turned to dust, and what had the Revolution accomplished thus far? We had gotten rid of the warlord Wu Peifu and also chased away his running dogs. May this be a consolation to our martyrs. But we must strive on, we were going to Henan, we must take the cities of Zhengzhou and Luoyang, which used to be the base of the striking workers—now the base of the warlord Wu Peifu. We must also take Peking, and lead the oppressed masses of the whole world to Liberation.

When in Wuchang, I had always wanted to visit the Jiang'an Railway Station, which had played such a heroic and tragic role in the history of the Chinese Revolution, but had never found the time. Now that I was right next to it, I decided to pay a proper visit to the site. The platform of the little station was packed with soldiers and groups of people hanging around. As I made my way into the station building, I saw that various branches of the Revolutionary Army had set up their offices within the building and many officers were milling around.

I made my way inside and met with my colleague Luo. Luo gave me the good news that our special train was on its way, and that we would certainly start off by three o'clock at the latest. The news made me happy, as I was eager to get going.

The office was packed, standing room only, so I left and walked around the platform, which was piled up with goods waiting to be shipped off. From their dilapidated state, it was obvious that they had been lying there for a long time.

An old worker at the station said that these freight containers had been there for over a year, waiting to be shipped to the North, but now that the war was on again, there was even less chance of them ever getting there.

I was surprised to see so many ragged locals crowding the platform.

"Are there any civilian trains coming?" I asked the old worker.

"Oh no, we haven't seen civilian trains these last six months. Last month we did see one reaching Xinyang, but nowadays you won't even see one going to Wusheng Pass. The warlord Wu Peifu has taken away the engines. Right now all we can do is to provide special trains for the army."

"Then what are these people doing here?"

"You mean this crowd? Oh, they are hoping to catch a ride, a passenger train or a military convoy, anything that moves. They know that the Revolutionary Army will not hurt them, so they are not afraid."

The old worker was called away, and I turned to the man next to me.

"Where are you going?"

"I am hoping to catch a ride into Xinyang, Your Excellency. When the train arrives, please let me climb up, I will be very grateful."

"I don't know if there will be space in the special car."

"Oh no, not in the car, Your Excellency. I am only hoping to climb onto the roof of the car."

"Can you do that?"

"What else can we do? Since the war, the trains have stopped running. All we can do is wait for military trains and climb to the roofs of the carriages. No one tries to pull us down. But if I am not quick enough, all the space on the roof will be taken."

I asked the old man about things in Henan; he only shook his head and sighed.

The smell on the platform was unbearable, not only coming from people, but also from the cargo goods, some of which were rotting. I left the platform and wandered to a primary school nearby to take a look, but the school was closed.

I went back to our retreat in the woods. Since the train was still on its way, we had a meal, then sat and rested in a little pavilion nearby as we listened to the warbling of the thrushes.

It was a wonderful cloudless day, and sitting in the pavilion, I drifted off to sleep. When I woke up, it was close to three in the afternoon. The others in our group were spread out here and there in the wooded area, dozing next to their luggage. Obviously the train had not yet arrived. *Looks like we are stuck here for the day! Such a nuisance!* I said to myself.

I got hold of Ye of the Organization Department, and the two of us went to the train station for an update. Fortunately we ran into Luo. "Officer Luo, you said the train will arrive at noon, but it is three already . . ."

"It is definitely coming by five at the latest. We are leaving tonight, that's for sure."

"Leaving tonight? You'll be lucky to leave tomorrow! The train is stalled in Zhumadian station . . . ," a staff officer with the Military Affairs Department butted in. But I had more confidence in Luo, since he was in charge of coordinating transportation.

I returned to the pavilion in the woods and chatted with my boss, Liao Qianwu. He asked me to join him for a drink, and then we were joined by staff officer Li Renyi. The three of us went to a small place near the station, a Tianjin eatery which usually catered to railway workers and peasants. Seeing that we were armed and followed by orderlies, the owner found us a clean table and treated us with excessive respect. Liao's two orderlies and my own young orderly, all three fully armed, stood at attention outside the restaurant. The restaurant's regular customers were too frightened to enter. When I realized this, I ordered the three of them to go and wait at the railway station.

The three of us took our time drinking—we were still awaiting some dishes. The cooking was excellent, topping some of the bigger restaurants in Wuhan. One really should not judge by appearances alone.

We sat drinking until past five. There was still no news of the train. Obviously we were not going to leave.

The steamboat which brought us here had returned to Wuhan, and our train still had not arrived. There was barely standing room at the station, and no public facilities around, so where were we going to spend the night? We had a meal in the woods; then night descended and we started to worry about sleeping arrangements. Finally, we handful of senior officers took the pavilion while the younger ones made do in the open.

As night descended it turned cold. A new moon cast down a pale light. We put out our lanterns and started chatting. We four in the pavilion represented the four corners of the country: Director Liao was from Shaanxi, representing the North. Ye of the Organization Department was from Canton and represented the South. Liu of Administration was from Hunan, representing the Center. I myself was from Zhejiang, representing the Southeast. We chatted about the special features of our own localities, and then went on to talk about the Revolution.

As we were close to the site, our conversation inevitably drifted to the February Seventh Massacre of 1923. Actually Director Liao had been an actor in that event. After the collapse of the [railway workers'] movement, Liao himself almost suffered the same fate as the martyr Lin Xiangqian. He had first hid in an opium den in Wuhan, then managed to reach Xiang Zhongfa and hide on a raft before finally fleeing to Canton. Liao made light of the dangers as he told the story.

When we young people get together, the topic of conversation inevitably turns to the subject of women. On this occasion, however, Director Liao was close to sixty, Liu was close to forty, while Ye was over thirty. I was the only young man. Besides, there was a strict sense of hierarchy within the army; our orderlies were sleeping nearby so we were guarded in our speech. Finally, after chatting for two hours, I could not hold off any longer and said: "Say, Director Liao, we at the Political Department should hire some female staff. Management has female staff, Organization has female staff, why shouldn't we in Propaganda hire some female staff?" Ye from Organization immediately jumped in, saying that women were indispensable to his Department. Liu from Management also stressed that women were indispensible in secretarial and financial services, because they were more careful and reliable.

We were actually arguing for argument's sake, since we all knew that Director Liao would never agree to hire female staff. The fact is, he had an aversion to women, referring to them in outrageously sexist terms. It was known that he had never had a romantic relationship. He maintained that women stood in the way of a man's devotion to the Revolution, and that he had kept away from women for the sake of the Revolution. That did not make sense of course, since humankind would come to an end if everybody followed his example. Back at the office there had been talk about the real reason for Director Liao's aversion to women. One explanation was that he had been disappointed in love in his youth. The other explanation was that he could not perform. The general consensus was that his physical disability lay at the bottom of his misogyny.

Chatting on about this and that, we didn't fall asleep until the wee hours.

III

It was only by noon of April 24, one whole day after our arrival at Jiang'an Station, that our special train finally arrived to pick us up.

There were about twenty or so carriages altogether, no second-class carriages, and only two third-class carriages. All the rest were fourth-class and freight cars.

The train itself was a living example of the dilapidated state of our railway system. These twenty plus carriages were a motley collection. To judge by the destinations painted on their sides, only two carriages were from the Peking-Wuhan line. As for the rest, they were from all over the map of China: Tianjin-Shanghai, Peking-Fengtian, Peking-Suiyuan, Gansu-Qinghai . . . whatever. Others ran locally within the provinces of Shandong, or Henan . . . wherever. It seems that all the trains running between south of the Great Wall and north of the Yangtse River were represented.

The engine for our train was presumably from the Gansu-Qinghai line and was as fast as a lame cow.

The train started off from Jiang'an Station at five o'clock in the afternoon. This expedition had been so hastily put together, it seemed as if we were fleeing. There was no send-off party. Forlornly, our train left the station.

When waiting for the train to arrive, we had been so impatient, but now that it had actually arrived and was taking us north, I felt a kind of nostalgia for Wuhan. Compared to the first Northern Expedition,[5] this second Northern Expedition[6] was more dangerous, more risky. The reasons being as follows:

Nowadays, the population in the north is unorganized, unlike the situation during the first Northern Expedition, when there was wide popular support.

The Northeastern warlords, target of this current expedition, are much stronger than the Southern warlords overthrown in the first Northern Expedition.

Due to the rift within the GMD between the Nanjing faction and the Wuhan faction, we were weakened and isolated, unlike the first Northern Expedition when we had been strong and united.

The machine guns of the Northeastern warlords were formidable. For all we knew we could all end up as cannon fodder. For myself, I

---

5. See Spence, *The Search for Modern China*. "The strategy for the Northern Expedition called for three armed thrusts: one up the completed sections of the Canton-Wuhan railway, or along the Xiang River, to the key Hunan city of Changsha; one up the Gan River into Jiangxi; and one up the east coast into Fujian . . . The Canton government named Chiang Kai-shek commander in chief of these hybrid forces in June 1926, and the official mobilization order for the Northern expedition was issued on July 1 . . ." (pp. 328-330). The objectives were achieved and Wuhan fell on October 10, 1926.

6. Ibid. "These victories brought the debate over the next phase of Guomindang strategy. Chiang Kai-shek, at his Nanchang base, had decided on a drive to Shanghai by two routes . . . The Guomindang leaders in Wuhan . . . supported instead a northern drive up the Wuhan-Peking railway . . . hoping to effect a junction with several northern warlords . . ." notably Feng Yuxiang (p. 331).

had no fear, I actually felt that instant death has its advantages. Before starting out, I had written to a female comrade in Wuhan saying: "I hope to die on this expedition. All questions of love and revolution will then be resolved." Only in death would everything be thoroughly resolved. Living, nothing can be simple and clear-cut.

We at the Political Department occupied one third-class carriage and two freight cars. Before starting out, we were told that we might get first-class carriages, but now even third-class carriages were a privilege. Our orderlies and service people, along with our bags and supplies, were all crammed into the two freight cars, while we officers took the third-class carriage. It was very uncomfortable. But when I thought of the freight cars and those poor folks lying on top of the carriage, and still others clinging to chains *under* the carriage, I was grateful for my two seats where I could put my head down and get some sleep.

We young comrades were seated close together, and we talked about revolution and love and women, totally uninhibited. Director Liao treated us to beer and the dried beef he had brought along, and we enjoyed a hearty meal. The train chugged northward, and soon night descended. There was no lighting in the car, only a dim glow from our lanterns.

I had not read the papers since getting on the train. A comrade from the Secretariat got hold of a copy of the *Republican Daily*. When I saw editor Chen Qixiu's article, I put the paper aside, not even caring to skim through the news. Chen's article completely put me off. His name absolutely polluted the paper. He had dragged it down and turned it into a bureaucratic rag, a disgrace to our Party. I was not alone in my aversion. Everyone in Wuhan agreed with me on this point. It was nothing personal, I don't know the man; he and I had never met. But I firmly believe that someone should take two tanks of petrol to the *Republican Daily* building and burn it to the ground. If Borodin or Wang Jingwei won't do it, the only option left is for the Northeastern warlords to do it.

The train continued on its way, and we all drifted off to sleep. When we woke up the next morning, the train had reached the Li Village Railway Station. It was a relief to take a walk and breathe in some fresh air. The train had stopped to fill the water tank. From where we were at the station, we could see Jigong Mountain in the distance, a wonderful summer retreat. Jigong Mountain was not as tall as Lushan, but more imposing. Colorful villas dotted the slopes—retreats of warlords and foreign bigwigs. The warlord Wu Peifu used to visit his villa there periodically, before he was brought down. The train started off shortly after this brief stop; there was no time hike up the mountain.

Now that we were in Henan territory, I suddenly felt the difference—we were truly in the north now, with Wuhan long behind us. Tragedy struck as the train was passing through the tunnel at the Wusheng Pass. A man clinging to the chains under the train fell and was crushed. And there we were, sitting in the train, totally oblivious.

We were supposed to arrive at Xinyang around five in the afternoon, but at three, the train suddenly stopped at a little station. We thought that we had arrived ahead of time. But when we poked our heads out the window, it was clear we were not in Xinyang—we were in trouble. We were surrounded on all sides, not by soldiers, not by students, not by ordinary folks.

"It's the Red Spears!"[7] my young orderly exclaimed. Indeed, we were surrounded by members of the Red Spears. They were able-bodied peasants, armed not with rifles or machine guns, but with spears sporting a red tassel at the top. We had read about them in the papers, now they were right in front of us!

It was an imposing sight. Most eye-catching, of course, were the spears held erect in their hands. The long handles seemed to be made of wood, but tipped with iron. Taking it in at a glance, it was like a scene from a Chinese opera.

We had heard about the atrocities of the Red Spears, about how they would kill government soldiers and take their arms. Sitting in the train, I thought to myself, "Oh no, they're coming to grab our weapons . . ." There were few soldiers on our train, only a battalion

---

7. The Red Spears, a secret society in Henan formed to resist taxation. The group owed its growth to an alliance with the reigning warlord Wu Peifu, who controlled the railway network. See Graham Hutchings, *Modern China: Guide to a Century of Change* (Cambridge, MA: Harvard University Press, 2001), p. 191.

from the special force. If the Red Spears started to make trouble, we would be very vulnerable. Instinctively I looked down at my revolver, and asked my orderly "Is your gun loaded?" "Of course," he said. "Keep your grenades close to hand!" I ordered, and made sure that my own revolver was loaded.

I got off the carriage with some younger colleagues, followed by my orderly, to investigate the situation. Fully armed, we walked gingerly toward the crowd. From what I could see of their facial expressions, the Red Spears were not here to fight or to snatch our weapons. Personnel from Army Headquarters were talking to them. It turned out that they were heading for Xinyang to attend a General Congress, and they wanted a lift!

It seemed a reasonable request, but for us it was a real dilemma. Seeing as how crowded we were already, how could we possibly fit them in? But we could not refuse; we could not afford to offend them. What's more, we should try to make them understand us, to win them over to our cause! Thus we should try to accommodate them to the best of our ability, especially as their demand was not unreasonable. From where we were at this little station called East Double River, it was a mere fifty kilometres to Xinyang, where they were heading.

After some negotiation, we allowed them to board our train.

A dozen or so were assigned to my car. One of them took my extra seat, a young peasant, strong in body, but with a worn expression on his face, a witness to his miserable life.

We had a short conversation.

"May I ask your name?"

"My name is Wang, Wang Azeng."

"Are you a native of East Double River?"

"My home is farther east, Wang Village."

"How long have you been with the Red Spears?"

He counted on his fingers: "One year."

The Red Spears are good, I would also like to join."

"You, gentleman, you are joking."

"No, I mean it. What do you do in the Red Spears?"

"The first thing we do is to fight the Old Shaan gangs." He meant the army of Shaanxi Province, led by Yue Weijun, who had been stationed in Henan. The Shaanxi army was undisciplined, and to fight them, the local peasants had organized the Red Spears. For the latter, any army which was undisciplined was now called the "Old Shaan gang."

"Will you also fight the Revolutionary Army?"

"I have heard it said that you Southerners are not bad."

"We are not the Southern army, we are the Revolutionary Army. Among our ranks, there are Southerners but there are also Northerners including some from Shaanxi. North or South, no matter, we of the Revolutionary Army do not harm peasants. We are on the side of the peasants and help to right their wrongs."

"Whatever you say, Sir."

"Are you on the side of the Revolution?"

He hesitated and then said: "So long as the truly mandated Son of Heaven does not appear, things will always go wrong."

"There is no Son of Heaven," I told him, "That's just talk. We the people, we are the Son of Heaven."

"How can you say that, Sir?" The young fellow shook his head disapprovingly. Then he brightened up: "Fortunately the Son of Heaven has appeared, and there will be peace on earth."

"How do you know?"

"Lord Guan[8] has announced it: the Heavenly Star has descended to earth, in Jinan of Shandong Province."

"Oh no, this is a joke."

"What did you say!?" his eyes blazed in anger, challenging me.

So these are the Red Spears, I said to myself. I also talked to several other members of the band, and their responses were similar. How pitiful they were, these oppressed masses. I felt more keenly than ever the meaningfulness of our current expedition.

At about six in the evening, our train finally made it to Xinyang. The water tank had to be filled again, and the workers stopped for dinner,

---

8. Guan Yu, or Guan Yun Chang (160–219 CE), a general of the Three Kingdoms period, renowned for military prowess and loyalty, as described in the classical novel *Romance of the Three Kingdoms* (San guo yanyi). Guan Yu was later popularly deified as Guandi.

so we had some time to take a look around the town of Xinyang.

In the growing dusk I got off the carriage with a couple of young colleagues and took a walk around the platform. Sickly looking peddlers some selling tea, others selling steamed buns, lined the paved path next to the station. An older man stood behind a braised beef stall, carving meat and hawking his goods in a strange accent. A welcome aroma greeted us as we approached his stall. We bought some beef and found it very good. We also bought steamed buns at the other stall, and they were equally satisfactory. We controlled ourselves, however, as we were hoping to find a proper restaurant in town. Rickshaw pullers offered their services, but we disappointed them.

Leaving the railway station, we approached the town gate; to judge by the directions we were given, it must be the east gate. The walls of the gate were thick, the whole edifice very imposing, befitting the gate of an ancient citadel on the northern plains. As we passed through the town gate, we were shocked by the desolation within. There were no restaurants, not even small food stalls. We stumbled onto the premises of the Provincial Second Girls' Teachers' College. It was being occupied by part of the Eighth Army, which was stationed in this area. We went in and saw some young comrades whom I had known in Canton. They had just arrived from Wuhan a few days earlier. Meeting here in a strange place was a pleasure, and we stopped to chat.

General Wei Yisan's troops were stationed here in Xinyang, and we wanted to call on this former Northeastern warlord who had crossed over to the side of the Revolution. But time did not permit. We thought we heard the faint sounds of a whistle. To be on the safe side, we made our way back; there was nothing to see anyway. Comrades from the Eighth Army saw us back to the station. Those who had stayed put had just had their dinner, but our stomachs were still empty, since we had found nothing in town. Fortunately we could fall back on the peddlers for beef and buns.

Soon we were back on the train and moving farther north. Although I was born and bred in the scenic part of south China, I had always loved the austere beauty of the North. But having had only two short hours in Xinyang, when would I see it again? When the train started, it was already late, but I was unable to sleep, and passed the time reading a bit of a Guo Moruo translation. After leaving Xinyang, our train seemed to be moving more slowly. But one thing was certain, we would surely reach Zhumadian the next day.

When I woke up the next morning, the train had stopped, and I presumed that we were in Zhumadian, but it was only a small station. We had stopped to make way for a train coming down from Zhumadian, carrying Tian Weiqin, Jin Yun'e and company heading for Wuhan. [Their forces were part of the Third Column, on the Left Wing of this Expedition.] We had hoped to catch a glimpse of these former Northeastern warlords who had come over to the side of the Revolution, but their train steamed by without stopping.

After the southbound train had passed, we continued on our way north passing through several small stations, until we reached the town of Zhumadian.

IV

The Political Department of the Twelfth Division had arrived at Zhumadian earlier; they were at the station to greet us and take us to their headquarters for a break. They were in a Catholic church, a remarkable piece of architecture for such a small town.

Our Political Department was to be housed with Army Headquarters in a missionary hospital, a short distance from the town proper, and reputedly the best building in the area. Before settling down in our quarters, we decided to take a stroll around the town.

Zhumadian was a stronghold in southern Henan Province. Strategically important, it had been the site of many wars and had been completely devastated. All that was left of the city wall was a stump of beaten clay. The town itself, boasting three streets, would have been nothing compared to a small town in the South, but here it was not only strategically important—it was also a commercial center, the whole area being so pitifully backward. There was a pharmacy, a dried foods store, a little eatery, a little teahouse, a sundries store and such like, but no modern department stores, no industry.

We went to a restaurant for dinner and drinks. I actually prefer Northern-style dishes over Sichuan or Cantonese dishes—excluding the Cantonese gourmet dishes of several hundred *yuan* apiece of course. Our group consisted of [former] colleagues from the Army Affairs' Political Department, as well as leaders from the Political Departments of the Twelfth Division and the Twenty-fifth Division, eleven of us altogether. Having been cooped up in the train with no decent food, we enjoyed the dinner immensely.

After dinner we made our way to where we were quartered in the missionary hospital—a remarkably impressive building. Those upholders of imperialism, they arrive mouthing words about the Garden of Eden and so on, but relying on imperialists' support, they really take good care of themselves. Wherever you go, the church and its annexes are always the best in town. These imperialist running dogs, preaching the gospel of the ruling class, molding the masses into willing slaves of capitalism, they themselves were living it up—they should be lined up and machine-gunned, one and all.

Now that the Revolutionary Army had arrived, those defenders of imperialism saw their luck running out. In the past, they used be so high and mighty—even the warlords, who were in awe of foreigners as a whole, treated the missionaries with special deference. These warlords take over ordinary people's houses and wreck their livelihoods. But obviously acting on the principle of "love me, love my dog," they never lift a finger against church property, Protestant or Catholic. Deferring to these running dogs of imperialism, the warlords never confiscate church property as barracks for their soldiers. But not we. Wherever we arrive, the first thing we do is to take over church buildings and missionary property—we were not afraid of offending the imperialists. We not only take over their churches, we chase them away, and publicly expose their crimes. They are a clever lot; these church people—before our arrival, all of them had made themselves scarce. We take over their buildings as a matter of course, our only regret being that we did not catch a couple of them to make an example of.

The Army Political Department called a meeting of the political departments of the Twelfth and Twenty-fifth divisions. At the meeting it was decided to entrust to the former the work of mobilizing the townspeople of Zhumadian, while mass mobilization in the surrounding countryside was the job of us people under the Army Political Department. As for the Twenty-fifth Division, it was heading farther east.

I divided my propaganda team into small groups, four people to a group, and I alternated between them as we headed out into the countryside of Zhumadian for propaganda work. Over the days, we covered a total area of twenty square *li*. At first the peasants were suspicious of us, but after explaining ourselves, the distance between us disappeared.

News from the front lines was tense.

Our enemy, the northeastern warlord's advance troops, had pushed down and taken the town of Xiping [roughly one hundred *li* north of where we were].

Lying between us in Zhumadian and the enemy in Xiping was the town of Suiping, defended by Zhang Wanxin's newly incorporated Sixteenth Division. They had been part of Yue Weijun's "old Shaanites" [detested by the Red Spears], later incorporated into the warlord Wu Peifu's forces, and after the fall of Wu finally incorporated into our Revolutionary Army. Obviously their loyalty could not be counted on.

Close by the town of Suiping was the Suiping Railway Station, defended by the newly incorporated Third Army of Liang Shoukai.

Farther south, closer to our position, was Liu Village, and a little railway station attached to it, defended by the newly incorporated Fourteenth Army of An Juncai—all equally unreliable.

We felt honor bound to dispatch some advance units to go beyond the defense line for propaganda work, to mobilize the masses, and to scout the enemy area. Director Liao warmly supported my suggestion, but Army Headquarters deemed it as too risky. Our orders had been to reach Suiping first, and from there to move north depending on circumstances.

But the fact was, we did not have any force of our own in Suiping; the troops there were a mishmash of former bandits, totally unreliable. Or, I should say, perfectly to be relied on to turn against us. Besides,

Suiping was only forty *li* south of Xiping, and the latter, as mentioned before, was already in enemy hands. Actually there were already enemy scouts barely ten *li* north of Suiping [the buffer between us and the enemy]. One can safely assume that the minute the enemy's guns started booming, these troops would promptly turn against us.

But isn't it true that if there is meaningful work to be done, shouldn't we go ahead and do it? Isn't revolution dangerous by nature? How can one hesitate because of danger? Thus, we decided to dispatch advance units, led by me. On the morning of April 29, we—twenty-one stalwart young men with ten orderlies and four carriers—left our base in Zhumadian, heading north.

We were heavily armed, with nineteen Mauser pistols, three revolvers, two carbines, and several grenades. We advanced along the railway line. We stopped for propaganda work along the way, and reached the Liu Village Railway Station by three in the afternoon. It was out of the question to try to reach Suiping the same night. Besides, we had our work cut out for us in Liu Village, so we decided to stop there for the night.

Fourteenth Division Headquarters, defending the Liu Village Railway Station, was set up in a railway car. I called on An Juncai the Division commander, but he was away in Zhumadian. I stayed and chatted with some of his staff and learned something of the sufferings of those newly incorporated forces, hastily patched together. Within our Revolutionary Army, a battalion Headquarters would be well set up, a division Headquarters would be downright princely. But Division Headquarters here was in a discarded freight car, like a vagrant's hideout. The freight car, probably used to transport cattle, now doubled as the commander's office and bedroom. There was no bed worthy of the name, just two naked boards hitched together with a moldy blanket thrown across, obviously the commander's only protection against the cold. There was a rickety table with one broken leg—the commander's desk. Nondescript rubbish was heaped up to be sat upon.

One of the staff tried to do the honors; he ordered a soldier to "bring up some tea," and the fellow came up with a cup of, not tea, not even boiled water, but some muddy liquid which obviously had not been brought to a boil. If one did not know their real situation, it could have been taken as an insult.

The staff officer was dressed in a coarse blue short jacket, dirty and worn to tatters, as if he had just been released from jail. If the orderly had not told me so, I would never have taken him to be an officer. His yellow complexion and dark splotches were clear indications of malnutrition. We had a long conversation, and I began to understand the plight they were in. Over a two-year period, their army had never seen any pay, not even money for food. Officers and soldiers survived as best they could. When they could not afford noodles, they would survive on soybean dregs, stuff which we in the South use for pig feed. When they could not even afford that, they would turn to the locals to raise money. The locals had been squeezed dry, so they would kill farm animals—at one point they had even killed dogs for food. There were richer areas, but those had been picked clean by more powerful forces, against which they were no match. They were continually struggling with hunger. Division Commander An Juncai had gone to Zhumadian to beg money for food.

At Liu Village, our top priority was to find somewhere to lie down and rest, but it had been quite a challenge. We had assumed that since there was a railway station, there must at least be a township. In reality, however, except for a little station building, there wasn't even a village. We finally had to lie down in an abandoned hut near the tracks.

It was a low-ceilinged two-room hut, with its door torn off, probably used as firewood. There was nothing inside, no bed, no table or chairs, no stove, no cooking utensils, nothing except a heap of moldy straw. Moreover, rural dwellings in Henan traditionally are never fitted with windows. Thus the two rooms were pitch dark, the four walls gray-black. The earthen floor was damp although it had not rained. Stepping on the damp floor in our straw sandals was very uncomfortable. Worse was the smell. Fortunately I had eaten nothing except a bit of Chinese pancake; otherwise I would have thrown up then and there.

Who knows where the people who used to live here had got to. Perhaps all dead. We should have come earlier. We were too late. If we had been here three years earlier, this house could have been a happy home for a family. But now, three years later, probably even their bones were scattered. We had no choice but to stop here for a break. Our orderlies cleaned out the floor as best they could and spread out the oilcloth and raincoats which we had brought so that it was possible for us to sit down. We were dead tired. But it was only four in the afternoon; so we went off to work again.

We explored the surrounding area within a radius of five or six *li*. The countryside was devastated, even worse than Zhumadian. We went through several villages, and what we saw was similar to the hut that we had just taken over: empty shells with no doors, the owners probably dead. Some were occupied by the very old. Not a single youth and not a single woman—the most sought after prey of any army, even older women were not spared. As for men, anyone from fifteen to fifty was not safe from the press gangs. If they were not dragged off to war, the army passing through would rob them of their last handful of grain. The few surviving villagers that we met looked more dead than alive. They had lost their families and now were struggling for sheer survival. Grain was out of the question; all they had to live on were soybeans or half-rotten pumpkins, sometimes just tree bark and grass roots.

Moving among these cadavers, the only thing we could do was express our sympathy. The only other thing we could do was to share some of our food. Thus, instead of doing propaganda, we had turned into charity workers.

We went back to the hut after dusk; fixed a hasty meal, and planned the next day's work. We had previously wanted to move north to Suiping, but we heard of a major stronghold in the vicinity and of the growing influence of the Red Spears. So we decided to stay on a couple more days to check out the situation.

The twenty or so people in my group joined the pieces of oilskin and raincoats to form one big communal bed and we lay down as best we could.

Between the smell permeating that small space, and the dankness of the earthen bed, I couldn't help wondering what were we doing after all? Weren't we comfortably off in Wuhan? But I immediately dispelled the thought. "Who should venture into hell if not I?" I would be a charlatan if I limited myself to revolutionary talk but did not take a bit of hardship.

Since there was no door to the hut, we could hear the slightest sound coming from outside. At first we all lay down unsuspectingly, but shadowy figures seem to be hovering close by. A comrade suddenly remembered the advice of a local: the man had told him that the hodgepodge army, bandits actually, had their eye on us. They had noticed that we pale-faced scholars were not only supplied with food, but that we carried arms, and the man had advised that we should be on guard, especially at night. This warning was very important, as the vagrant soldiers around here had indeed been quite hostile. Then an orderly also remembered that a beggarly soldier had said that the Red Spears were unscrupulous and might attack us that very night to snatch our weapons. This new information was also important, as the Red Spears had been known to rob officers and soldiers of their weapons. I realized that I had been remiss and immediately ordered everyone to get up and get dressed.

They moved as one—the twenty-one brave young men respected me. Our average age was twenty-one, the oldest twenty-four, the youngest seventeen. I was twenty-one by the lunar calendar; actually I had not yet passed my twentieth birthday. We were inspired by a spirit of sacrifice, and feared no danger—we all got up and dressed and armed ourselves. Suddenly the air in the room was charged with tension.

We began to discuss methods of defense. We were faced with dangers from two sides: the soldiers of the Fourteenth Division and the Red Spear band. How should we deal with the first? Give in? Resist?

One comrade said that whatever the circumstances, the Fourteenth Division officially was our ally, that if the men tried to snatch our weapons while their commander was away, we should give in: we were going to see action very soon, and if we start fighting within our own ranks, it will be bad for morale. He added that even a minor incident might sow suspicion within the newly incorporated army and adversely affect our military plan for this expedition. Finally, he added that the Fourteenth Division stationed in Liu Village numbered more than seven hundred men, that any resistance would be futile and a meaningless sacrifice on our part.

I was impressed by his line of thinking, but still we unanimously opposed his position.

[First we] decided to fight to the death in case the Fourteenth Division tried to snatch our weapons. This was the first time the Revolutionary Army was heading north, we were the vanguard. Compared to the old-style army, we were equipped with political workers,[9] and this was the first time that political workers were coming up north. If we gave in to violence, it would be loss of face for the Revolutionary Army. We must show our mettle; even if we were all killed, it would be worth the sacrifice. It would show the spirit of the revolutionary soldiers and revolutionary political workers, and our enemies would be intimidated.

Second, the hastily incorporated new forces were not reliable; our retreat would make them despise us; only resisting to the death could impress them.

And finally, when we first started out from Zhumadian, we had been filled with the spirit of self-sacrifice. If we backed down at the first challenge, it would be a lifelong disgrace for ourselves as well as demoralizing for our comrade political workers.

Having arrived at this unanimous decision, we made ready for battle. The comrade who had advocated retreat also agreed with us. We knew that he had advocated retreat not from cowardice, but from his own line of thinking; he was a brave comrade and we never suspected otherwise.

Having arrived at a unanimous decision, we immediately prepared ourselves for action, and sent two comrades to stand on duty outside the door.

"Perhaps we will all lie bleeding here within a few hours . . ." an eighteen-year-old comrade said. I laughed. In my heart of hearts, dying was for me not a tragedy but a welcome release. In any case, we were all extremely tense.

Our next problem was how to deal with the Red Spears. They were

9. "Conventional battlefield victories only partly explain the Northern Expedition's early success. Equally important were the political campaigns waged by Communists and the Kuomintang Left-wingers who organized strikes, boycotts, protests, trade unions and peasant associations in the wake, and sometimes even ahead of, the National Revolutionary armies." See Hutchings, *Modern China*, p. 318.

not the hodgepodge army, they were part of the ordinary masses, and they did not carry regular arms. We should not deal with them as enemies, but there were two sides to the question. If the Red Spears attacked us, we would not retaliate, since politically we were trying to secure their sympathy and support. We absolutely must not kill any Red Spears. But we should not give up our arms either, because once we started down that road, we, the Revolutionary Army, would never find footing in Henan—we would just be treated as easy prey. We should take proper defense measures if attacked, but avoid indiscriminate shooting, the best solution being to take them prisoners and release them after some education.

The wretched hut was filled with the smell of war as we discussed the pros and cons. In fact, all our arguments had been wasted: neither the Fourteenth Division nor the Red Spears attacked. The only thing that happened was that we spent a sleepless night.

The next morning, I divided our advance force into four groups: two groups were to attend two market fairs, one each, and I would lead the two other groups to the Chai Family Stronghold.

The fields were green with young wheat. That year's crop was good; but for the war, the peasants would have gathered a good harvest, but right then horses trod freely in the untended fields. The farmers had all fled for fear of conscription. After walking about ten *li*, my group saw several Red Spear members picketing on the roadside. As soon as they saw us coming, two ran back, while the other two stood their ground. To avoid misunderstanding, I dispatched one comrade to approach and explain the situation, while we followed behind. The explanation didn't seem to work: our comrade was still talking to them as we approached.

The two peasants standing on duty each held a sabre, not the red-tasseled spear. A streamer was draped by the roadside, announcing the XXX group of XXX Village of XXX County. According to the information of the two young men standing guard, it was not a market day at the Chai Family Stronghold—fairs being held on the second, the fifth, and the eighth day of each lunar month—thus the gate was closed, and there was no entry. We repeatedly asked the two Red Spear guards for permission to enter the Stronghold, explaining our mission, but to no avail. Finally, they allowed us to go up to the gate and do our own negotiation.

We walked a few more *li* toward the Stronghold. As we approached, we saw that the wall of the Stronghold was of beaten earth and that the gate was tightly shut. There was a moat with a drawbridge drawn up. Many people stood atop the wall, holding spears and sabers which flashed in the sun against a background of colored pennants. It was like a scene from a historical novel, with us as part of the scene. To think that ten years after the Great European War, when chemical weapons had been used, there were still strongholds defended like medieval castles! We would not have believed it if we were not seeing it with our own eyes.

Standing outside the gate, we talked to the people on top of the walls until the chief of the Stronghold was convinced that we meant no harm and allowed us to enter. The drawbridge was let down, the gate to the Stronghold opened, and the chief and other elders welcomed us in. Men, women, and children crowded around us. I seized the chance to do some propaganda; unfortunately my southern accent got in the way, but Comrade Yang did some "translation," so the message got across and people seemed quite receptive. We had not gone to all that trouble for nothing, after all. Apart from making speeches, we also dispensed pamphlets and propaganda sheets, which the people accepted gladly.

After our propaganda work was done, the chief of the Stronghold invited us to dinner. He took us to a hall, which seemed to be a place for public consultation, and we were joined by several elders. I did not want to have anything to do with these people, but then thought better of it.

The chief of the Stronghold began by listing the sufferings of the locals. He took out a pack of documents, mostly orders handed down by the county authorities or by warlords, such as Wu Peifu, for contributions of grain, or fodder, or vehicles, or draught animals. These orders also carried deadlines and threats of punishment if the orders were not obeyed. For our part, we tried to help them understand the aim and meaning of the Revolution, and the reason for this Northern Expedition. We also tried to extract some information about the Red Spears. The conversation was genial on both sides, and an hour later, they insisted on treating us to dinner.

They set out two tables and very politely put me at the head table. Five dishes were set on each table: the first a dish of uncooked tofu sprinkled with coarse salt, the second a dish of soybean sprouts, the third a dish of barely cooked vegetables, the fourth of dried turnips, and the last and best—four fried eggs. I found these five dishes hard to swallow, though they had done their best. The chief of the stronghold kept apologizing: "Our abject apologies to Your Excellencies"—they insisted on addressing us as "Excellency," which gave us the creeps—"please understand that this is the best that we can do. We usually survive on coarse baked buns; vegetables have been scarce for the last several years . . ."

Another elder added: "When his highness Wu [Peifu] left the area, he wiped us out, draught animals and all. Right now we have two chickens left, but there was not enough time to kill and cook them for Your Excellencies . . ."

I was sure they were telling the truth.

It was almost two o'clock in the afternoon when we left the Chai Family Stronghold. We went to other villages and only returned to Liu Village in the evening to spend another night on the damp earthen floor. The next morning we headed for the Suiping Railway Station.

V

We had been exhausted those last couple of days, but we were in good spirits. Shod in straw sandals, shouldering our guns, we sang revolutionary songs as we walked along the railway tracks, heading north. As the sun rose higher and higher, we took out our bamboo hats to ward off its heat. Beads of sweat rolled down our backs, but we kept marching and singing and arrived at the Suiping Railway Station by noon.

I called on Liang Shoukai, commander of the Provisional Third Army, who was stationed near the railway station, and met my former colleague Li from the Army Affairs Department. Commander Liang was robed in a long gown, originally gray which had turned a dirty black, and his hair was long and matted. No one would have guessed that he was an army commander who had led thousands of soldiers in his day. Now he looked more like one of those rascally fortune-tellers on old Shanghai's street corners. Aside from Liang, present were his chief of staff Geng and his secretary-general. Liang was very genial, unlike my idea of an old-style army man. Or was he just acting polite to me? His chief of staff Geng was thirtyish and seemed full of energy. The secretary-general was an elderly man who retired discreetly into a back room after greeting me briefly.

Commander Liang and chief-of-staff Geng told me about their poverty and grievances. This could be seen from the state of their headquarters, which was almost as shabby as that of An Juncai in the freight car back at the Liu Village Railway Station. Liang's headquarters was in a low-ceilinged dilapidated house. The so-called office was furnished with two rickety tables and a couple of stools. The commander's bedroom, which he shared with his chief-of-staff and secretary-general, was in the back room. Old boards and broken down doors were placed unevenly side-by-side to form their communal bed. Ragged bedding was thrown about haphazardly. They treated me to a meal of noodles and buns (there was no rice in Henan) and three dishes, which were even worse than those at the Chai Family Stronghold.

The area around the Suiping Railway Station was sparsely populated; there was not much work for us around there. We decided to head for Suiping, which was about eight *li* away from the railway station where we were. Commander Liang Shoukai asked his chief-of-staff Geng to make a call on the military line to Zhang Wanxin, commander of the newly integrated Sixteenth Division, which was defending Suiping, asking him to help us find temporary quarters in town. Liang also wrote a personal letter to Zhang, asking him to do what he could to help us. I took the letter and we continued on our way north. Along the way, we saw many air-raid shelters. There was an air of impending war.

A few *li* away from the Suiping Railway Station, which we had just left, we came upon the banks of the Sha River, and started to walk along the path parallel to the river. The banks on both sides were overgrown with reeds so that we could barely see the water. Crows hovered over trees and the reeds—I had never seen so many crows in my life, and could not understand why they converged in that particular place at that particular time.

We saw straggling groups of beggarly soldiers on the road, probably from the Sixteenth Division. They seemed surprised to see us, and I noticed that their eyes were full of malice, which made me very uncomfortable.

The town appeared in the distance; it got closer and closer until we finally reached the outskirts of Suiping. The Sha River flowed quietly on the edge of town. A stone bridge spanned the river. Once across the river, we found ourselves at the Suiping gate. The Sha River flowed by the town gate and widened out, with sand banks and reeds on either side. One could see the bottom of the river, the water was so clear. The town wall presented an imposing sight, with a huge colored pennant perched on top. Crows, hosts of crows, circled around, creating a singular background to this ancient town. There was a stone tablet by the gate, though I do not recall the inscription.

After we were harshly questioned at the gate, we were guided in by a soldier, who escorted us to the county public office. It was now used as the headquarters of the Sixteenth Division. As we walked down the streets, I noticed that most doors were closed, but there were people about—or beggars rather, as all the people looked so wretched.

We arrived at the Suiping County public office, a temple-like building. Once we went through the outer gate, a "wall screen" decorated with the drawing of a birdcage, shielded the visitor from a direct view of the building.

Our guide led us past the screen into a waiting area and went in to announce our arrival. Suddenly there was a shout of "Please!!!" which made us jump. We were shown into the main hall.

Wow, what a shock! We had walked into the scene of a traditional opera!

We were in the main hall. Facing us was a huge old-style "judge's desk" with a crimson apron draped along the edges. On the desk stood an old-style rack, stuck full of "authorization tokens," consisting of carved wooden slats [conferring "authorization"]. There was a huge brush-pen rack and two huge brush-pen holders, one crimson brush pen for writing out death sentences, a huge ink slab, and a long "disciplinary ruler."

Behind the "court desk" stood an imposing high-backed chair. Huge, intimidating "admonition placards" stood on each side of the room, painted respectively with the words of warning "Silence" and "Refrain." Most outrageous were the two huge "weapons racks," standing on either side of the hall. On the racks were displayed varieties of ancient weapons only seen on stage in Chinese opera nowadays—sabre, axe, spear, halberd, and the multi-edged sword attributed to ancient heroes. To cap it all, there was a huge drum, beaten to announce the arrival and retirement of the judge, according to ancient practice. Our jaws dropped at this apparition of a typical Chinese opera scene which had been preserved through Republican China.

Commander Zhang Wanxin of the Sixteenth Division and the town official Zhao greeted us at the entrance of the hall. Commander Zhang—dark, thin, haggard, hollow-eyed—wore a ragged gray cotton coat, while Zhao, clothed in a traditional short jacket over a long gown, was plump, a typically corrupt official who was always assured of a good meal.

Commander Zhang drew me to his bedchamber for a conversation. Zhang's bedroom was not much better than that of Commander An Juncai's in the freight car, or commander Liang's in the decrepit hut. Zhang, like the other commanders, also began with a list of his grievances, and asked me to convey his request to the Wuhan government for cash to take care of immediate needs. I was not in a position to do anything, though I was sorry for them.

Commander Zhang also talked about the situation at the front. According to his report, the Fengtian warlord's forces were just seven or eight *li* north of Suiping, where he was: their cavalry had showed up now and then, and their planes often flew over Suiping scattering leaflets, though they had not dropped bombs.

Zhao, the local official, answered my questions regarding local conditions.

They had wanted to put us up in a county accommodation, but we politely refused, as that would inhibit our freedom of movement, and separate us from the masses. We rented the back rooms of a local pharmacy.

The pharmacy occupied two connected front rooms, and was closed for business. The back rooms we rented faced a little courtyard. There were two pomegranate trees and a poplar, and a bird nest with birds chirping away cheerfully. The three connected rooms were dark, but quite comfortable by Henan standards. The middle room had a shrine dedicated to the god of wealth set on a traditional-style square table. There were folding beds in the two adjourning rooms on either side. They used to be the storeowner's living space, but he gave them up to us. Compared to the misery of the ramshackle hut in Zhumadian, this was luxury indeed.

The owner of the pharmacy was a mild-mannered, middle-aged businessman with a scholarly air, instead of the petty trader's crafty looks. After settling down in our new quarters, all our comrades were dispatched to different parts of town, while I sat down for a conversation with the owner. At first the man was afraid, but after some explaining, he was relieved and gave me a lot of information about what was going on. The county official Zhao, it turned out, had formerly been Commander Wan's military adjunct, and was a downright rascal. The owner was hesitant to go on, but after being assured that I was not on their side, he gave me case-by-case particulars of Zhao's corruption. He also painted a broad picture of the wicked local gentry. I was very grateful to him for his confidence.

My comrades returned one by one, and by pooling our information, we pieced together a general picture of the social-economic-political situation of Suiping:

One. The newly integrated Sixteenth Division stationed in Suiping has about fifteen thousand men within the city and fourteen to fifteen thousand scattered in the outskirts. Of these, seventy percent are armed, though everyone in town carries arms. The division has two cavalry regiments, one of which is stationed within the city. Also, there are six cannons in the city. Officially they are under the Revolutionary Government in Wuhan; but in fact they are flirting with the Fengtian warlords and could turn against us at any time. In a word, Zhang

Wanxin's Sixteenth Division's capacity is not to be underrated, and they are absolutely not to be trusted.

Two. Advance units of the enemy force are stationed in Xiping County, forty *li* west of where we are, but their scouts have come as close as within fifteen *li*. The enemy's cavalry has even ventured to the outskirts of Suiping; confronting the Sixteenth Division. Neither side fired, as if they had an understanding. The planes scattered two kinds of leaflets, which our comrades have secured. One titled "To the Northern army" reads as follows:

> We are all northerners. The southerners are coming to attack us northern brothers. We should band together and disarm them, and kill them one and all. Our great leader is the best. He never holds back our monthly pay. Join us. We have silver coins, meat for every meal, and clothes. Join us for the good life . . .

This kind of leaflet can be very effective among a ragtag army. The second kind of leaflet does not specify its audience:

> The southerners are out to kill all the northerners. Once the southern army arrives, property and wives will be shared in common. [Chiang Kai-shek] is keeping seventeen concubines, and has collected a fortune of millions and millions.

This latter piece of propaganda was so ignorant as to name XXX (Chiang) as part of the Wuhan government! But it could still be effective with the populace here, because—

Three. The general population is suspicious of the Revolutionary Government in Wuhan and of the Revolutionary Army as a whole.

Four. The socio-economic structure has collapsed, and Suiping is overrun with peasants taking refuge. The town has enough grain to last only two or three months.

Five. There are no revolutionary mass organizations in town; actually there are hardly any progressive elements. But the majority of the population has a potential for revolution. The educated people are sympathetic to the revolution, though they are in the minority.

Six. The local despots and landowners in control are hand in hand with warlords and officials, and they have squeezed the people dry.

We held a meeting to discuss how to carry out our work in Suiping. I felt that the situation was urgent, and that our task was daunting and should not be limited to propaganda. Taking all aspects of the situation into consideration, our meeting unanimously passed a resolution:

First. Immediately form an undercover work group to be headed by a comrade familiar with the situation at the front, hire trustworthy locals to slip behind enemy lines in Xiping and bring back information.

Second. Designate several comrades to carry out propaganda work exclusively among the soldiers of the Sixteenth Division, mainly to explain that within the Revolutionary army, lines should not be drawn between north and south. Apart from propaganda, the comrades should sound out the attitude of the Sixteenth Division.

Third. Make every effort to mobilize the masses. In practical terms, it means—

a. call a mass meeting within the next few days to whip up a revolutionary spirit;

b. call a meeting of students, educated people, and others sympathetic to the revolution, and form a Federation of Educated Youth;

c. set up a businessmen's association, a peasants' association, and a workers' union;

d. openly solicit people to become members of the GMD and set up a Suiping GMD provisional branch as soon as possible;

e. carry on work among the Red Spears.

Fourth. Considering the dangers latent in the situation—the Sixteenth Division may mutiny at any moment—we should do the following:

a. secretly sound out locals who are reliable, set up secret organizations in town to provide safe haven in the event of sudden reversals;

b. set up similar secret organizations in the countryside;

c. immediately dispatch comrades to the railway station and contact the Railway Workers' Union to request that two special mechanically operated rail cars be reserved exclusively for the officers of our group. In case the Suiping Railway Station cannot provide such rail cars, they should immediately contact Zhumadian station and ask Army Headquarters to requisition two such rail cars to be sent over to

Suiping, ready for our use at a moment's notice;

d. every comrade must be provided with a set of civilian clothes. This must be done discreetly so as not to arouse suspicion;

e. the Provisional Third Division led by Liang Shoukai [at the Suiping Railway Station] is comparatively more reliable than the others; a liaison officer should be permanently stationed within his army;

Fifth. immediately dispatch someone back to Zhumadian to report confidential information to the Political Department.

Sixth. It is advisable to keep in touch with the Sixteenth Division, but to deal severely with local despots and landlords, so as to secure the support of the masses.

After having passed this resolution, we set off, each to his designated task.

VI

That very same day, I called a meeting of all the local notables: the head of the Merchants' Association, the head of the Peasants' Association (the old one), the head of the Education Association, the chief of the Self-Defense Regiment, the chief of the waterworks, the head of the Charity Association, the president of the Self-government Association, the director of the Public Welfare Association, and so on, some seventeen or eighteen in all. Those individuals were old hands at finding their way around, treating me with exaggerated respect. Their tricks would never work with me—even if they kowtowed and called me their own ancestor, I would not be moved one inch.

I listened to their reports—biased in their own favor, of course, but still one could garner some useful information. I then proceeded to lecture them most severely, and all they could come up with were repetitions of "As you say, Sir," "As you say, Sir!"

The next morning, I called together all the progressive-minded young people of the town, thirty-one in all. Some were teachers at the public elementary school or students of the graduating classes, some were teachers of the junior elementary school, and others were those who had returned after graduating from schools in neighboring towns.

All in all, they formed the local educated class and were very receptive to our propaganda. They immediately passed a resolution to set up a Provisional Committee for the Suiping Association of Revolutionary Youth and set to work right away. On the basis of the above Provisional Committee, they set up a Provisional Committee of the Suiping branch of the GMD and immediately set about recruiting Party members. The placards of the two Provisional Committees swiftly appeared at the gate of the local school. With a bit of help from our discretionary funds, these young people, long stifled by the stagnant atmosphere, were now all fired up. I saw the need for another project, which was to start a newspaper. Suiping was so backward, newspapers and periodicals were simply unknown. Now that the revolutionary fire was being ignited, a periodical was indispensable. A printed paper was out of the question, but we could use a lithograph, and in fact there were two stores in town engaged in the business. I designated two comrades to undertake the job. Distribution and copy work was allocated to the Association of Revolutionary Youth. The first number appeared the very next day, with a run of 600 copies which were snatched up in a twinkling. Our paper, called the *Revolutionary Daily,* explained the basics of the Revolution, and carried news of the Revolution in neighboring towns and provinces.

Another aspect of our job also went very well, and that was to set up a union of cart drivers, as there were many people in Suiping who made a living by driving horse-drawn or mule-drawn carts. We also had success with the carpenters' union and the barbers' union. The apprentices' union was the only item not moving forward, though we had spared no energy. We had been in Suiping but three days, and generally speaking the town was already swept clean of the old malaise and bubbling with revolutionary excitement. The Association of Revolutionary Youth, under our guidance, has set up its own propaganda team and was active in town and countryside. They relied on the outline designed especially to target the Suiping situation, while the propaganda material brought down from Wuhan also proved useful.

One of the most effective forms of propaganda were periodicals, but our periodicals were pitifully few. I had had a difference with the leadership at the General Political Department over this issue. They had spared no expense to print great numbers of photographs of our revolutionary leaders, namely, photos of Wang Jingwei, Sun Fo, Tang Shengzhi, Zhang Fakui, Deng Yanda, and the rest. I was utterly opposed to distributing those photographs. As I saw it, we could only be sure of those leaders who had had the last word passed on them after death and only then could their photos be used for publicity purposes. As for the living, no one was a sure bet—they may be revolutionary today but who knows what they would be tomorrow. We hold the materialistic view that man is the product of his environment and that as the environment changes no one can tell how a revolutionary leader might be affected. We should not make idols of the living. Our propaganda work is supposed to help the masses understand our program, not to make the masses worship our leaders. But my line of reasoning did not stop the General Political Department from printing myriads of photos of the above-mentioned leaders. When my objections could not stop the printing, I decided that the Fourth Army should boycott the pictures. My boss Director Liao did not support me; he affirmed their usefulness in propaganda. So on the day we started out from Wuchang on this expedition, I had no choice but to order the packages of these photographs to be "distributed" into the river. Everyone at the propaganda team was on my side, though I was censured for "insubordination." I took great satisfaction in the fact that not one single copy of those photographs passed through the Fourth Army Political Department for distribution to the masses.

To sum up, in the rural part of Suiping, the work of the Association of Revolutionary Youth was extremely helpful in opening the way for us.

We had also discovered that the Red Spears could be our allies if rubbed the right way. We could lead them onto a shining path if only we could stay on in Henan. One problem that confronted us after the Red Spears had come to understood us better, however, was their request for arms. Of course we could not give them arms, but we did not want to disappoint them either. We would give you arms, we said, if we had them, but now we only have enough for ourselves. If you want arms, come join us in fighting the Fengtian warlords.

One of the hardest jobs in rural work was social investigation at the grass roots. It was impossible to get straight answers. If you asked the head of a household for the number of people in his family, he would suspect you of trying to collect the head tax; if you asked how much land he owned, he would suspect you of trying to collect the land tax; if you asked how many men and women were in his family, he would think you were planning communal marriage. Whatever question you asked, you'd never get a straight answer. But of course this did not mean that we could not make any headway in rural work. On the contrary we immediately started to organize peasants' associations at the grass-roots level.

The air was filled with revolutionary tension; the local warlords, corrupt officials, despots, and evil gentry became alarmed and scurried to Commander Zhang Wanxin, begging him to interfere on their behalf. And interfere he did. He delegated the county official Zhao, he of operatic splendor, to advise us not to overdo it, or there might be consequences. It was more threat than advice, I would say, but I was ready for them. I said, the masses are rising up in revolution due to the force of circumstances, and nothing can stop the momentum. The warlord Wu Peifu tried to stop them, and see what happened to Wu? He is out. I pointed out to him that seeing as how the peasants were aroused, what we should do is lead, not suppress. As for the fear of complications, that is pure rumor cooked up by the evil gentry. Even if something did happen, I added, the government in Wuhan would take full responsibility.

While firmly rebuffing them, we on our part did take precautions, as the situation was indeed growing more tense. The army of the Revolutionary Government in Wuhan had completed its move to Zhumadian; Tang Shengzhi and Zhang Fakui had arrived, and the enemy was on full alert. The Fengtian warlords' planes flew over us regularly, sometimes getting as close as Zhumadian. The inhabitants of Suiping, caught in the middle ground between the two sides, lived in daily terror. Commander Zhang Wanxin of Suiping was clearly leaning toward the enemy. Director Liao ordered us to leave Suiping and return to our base in Zhumadian in case of complications. But our work in Suiping had just got underway: we needed to lay a firm foundation and see the work through to the end. The revolutionary spirit which we had nurtured would be in danger of petering out if we left precipitately.

On the morning of May 4, we called a mass rally. We decided to hold the rally outside of town as it was unsafe in town, given the curfew and the constant danger from the now hostile Sixteenth Division. We held the rally outside the east gate to make it convenient for the masses outside of town, as all three of the other gates were closed. At about ten in the morning, roughly a thousand people gathered and loudly applauded our speeches. We did not notify Division Commander Zhang Wanxin or official Zhao or any local gentry. In their absence, the masses loudly abused these rascals without restraint, and feelings ran high.

But the situation was indeed fraught with danger. Just the day before, Commander-in-Chief Tang Shengzhi had arrived on an inspection tour at the Suiping Railway Station. Commander Liang Shoukai of the Incorporated Third Division, who was posted at the Suiping Railway Station, had been ordered to move elsewhere, and Suiping was now isolated. Meanwhile, Commander Zhang Wanxin was showing growing signs of insubordination as the northeastern warlords made further headway down south. According to the report of our spies—Zhang Wanxin had placed a representative within the northeastern warlord's camp—we had to be on guard against him.

As our rally was proceeding full steam ahead, one of our spies in Zhang Wanxin's camp arrived in haste to report that Zhang, hearing of our rally, had called a meeting of the local notables and that Zhao was all for rounding us up and secretly executing us. Zhang, though not going to that extreme, was all for taking us into secret custody. Just as the rally was winding down, a messenger from Zhang Wanxin arrived, asking me to join him in a conference. I knew it was a trick, so I scribbled a few words on my card, stalling him. The minute Zhang's man left, the Association of Revolutionary Youth took charge of the meeting. Our group took a circuitous back road and reached the

Suiping Railway Station after walking for two hours. Someone from the Youth Association was there waiting. He told us that as soon as Zhang Wanxin realized that we were gone, he sent his men in hot pursuit along the main road. Having missed us, he closed all the town gates and conducted a search. Now that this young man had drawn to himself the hatred of the local despots, he could no longer survive in Suiping and therefore he threw in his lot with us.

We have to thank the comrades of the Railway Workers' Union. They had scrupulously followed our previous request and had reserved two "mechanically operated" special carriages for us. So the minute we arrived at the station, we hopped on board and made for Zhumadian. The carriages were almost as fast as the regular trains, and we reached Zhumadian within the hour. If not for these carriages, Zhang Wanxin could easily have pursued us along the railway line and taken us captive.

VII

On our way from Suiping back to Zhumadian, we came across a heartbreaking scene. As we sat in our train heading back, we saw the so-called Propaganda Train of the General Political Department coming our way on the other side of the track. The train was decked out in royal splendor; the propaganda personnel likewise were spruced up in their uniforms and shiny leather shoes and leggings. Unlike our group risking our lives to work inside Suiping, all they did was to stay in the safety of the train and throw boxes of propaganda material out the windows. Whether these boxes reached the masses, whether the masses could understand and profit by these materials, was beyond their concern. All they cared about was scattering the materials, using up their budget, and feeling good about themselves as genuine revolutionaries. These so-called propaganda materials accomplished nothing positive, they would probably lie exposed beside the tracks until they rotted, never noticed by the village people. Actually they would do damage if discovered: "Wow, look, the Revolutionary Army folks are really living it up! We can hardly feed our bellies, yet they throw away these expensive gizmos! Won't the heavenly gods pass judgment?!" Those were the exact words that we heard from the peasants while doing social investigation in Zhumadian.

Speaking of the General Political Department, it was heartbreaking to see how the situation had deteriorated since the February Reorganization. Before that, there were still some people taking their jobs seriously. But after the Reorganization, it was a complete shambles, especially Zhang Bojun's Propaganda Section, which merely kept up the pretence of work while enjoying a completely corrupt lifestyle. I can state with certainty that there was no other department under the Wuhan Revolutionary Government which was as corrupt and degraded as the General Political Department.

Deng Yanda was the director; his deputy was Guo Moruo. Deng was very capable, and worth watching. I personally think he will be China's Kerensky[10] one day. The Wuhan government, being very short on talent, was perfectly right to promote him. But Deng, though responsible and astute, was not up to the job of director of the General Political Department, and it is a fact that the General Political Department was not well run. Before leaving for Henan, I had given my opinion that the government should set up something like a Presidential Division and appoint Deng Yanda commander; I had always thought that Deng was cut out for a military career. But what does it matter what I think, a lowly person like me.

As for Deng's deputy Guo Moruo, he was but a romantic poet, crooning on about how he "loves the crocus but loves the plum rose too," or how he "walks beside West Lake, and drinks its sparkling waters." He writes love letters pretending to be novels, good enough to attract decadent youth but having nothing to do with political work. The Political Department's Nanchang Branch, which Guo used to run, had been a bog of bureaucracy.

10. Kerensky (1881–1970), leader of the Russian February Revolution in 1917, was a dominant figure in the newly formed liberal coalition government until the outbreak of the Bolshevik's October Revolution that same year. Kerensky died in exile in the United States.

Zhang Bojun,[11] head of the Propaganda Section, was a returned student from Germany. Before setting out on this current expedition, I had called on him over something involving our work. To me, he was just a scholar attached to an educational institution and could not be less suited for the job of propaganda chief.

As for the staff, including the section personnel, I have never seen a more hopeless lot. All they did was dress up, sport their briefcases, and swagger all over town, the last word in depravity. Back in Wuchang, when we were about to leave on this expedition, I had said that if something drastic was not done about this demoralizing situation, the Wuhan government would not last beyond a year.

As for myself and my group, I feel that we had done our duty. Our work in Suiping had not amounted to much, but at least we had spread the spirit of revolution among the masses. If the General Political Department people on the propaganda train that had arrived ahead of us had done their job as we did ours and gone down among the masses in Suiping, our combined efforts would have amounted to something.

Our group finally arrived at the General Political Department at our base in Zhumadian, just in the nick of time to start off with Army Headquarters the very next morning. Director Liao was about to send for us.

The next morning, we left Zhumadian to set up headquarters at Shuitun Township twenty *li* away, but our group had to stop and do propaganda work en route, so we only managed to arrive late in the afternoon. Shuitun was an ancient fortified township, protected by a wall and a moat. There were many such in Henan, but to us from the South, it was always something of a novelty. Passing through the gates of Shuitun, we went down several alleys, finding only a teahouse

11. Zhang Bojun (1895–1969) was involved in progressive politics since early youth and had spent three years in Germany studying philosophy. On returning in 1926, Zhang joined the GMD-CCP Allied Revolutionary Government and took part in the march south after the collapse of the alliance. Zhang opposed Chiang Kai-shek's civil war, and worked to promote democracy. He was given position and titles on the mainland after 1949, but was labeled a "rightist" in 1957.

and a pharmacy, which doubled as a general store. We at the Political Department stayed at the pharmacy, while Army Headquarters was put up in the Catholic church.

We were about to march off the next day, so apart from some propaganda work and investigation among the town's population, we had not done much.

But a storm had broken out within the Political Department itself. There were no political factions within the Political Department, but as far as attitude toward daily work was concerned, one might say that there were indeed two camps. We comrades in the Propaganda Section and the Propaganda Team were active and hardworking, while those people in Management were a laid-back bunch. Take the dining plan for instance. We each payed twelve *yuan* monthly for food, but the meals they served up were not fit for humans. We did not expect anything special, of course, but we did not like the idea of our money filling the pockets of those in Management. Now that we were on the march, the quality of the food would be crucial: meals would not only affect our health, they would affect our campaign. Our comrades in the Propaganda Team had suffered enough from their mismanagement, and often complained to me. So did comrades from the Organization Section. Back in Zhumadian, I had suggested a shake-up of Management, but as far as Director Liao was concerned, it was anything for a quiet life, so nothing had been done. Now in Shuitun, faced with the coming campaign, something had to be done, or the success of our mission would be jeopardized. I was determined to get rid of the head of Management, Liu. Liu was a mild-mannered man, so mild that his underlings controlled him. Nothing could be done at Management without first getting rid of Liu. I got together with Ye, head of Organization, and all the cadres under Propaganda and Organization. At a general meeting of the Political Department, I launched an attack against Liu and easily got him ousted. Then at my suggestion, Ye of Organization was recommended to double as head of Management, and with Director Liao's approval, he got the job. And thus we accomplished our internal revolution.

The next day, May 6, we headed east from Shuitun and stopped in Zhu Village. This last was also a fortified township, smaller than Shuitun. We stayed at a pharmacy again; there being no beds, we slept on the floor.

Zhu Village held a market on the first, fourth, and seventh day of the lunar month. We arrived just as the market was in progress: dozens of peasants had brought their goods on shoulder-poles—old clothes, dried tofu, bean sprouts, vegetables, raisins, vegetable oil, buns, cherries, and the like, all for barter. There was no sign of meat or fish, and one seller of eggs came only when he heard of our arrival. It seemed that bartering was quite prevalent. I saw a man exchanging old clothes for buns, another exchanging tofu for spinach. They did not trust any kind of printed currency; it was said that some people lived most of their lives without seeing any paper currency. We also noticed that there were no matches—people made fires the old way, lighting them with a flint and thread soaked in vegetable oil.

From an economist's point of view, one might define the local economy as medieval. This state of affairs was not limited to Zhu Village, but was true of almost all of Henan Province. Actually, some places were even more backward than Zhu Village, which was at least close to the railway.

Since leaving Wuhan, we hadn't had any fruit. Now here in Zhu Village we saw fresh cherries for the first time. We bought a big basket of cherries, which were immediately snapped up by the comrades. The old man who had sold us the cherries cherished us like the god of wealth himself. He promised to go back to gather more, and indeed came back that same night with two big baskets of cherries, which we thoroughly enjoyed.

There was no post office in the village, only a box at the pharmacy. A man from Zhumadian arrived every other day to collect mail. I took a chance and sent out a lot of letters. Our front lines were already going into action, and we were supposed to follow within the next two days.

Before leaving, several of us from the Propaganda Section and the Propaganda Team decided to pay a visit to the commander of the Red Spears, a man named Fierce Tiger Zhao; his residence was across from the pharmacy where we were bivouacked. Fierce Tiger—the name itself was intimidating, not to mention the fact that he was the head of more than two hundred thousand members of the Red Spears spread out over an area covering five counties.

All the peasants lived in houses of beaten earth, Zhao's was the only exception. Seen from the outside, his was a large and strongly built brick house with a garden. All the available housing in the village had been taken up by our men, but not Tiger's. Commander Zhang Fakui's own orders were posted on the gate of Tiger Zhao's residence: "No part of the army may be quartered here." And indeed Tiger's house was not disturbed. Such was the might of Tiger.

The gate was tightly shut. We knocked and asked to see the master. The man who opened the gate said: "The Master is not up yet, come back later" and was about to shut the gate on us. It was really as the saying goes, even the lackeys of great man carry themselves with airs, and this one was no exception. I looked at my watch, it was a quarter to eleven! "Why is your master not up yet at this time of day? Go tell him to get up. Their Excellencies need to see him!" I said severely. This lackey had been so rude that I felt I must take him down a peg or two. Since he had emphasized Master, I threw in Excellencies to top him. What's so special about these people, anyway, just a bunch of lousy landlords and evil gentry. Actually that was the first time I had referred to myself as "Excellency." Thinking back, it was ridiculous. I have never shaken off my childishness.

My ploy worked after all—the man explained meekly that his master's orders had been that his sleep must absolutely not be disturbed. Since he was too scared to wake him, we decided to return in the afternoon to catch sight of this formidable Tiger.

In the afternoon, it was that same old retainer who opened the door. He showed us into the study and went in to announce our arrival. His master was at his opium, we were informed, and we must wait in the study until he has had his fill. "So the Tiger cannot do without opium?" We laughed at the idea.

There were a few books lying about in the study: a copy of the *Chronicle of the Three Kingdoms* [San guo zhi] with many missing pages; an episode of *Xue Rengui's Eastern Expedition* [Xue Rengui dong zheng] from the *Sui-Tang Chronicle* [Sui-Tang yanyi], a tattered *Biography of General Yue Fei* [Yue Fei zhuan], a few pamphlets on palm reading which we could not decipher, and finally a copy of *Heroes of the Marsh* [Shuihu zhuan], the only intact volume in Tiger's collection.

Tiger finally appeared in person. Before seeing him, we had imagined Tiger Zhao as a man of Herculean stature, ten feet tall, ten clasps in width, head like a "wine bucket" and eyes like bronze balls, as they say of ancient heroes. But the Tiger standing in front of us was a wizened little man not quite five feet tall and sickly looking as if he were suffering from consumption. With bleary eyes, dripping nose, lips and teeth darkened by opium, Tiger looked like a mangy dog.

We remembered the old adage not to judge a man by looks alone, so we started a conversation with him—what a shocking disappointment! We learned that he was made commander of the Red Spears of five outlying counties not for any credit on his own part, but solely because he had a lot of land! A typical despot landowner, he should have been taken out and shot!

VIII

May 8: we started out from Zhu Village; from then on we were steadily on the march.

Being part of the First Column, we were on the right flank. Commander Tang Shengzhi himself directed the action from a position along the Peking-Wuhan railway, though we were not in touch with the left flank or the center. In Suiping, it was confirmed that Zhang Wanxin had turned against us and was pounding the Suiping Railway Station with his artillery.

Our Twenty-fifth Division had surrounded Shangcai, at the time defended by the Fengtian warlord Fu Shuangying, who had secured himself behind the town gates. Fu was a hard nut to crack, but our troops moved victoriously through Ten Mile Village, Crouching Dragon Hill, and the East Bridge and West Bridge areas. Throughout the action, we comrades of the Propaganda Section and the Propaganda Team were side by side with our soldiers. Our work was not limited to propaganda; we scouted, we administered first aid, and helped the medical staff, but most of all we threw ourselves into the political work of boosting morale, and we were very effective.

Among other troops, political workers were derogatively called "medicinal plaster," meaning useless, just there for show. But we at the Political Department of the Fourth Army were warmly appreciated by the officers and men—our selfless dedication would have moved a heart of stone.

The battle of East Bridge and West Bridge was fiercely fought: we were constantly running between the front lines and the rear; one moment we would be chatting with the soldiers to keep up their spirits, the next moment we would be at the rear helping the wounded. Stretchers were in short supply, and we of the Political Department went to the local peasants for help. We did not need to coerce them: men and women rushed to help move the wounded, made soup, and offered their carts and planks and ropes for our use. Officers would always come to us when they couldn't buy firewood or find porters. Whenever the peasants saw us waving the white flag of the Propaganda Team, they would flock to us, asking us to give them a "talk." In a word, whenever there was a problem, officers and men would turn to us. We enjoyed great prestige among the troops and the people. Over and beyond the above, we of the Political Department had caught spies and had dispatched our own spies to enemy-held territory. Our work in this respect actually overshadowed that of the professionals.

The troops were wonderful; even lying on stretchers, they would try to read the pamphlets that we had distributed; passing us as they were being taken to the rear, they would struggle to salute.

After the battle at East Bridge and West Bridge, Commander-in-Chief Zhang Fakui called a meeting of the higher-level officers from the Fourth and the Eleventh Divisions. At the meeting, Zhang expressed deep appreciation for our work. He said that we had opened up wasteland where there had been no hope of growing anything, and that we had reaped a rich harvest.

At Huapo Township, under the jurisdiction of Xihua County, we had a surprise achievement which gave us great satisfaction. As our troops were passing through Huapo Township the chief of police, a certain Mr. Feng Guobi, had treated us leading officials to a seafood dinner, and our commander, Huang Qixiang, had praised the man as a very effective leader.

We conducted some secret investigations, however, and learned that this Feng was a downright rascal, who had squeezed the local people dry, and was universally despised. But he had arms in his possession and he had powerful backing at the local garrison, where the commander, a certain Zhao, had adopted one of Feng's sons, thus cementing the relationship between the two rascals. The locals wanted nothing less than to get rid of this police chief. But Commander Huang Qixiang put his foot down, saying that it was not appropriate, that we were not authorized to oust the man, and so on, as if it had nothing to do with Feng's seafood feast of the day before.

Huang Qixiang

But we could not afford to disappoint the masses, lest we be accused of making empty promises. The very next day, Army Headquarters was scheduled to leave Xihua and move on. We comrades of the Propaganda Team decided to hold a mass meeting before leaving.

The mass meeting was held as scheduled, and I dragged the much-hated Feng Guobi along, though he was reluctant. I posted a few comrades at the police station to keep an eye on Feng's confederates, who were all armed. We had to take precautions—if things went wrong, it could be messy. When we arrived, there were about four hundred people at the rally. I had hinted at what was about to happen beforehand, so the atmosphere was quite electric. Feng, of course, was no fool; he was armed and had secretly placed two armed policemen on site. I left Feng among the crowd while our comrades kept an eye on his policemen. I myself mounted the stage to give the first speech. I began by saying that because our Revolutionary Army was there to alleviate the suffering of the masses, whoever had made the people suffer should be punished and the people themselves should rise up and overthrow their persecutors. My speech was inflammatory; before I had finished speaking, the crowd was aroused and several young men had pushed Feng to the ground. His two policemen tried to intervene, but I immediately ordered my men to disarm them and also take away Feng's gun. By then Feng himself was already bloodied by dozens of fists pounding him, and was groaning in pain, unable to get to his feet.

How was this going to end? The crowd was screaming for his head. I was not afraid to go all the way, but I understood that it was neither the time nor the place. All I could do was promise to let him go on condition that he give up his weapons and the public funds in his control. We had already taken his weapons, but Feng would not give up the funds. We found 3,570 *yuan* in his bedroom and distributed the money to the poor people, then and there. We handed over the twelve guns to the Red Spears, entrusting them with the responsibility of policing the place. This was at the request of the four hundred people present at the meeting. As for Feng's personal revolver, to be quite honest, I pocketed it myself. My old revolver was too unwieldy, while Feng's was a smart German make. As for Feng's police, several joined us; others went home, and we gave them five *yuan* apiece severance pay.

And thus we could claim that we had done something substantial for the local people. We left the township amid a chorus of thanks and good wishes and headed for Happy Township, our next stop.

IX

We expected serious fighting at Happy Township, but to our surprise, the defending army under Zhao Enzhen of the Fengtian warlord faction had left before we arrived. There had been a brief skirmish, and Happy Township was quickly taken by our troops. General He Long's Independent Fifth Division had already been there and fought through the streets, leaving many dead bodies exposed.

He Long

As we neared the city, we proceeded very cautiously, in case of ambush. A new moon peeped out now and then from behind the clouds, giving a feeble light; otherwise we walked in pitch darkness. We dared not light our lanterns or turn on our flashlights. We walked gingerly along the narrow uneven road between a river on our right, and a bog on our left.

After walking and stopping, stopping and walking for two hours, we finally reached the town wall. Suddenly from out of nowhere a rumor spread that the retreating army had laid mines, so we had to halt. After an hour or so when the problem had been clarified, we resumed our march and entered the township without mishap.

By then it was already midnight. In the darkness we could discern the outlines of an imposing town wall and fairly wide streets, totally deserted. By the light of lanterns from some houses, we saw dozens of corpses lying around.

We were extremely tired. Once in town, we bivouacked in a deserted temple. I laid my head down and immediately fell asleep. When I woke the next morning, I discovered that I had been lying next to a corpse. There was a wound in his chest and his eyes were staring. He had probably crept here to die. Poor man, he was my enemy, but at that moment I felt sorry for him. I looked at his chest, which was clotted with blood, and tears welled up in my eyes.

But we had work to do: first of all we had to get settled somewhere. We found quarters at a pharmacy—we had settled ourselves in pharmacies all the way from Suiping, to Shuitun, to Zhu Village, and now here in Happy Township.

We summoned all the notables in the locality to a meeting—the magistrate, the heads of the clan, the garrison commander, and the local gentry, around ten of them, all showing up in rough peasant clothes, and addressing us as Your Honor, Your Excellency. We assigned them the job of cleaning up the aftermath of the battle.

We of the propaganda team received a secret report that the local self-defense regiment commander by the name of Zhao, a very wicked man, had a secret hoard of weapons. We immediately decided to conduct a search. He received us very politely. When we announced the intention of our visit he acted shocked and vowed that he was innocent. However, that did not prevent us from taking action. I designated two comrades to guard the man, while the rest of us searched the house from room to room. The house was big, with garrets and underground storage. We started at noon and kept working until five without finding anything. Zhao followed us with his eyes and smiled to himself with malicious glee. But we were not about to give up, as we had absolute faith in the peoples' report.

Coming up with nothing aboveground, we turned our attention to underground. One of our men noticed that the boards of the kitchen floor were loose. We pounded the floor with the butts of our guns, and found that it sounded hollow. Obviously there was something underneath. We felt that we had discovered the whereabouts of the secret hoard. Having searched in vain for five hours, we were now elated like Columbus discovering the new continent. But we were not good at digging underground. I wrote a note and got a couple of men from the engineer corps to help. Zhao's old mother was dead set against us opening up the floor, but we went ahead anyway. The engineers finally broke through. There was a plank, and under the plank, a coffin.

It was already twilight, and despite our flashlights, the kitchen was still in darkness. We were all shocked as the coffin was revealed, lying in the kitchen hiding place. We were used to scenes of death and destruction, yet the sight of the coffin still filled us with dread. For a moment, we were struck dumb.

The old woman burst into tears. Her cries actually brought us around; we quickly ordered her to stop and asked the people from the engineer corps to open the coffin. The old woman pleaded that it was her dead husband in the coffin, but we were certain that it was firearms. After a brief consultation, we decided to go ahead. The engineers lifted the lid, and—Oh Heavens! What an overwhelming stink.

We ran into the garden while the engineers replaced the lid of the coffin. So far our search had come up with nothing. We were wondering whether we should go on searching, when news came that Deng Yanda had arrived from Wuhan, and that Director Liao had sent for me. It was a signal to stop the search.

Our search had come up with nothing; moreover it was a hard blow for Zhao. Obviously he could not punish us by the ancient law that "He who opens a coffin without reason should be beheaded." He could do nothing. Having done so much evil all his life, he was now gnashing his teeth in frustration. But we were overjoyed. The local people having heard of the search felt that Zhao had gotten what he deserved. We had not overstepped the bounds; if I could have had my way, I would have dealt with the man most severely, whether he had hoarded arms or not, but I did not have the authority.

I went to see Deng Yanda in the company of Director Liao. Present at the meeting was Deputy Commander-in-chief Zhang Fakui. Deng first of all assured us that all was well in Wuhan. That was good because for the last couple of days, bad news from Wuhan had been leaking out. But now the air was cleared. Deng Yanda dispelled these rumors one by one.

One. Regarding Xu Kexiang's mutiny in Changsha, it was no big deal; he was just a regimental commander and was now being severely dealt with by Commander Tang Shengzhi. Order has been restored in the city.

Two. Regarding Xia Douyin's mutiny, it was true that Xia had mutinied and fought his way to within forty *li* of Wuhan, but he had been dealt with by Ye Ting's Twenty-fourth Division and Hou Lianying's Central Independent Division (made up of cadets of the Wuhan branch of the Central Military Political Academy). As for the news of Ye Ting's airplane accident, it was a pure fabrication. Ye was alive and kicking.

Three. Regarding Yang Sen's mutiny, it happened to be true, but Yang Sen's was just a ragtag army, so his mutiny didn't amount to much.

Four. Regarding the news of Zhu Peide's mutiny, it was a piece of misinformation. The fact was that Zhu had had a run-in with the CCP, thus giving rise to the rumor.

Five. Regarding the Red Spears' harassment of our rear in Xinyang and the bombing of the Peking-Wuhan railway line—all rumors. The Xinyang problem had been solved, the Peking-Wuhan train was running, and supplies were pouring in from the rear. As for the Red Spears, the Party Central had decided to rename them "The People's Self-Defense Volunteer Corps." Tang Shengzhi was designated their commander-in-chief, and Yu Shude their Party commissioner.

Six. Regarding the situation at the front,

a. Feng Yuxiang had left the Tongguan Pass in Sha'anxi, and had just surrounded Luoyang, preparing to take the city.

b. Due to the Heavenly Gate Uprising in Hebei Province, the Northeastern warlords in the region would probably retreat north of the Yellow River, facilitating our rendezvous with Feng Yuxiang (the Second Group Army) in Zhengzhou and Kaifeng, two major cities of Henan. The fact was, Feng Yuxiang was leaning toward us.

Feng Yuxiang

Seven. According to Central Headquarters' plans, once Zhengzhou and Kaifeng were taken, the Second Group Army would cross the Yellow River and go north, first to take Shunde, next to take Baoding, and finally to take Peking. The Fourth Army would advance along the east-west Long-Hai railway line to take Lanfeng and then Xuzhou. At the same time, Wuhan would send out a newly formed Eastern Expeditionary Army to go east along the Yangtze River to take Nanjing, then join up with the Second Group Army and take Peking and Tianjin.

When talking about political work, Deng Yanda expressed his deep appreciation of the work done by the Political Department of the Fourth Army. He said that our unflagging efforts were exceptional; he even compared us to the Red Army. Zhang Fakui also expressed his approval of our work, but he murmured that we were sometimes extreme and may have offended the local gentry. He particularly expressed disapproval of our opening the coffin of the self-defense regiment commander Zhao's father, saying that it was offensive. Deng Yanda was noncommittal on the topic, but I made a heated statement emphasizing that what we at the Political Department had done was not only meaningful, but absolutely necessary. I pointed out that in order to win people over to our side, we must satisfy their demands, and their most pressing demand was to put down the local gentry and despots. We could not afford to compromise with the gentry and local despots, I added, or we would have lost favor with the people. I ended by stating that we had to choose sides, and we chose to side with the people. Deng Yanda basically agreed, but Zhang Fakui still maintained that offending the gentry could be risky. On the third day in Happy Township, we did not march, so we at the Political Department did some propaganda and organizational work among the people.

If one looks around with the eyes of a leisurely traveler, one may see that the scenery of Happy Township was quite attractive, especially the river running outside the North Gate, its water so clear one could see to the bottom. The town wall was reflected in the water. There was a hillock on the other side of the river, actually quite a rarity in [the flat plains of] Henan. Next to the hillock was a pagoda which faced the town across the river. Crows flitted from the tip of the tower to the town wall and then to the hillock in a graceful line. The pity was that the river was floating with dead bodies. They were the dead from the retreating Fengtian warlord's forces. After two days' soaking in the river, the bodies were bloated and emitted a terrible smell. I really could not bear the sight, but our comrades from the south loved water so much that they jumped into the river and started swimming right beside the corpses. Perhaps they had been in the army too long—to them dead bodies were a part of life, and they didn't give it much thought.

X

We reached Happy Township on May 23, and stayed the following two days. On the evening of the twenty-fifth, the Army headquarters passed down the order to march west. Our column was supposed to be the right flank, that is to say, the eastern flank. We thought that we would be heading for Kaifeng City. But the enemy was concentrated in the center, along the Peking-Wuhan railway. Tang Shengzhi's forces had been fighting them for the past few days and not making any headway, and now we were ordered to move to the center to join the battle. We started out on the morning of May 26. Passing through Song Village, we had a skirmish with the enemy and captured a lot of weapons. That same afternoon, we arrived in Lingyi County, a short distance from enemy lines. We stayed in some woods for a while. At six o'clock in the evening, we exchanged fire with the enemy in the environs of the twin villages of Tile Inn and Ten Mile.

The enemy at Tile Inn and Ten Mile villages was the cream of the Eleventh Army of the northern faction, known as the Invincibles. Moreover, some of Zhang Xueliang's[12] troops were also there, some fifty thousand.

The enemy's plan had been to destroy the center of our forces, sweep down the Luo River to take Zhumadian, to be followed by the fall of Xinyang, then pass through the Wusheng Pass to swoop down on Wuhan! So this battle [of Lingyi] that we were marching to was a life-and-death one. Since the first skirmish on the evening of May 26, we had battled all night and through the day of May 27. We threw all our forces into the battle but could not turn the tide. The commander of the Seventy-seventh Regiment, Jiang Xianyun, was hit. He was taken to the rear, but died on the way. His death was the greatest loss of this expedition.

I had known Jiang's name since I first arrived at the Whampoa Academy, but I only met him for the first time in Nanchang in January of 1927. Later we met several times when we were both in Wuhan. Before starting off on this expedition, the two of us had a long conversation. We talked over many things. He told me that he had just lost his wife. He had nothing to hold on to, he said, and perhaps would not return from this Henan expedition. And indeed he did not! Now he is really gone. He had died without regret—a revolutionary soldier should always be ready to give up his life.

Jiang Xianyun, a native of Hunan, had left school when quite young. Though the youngest in his class, he was exceptionally gifted and

12. Zhang Xueliang (1898–2001), son of Zhang Zuolin, was popularly known as "the young Marshal." After his father's assassination, he established his own power base in Manchuria. Zhang is remembered for unleashing the Xi'an Incident of December 12, 1936, when he kidnapped Chiang Kai-shek and forced him into a united front with the CCP against Japanese aggression. After that, Zhang lived under Chiang's house arrest for the rest of his life until his last years, when he died in the United States.

always stood out as a leader wherever he found himself. He had joined the Socialist Youth oganization as early as 1922. When working in the coalmines of Anyuan, Jiang became a leader of the workers. In 1924, he joined the Whampoa Military Academy, the most brilliant student in his class. The commandant, Chiang Kai-shek, held him in high regard and treated him as a younger brother; at one time, his friends had jokingly referred to him as the "Young Leader." Political Director Liao Zhongkai also thought highly of him. During the expedition[13] toward Fujian Province in the fall of 1926 Jiang had been appointed commander of the worst company in the whole regiment, right on the battlefield no less. Nobody had wanted to touch that hot potato, but Jiang managed to turn his company into a solid fighting force which excelled in the battle to take Huizhou, where Jiang was wounded. In 1926, after the Zhongshan Gunboat Incident, Jiang returned to Whampoa to become secretary at the Political Department. Then he followed Chiang Kai-shek on an expedition north as his confidential secretary. By then, public opinion was turning against Chiang Kai-shek, and Jiang's friends were dismayed that he was becoming Chiang's toady. Jiang Xianyun himself did not relish that position and wanted to quit, but he had been posted there by the CCP and it was not up to him to leave. Jiang worked conscientiously on the job until the split between Chiang and the CCP. After that, Jiang worked to train the worker security forces of Wuhan. On the eve of this current expedition into Henan, Jiang was promoted to commander of the Seventy-seventh Regiment, which was under the Twenty-sixth Division of the Eleventh Army and the worst regiment under Zhang Fakui. But again Jiang Xianyun managed to train and turn around his troops. The Seventy-seventh Regiment was on the front line in the battle at Ten Mile Village and had stood its ground for a full thirty hours. If it had given ground, our whole force would have collapsed. But Jiang hung on. He was shot in the left arm around noon of the twenty-seventh and continued to

13. The Northern Expedition had started off from Canton earlier and took Changsha (Hunan), Nanchang (Jiangxi) and finally Wuhan (Hubei) in October. The Expedition headed eastward toward Fujian and took Fuzhou, the capital, in December 1926. See map in Spence, *The Search for Modern China*, page 347.

direct the battle. He was shot in the leg at four o'clock in the afternoon and still stood his ground. Then at nine in the evening, Jiang was shot for the third time, this time seriously, in the chest. He collapsed and fainted as he was being taken away. When Zhang Fakui heard that Jiang was wounded, he went personally to the doctor and requested that Jiang be taken to a hospital in the rear, but Jiang died on the way. When Zhang Fakui got the news, he broke down in tears.

It was only when the Twenty-fifth Army threw in their forces that the tide turned. Even so, it was only after a whole night's fierce fighting that the enemy was routed on the morning of May 28. We took back the position but at a price. The Twelfth Division alone had suffered eight thousand casualties. The commanders Zhang Fakui and Huang Qixiang shed many tears over the loss. We political personnel had worked non-stop through two days and two nights, without sleep and without food, sometimes at the front, sometimes at the rear helping to care for the wounded.

On the afternoon of the twenty-eighth as we entered the town of Lingyi, the streets were littered with dead bodies too numerous to count. One might well say: "Corpses piled up like mountains, blood flowing like rivers."

XI

After Lingyi was taken, the Political Department was set up in a girls' school in town. The building was empty. Everyone, from the school principal to the doorman, had fled. Although we had not slept for two nights, we were exhilarated to enter this newly taken town, and started to work right away. We at the Propaganda Section immediately called a meeting and laid out the tasks ahead:

One, go into town for social investigation;

Two, talk to people and distribute propaganda materials;

Three, print a daily paper, the first number to appear the next day, May 29;

Four, hold a memorial meeting for the second anniversary of the May Thirtieth Incident which was coming up in two days;

Five, conduct organizational work, such as,

a. set up the provisional committee of the GMD Lingyi branch within five days,

b. set up the provisional group of the Lingyi Association of Revolutionary Youth within three days,

c. set up workers' unions and trade associations within the shortest possible time period,

Six, upgrade the news agency of the Fourth Army. Apply to Director Liao for additional personnel from the political departments of the various divisions,

Seven, suggest that Director Liao and Director Xu of the Eleventh Army's Political Department immediately call a general meeting of all political workers to correlate their work.

After passing these resolutions, we immediately went our separate ways to get to work.

At the time, there were many political departments at different levels within Lingyi. Apart from my group from the Political Department of the Fourth Army and the various political departments of the various divisions under the Fourth Army, there were the Eleventh Army's Political Department and the political departments under its various divisions. Moreover, there was the Thirty-fifth Army's Political Department, and there was the political section directly under the General Headquarters of the Fourth Front Army. Moreover, there were personnel under the [Government's] General Political Department. But among this crowd, only we at the Political Department under the Fourth Army were doing any real work.

All our work assignments went well and as planned. The dozen or so progressive young men in Lingyi, restless in the oppressive atmosphere, now attached themselves to us. The Provisional Committee of the Lingyi Association of Revolutionary Youth was quickly set up. These young fellows helped us in many ways, distributing propaganda materials, mobilizing the masses to attend the May Thirtieth memorial meeting, writing posters, and hand printing our daily paper. Furthermore, they went and encouraged other young people from among the apprentices, handicraftsmen (no industrial workers around), elementary school teachers, and others to join in our work. We always had fifty or sixty enthusiastic young people working together with us.

Our colleagues at the political departments of the Eleventh Army and the Thirty-fifth Army wanted to cooperate, and they were welcome of course, so we were never short of helping hands

By May 30, our work had borne fruit: the daily paper was out, the Committee of the Association of Revolutionary Youth was set up, the Businessmen's Association was to be inaugurated on June 1, the county Peasants' Association was to be formed before June 5. The people of Lingyi had overcome their fear—they now knew us and welcomed our presence. Our mass rally to commemorate the May Thirtieth Incident was a great success. It was scheduled to take place at noon in the Temple of the God of Fire, but by 11:30 AM the place was packed so we had to start ahead of time. After the meeting, we paraded through the streets.

But there were attacks against us, the most hurtful being those leveled against us by comrades from the General Political Department who were posted in Lingyi. They hinted that we were just out to "show off," and that we "disrespect the leading organs." According to them, all we had to do was to obey orders; anything else was "disrespect," anything we accomplished on our own was "showing off."

Isn't that outrageous?

It is true that we should work under the General Political Department, but what had they done? Nothing! Particularly obnoxious were those members who flitted to the front to "oversee" our work. They descended on us and put on airs, looking down their noses at us people working on the front lines—they were the ones who were trying to show off. Worse, they prevented us from working. We comrades in the Propaganda Team simply could not stand them and had a very dim view of the bosses at the General Political Department.

On the afternoon of May 31, the First Column called a meeting of all political workers. Every member of my group attended, making up almost half of the attendees, because by now our staff had swelled. The General Political Department did not even bother to attend but merely sent a representative, a certain Mr. Secretary. After Director Liao's opening address, this Mr. Secretary stood up and started to deliver a lecture. As I had said, we at the Propaganda Team had never been favorably impressed with the General Political Department, and now one of them actually stood up and started to deliver a lecture to us! Sounds of hissing could be heard from where my group was seated. I signaled them to respect the speaker. But this Mr. Secretary had no sense of reality, he actually picked on us, saying that our work had produced no solid results, though he could not give examples. If that was not enough, he went on to suggest that we improve our methodology, again not providing any specifics. That was the limit. My comrades looked at me—I had no choice but to stand up.

"We have just heard a lecture from our superior, the comrade from the General Political Department, and I am drowning in disgrace. The comrade says that our work is not solid. Very true. Army Commander Zhang [Fakui] has already made it clear that our work is opening up wasteland. Right? We have thrown ourselves into the work of opening up wasteland, we have gone down among the masses, we have gone down among the soldiers; we forgot about decking ourselves out in fancy outfits. Look at those of the comrades from the General Political Department! Look at their leggings, polished to a shiny sheen. Look at the face cream on their cheeks, thick and white and sensuous like that of a Peking opera singer. Solid indeed! (laughter from the audience). Look at us, look at our ragged straw sandals, look at our hair longer than a convict's. Of course we deserve a good scolding from the General Political Department. The comrade from the General Political Department finds fault with our method of carrying out our work. Of course he is right. Just take a look at how they carry out their work—they take out whole bags of propaganda material and scatter them onto empty fields. Then they report that they have 'distributed ten thousand propaganda sheets and ten thousand periodicals,' and have put up tens of thousands of slogans. This method of 'work' is of course better than ours, more solid. Besides, they are smarter. While we were fighting at the front, the comrades at the General Political Department stayed behind, lording it over the masses at the rear. Now that we have driven away the enemy, the comrades from the General Political Department descend upon us, take pictures, make speeches, and lecture us. We go to the front lines, we bring back the wounded, carrying them on our backs. In the eyes of the comrades from the General Political Department, this is violating the dignity of a political worker. Their highnesses at the General Political Department are more used to looking at beautiful ladies in high heels—the sight of wounded soldiers disgusts them. We share the life of the masses, we work in the villages and survive on tofu dregs. In the eyes of the General Political Department, this is degrading. They brought their beasts of burden, donkeys, to carry their smart suitcases, their face cream, their cologne, their canned meat, their cigarettes . . . they are on a pleasure trip . . ."

I could have gone on and on, but Director Liao stopped me. Mr. Secretary had stalked out in a huff. After the meeting, Director Liao scolded me for going too far, but my comrades at Propaganda were happy.

The very next morning, I learned that Mr. Secretary had reported to Deng Yanda, demanding that I be punished for insulting my superiors. I knew that Deng would never bother about such trifles. Indeed, just as I expected, nothing came of the matter.

We spared no pains when working among the masses of Lingyi, and things went well. While doing this work, I had a chance to get to know Mr. Zhou Fanxi. Although we had never met before, I was familiar with his novels and his poetry and had heard my friends talk about his work. A native of Lingyi, Zhou was currently with the political section of the Thirty-sixth Army. Older than the fellows in my group, Zhou was warm and friendly and very helpful to us.

XII

On the afternoon of June 2, I received a letter from the rear, forwarded from the Canton Office. It was such a happy surprise, I was seized by a desire to leave for Canton immediately to see her. Such a counterrevolutionary idea was of course a deterrent to my work and a damper on my spirits. I was afraid to get emotionally involved, but couldn't help thinking of her. Were revolution and love incompatible? Some people question this statement, or even assert that there is no conflict between the two. But I know for a certainty that love interferes with revolution. My article on the subject, published in the *Republican Daily*, had won wide support among the revolutionary youth. But I myself was now caught in the conflict between love and revolution.

In her letter the lady said:

> Lin,[14] come back to Canton. Right now the view at Lichi Bay is beautiful. Your favorite star fruit is in season, and Dongshan, your favorite haunt, has been upgraded. A cute little coffee house has appeared across the road from the Dongshan Restaurant, and Dongshan Park has imported new varieties of exotic plants and flowers from Southeast Asia. Lin, it has been too long, please come to me!!

I could not put the letter down and kept reading it over and over again. On the other hand, I could not bear to go on reading, as every word shook me to the core. I absolutely must not let anything stand in the way of my dedication to the Revolution!

Five hours later I received devastating news: on May 1, my beloved friend An Ticheng had died a martyr's death in Shanghai!

I first learned of An Ticheng's name from his writings in the pages of the *Weekly Guide*. At the time An's address, as listed in the publication, had been "c/o An Cunzhen, Academy of Politics and Law, Mapo Lane, Hangzhou." It was the spring of 1924: I had written to him, and that had led to our correspondence. We met in November of that year. That first meeting took place in his dorm at the Academy where he was teaching. I saw a man in his thirties, draped in a long padded silk gown, shod in northern-style fur-lined shoes, wearing thick spectacles. He shook my hand very warmly, expressing great pleasure that we had finally met, and then we sat down and started talking.

The room was large and sparsely furnished with only a table, a desk, two chairs, and a single bed, but because of the overwhelming number of books scattered everywhere, the place seemed crowded, and gave a sense of the kind of man who lived there. An's books were mostly thick volumes of Japanese studies on economics; he had returned from Japan and was now a professor of economics. There were also many periodicals in Chinese, Japanese, and English stacked from the floor right up to the ceiling. The desk was also piled high with papers.

An Ticheng was working when I arrived, although it was already

14. One of Zhu Qihua's ten or more pseudonyms.

midnight. I had taken the Shanghai-Hangzhou night train and gone straight to his place on arrival. I noticed that the bed was plainly furnished; apart from books, periodicals and papers, there were no other furnishings—so unlike some professors' rooms decked out like a lady's boudoir.

We talked like old friends. He told me about himself. He was twenty-nine years old, originally from Fengren County in north China, and he had studied economics at the Imperial University in Tokyo. After graduation he returned and taught for one year at the Academy of Politics and Law in Tianjin, spent some time in Harbin, and then moved to his current position in Hangzhou, while teaching a few hours per week in Shanghai. Later on, he had to give up the part-time job in Shanghai and concentrate his energies on Hangzhou. Apart from teaching, he was very much involved in current affairs. He was a member of the Standing Committee of the Hangzhou branch of the GMD, doubling as secretary-general and chief of Propaganda. An was editor of the magazine *Forward Together* and was involved in all the progressive activities of Hangzhou. He told me that he spent all his time in meetings, teaching and writing, and slept four or five hours a day. I stayed the night and we talked about everything under the sun. We became fast friends.

We met again during the 1925 New Year's celebration, hosted by the Forward Together Society, on West Lake in Hangzhou.

In March 1925, he came to see me in Shanghai in the company of a female comrade, Miss Huang Wenxia. At the time, they were delegated by the Zhejiang Branch of the "Committee to Promote the National Congress" to attend a conference in Peking. They stopped for one night and then boarded a ship on their way north.

That June, during the height of the protests in the aftermath of the May Thirtieth Incident, An Ticheng was again in Shanghai. I was chatting at the sales department of the *Central Daily* [Zhongyang ribao] when he walked in to get a paper. I had no idea that he was in Shanghai, and he did not know my new address. A most lucky surprise meeting it had been. He left the next day to give a series of lectures in the Suzhou area, while I left for Canton soon after, and we lost touch.

That December I met An Ticheng's brother An Tiren at the Whampoa Military Academy, and learned that my friend was with the Second Army of the Republican Army in Xi'an, but my letters to him were returned, since he had already left. Then, in February 1926, I heard that An was in Tianjin; I wrote to friends in Tianjin asking about his whereabouts, but didn't hear back.

One day in April 1926, I went as usual to my office at the GMD CEC, and picking up a copy of the *Republican Daily*, learned that my friend in the company of other notables had taken the roundabout route via Peking, Outer Mongolia, Siberia, and Vladisvostok to ultimately reach Canton, and that they were staying in a hotel. Seeing the news, I went immediately to look him up, but he was out. Having missed him, I went back to my office, and we finally met at my office. We had not seen each other for more than half a year, and he had aged a great deal, but his spirits were high. He told me that in the wake of the March Eighteenth Massacre[15] he was among the protesters. There had been a crackdown, he was hurt in the arm and the leg, his spectacles were broken, and his briefcase snatched away. He could have lost his life. He was on the warlord Duan Qirui's hit list, and had to leave Peking for Canton by that circuitous route through Outer Mongolia and Siberia. He told me of his observations en route, all very interesting. That same night I took him out to dinner. Soon after his arrival in Canton, An Ticheng became a political instructor at the Whampoa Academy, but continued to live in the city, and we often got together. At the time, Chen Qixiu was editor of the *Republican Daily*, and he had solicited An's article "A Sweeping View of Inner and Outer Mongolia." An had actually written this article sitting in my rooms. He became head of the Propaganda Section of the Whampoa Military Academy and lived on campus. But over weekends he would come to Canton and we would spend time together.

When I set out from Canton for the move to Wuhan, he had come to see me off, saying that we would meet in Peking. Who would have thought that before we reached Peking he'd be dead.

15. The March Eighteenth Massacre occurred in Peking in 1926, when forces under the warlord Duan Qirui killed demonstrators protesting against Japanese encroachments.

I have been on my own since early youth, having been to many places and making many friends, but there was no one to compare with An Ticheng for sincerity, dedication, and courage. During his years in Hangzhou, he worked seventeen-to-eighteen hour days and dealt with all matters big and small with the same sense of responsibility. During the fall and winter [of 1926] when he was with the Political Department at the Whampoa Academy, An Ticheng would be in his office from six or seven in the morning until after ten at night. His dedication would inspire the coldest heart. His generosity to friends was such that despite a good monthly salary of over a hundred *yuan*, he sometimes could hardly afford a few *fen* for food, all because he would give away the bulk of his salary to friends in need. Personally, he had no interests beyond the revolution and academic pursuits; he did not drink, did not smoke, did not play cards, did not care for entertainment, and did not care about clothes. No matter how hard the struggle, An Ticheng never gave up. He was forever filled with revolutionary zeal, always forging ahead. The word retreat did not exist for him.

Now An Ticheng was gone forever. Was I going to cry? No, I had no tears, only blood.

XIII

An Ticheng's death hit me hard, but sorrow only pushed me to strive on more resolutely. Our work at Lingyi was exceptional, the more's the pity that we could only stay a few short days and had to be on the march again, this time heading for Kaifeng, an ancient city of Henan Province.

The situation was evolving. We had won a decisive battle at Ten Mile Village in Lingyi County. At the same time, warlord Feng Yuxiang [leaning to our side] went east through Tongguan Pass, securing a great victory in Luoyang, another major city in Henan. The enemy has retreated north across the Yellow River. There were no more traces of the enemy in Zhengzhou, Kaifeng, Xuchang, or Luoyang [all major cities in Henan Province]. The first objective of our forces have been met. The troops directly affiliated with Tang Shengzhi left Lingyi and moved north along the Wuhan-Peking railway line, heading for Zhengzhou. The morning of June 4, we left Lingyi and headed for

Kaifeng, passing through many counties along the way; we were racing against time and could not stop to enjoy the view.

The morning of June 9, we in the First Column headed toward Kaifeng in eastern Henan. We passed through the famously scenic Zhu Fairy Township, and by five in the afternoon we saw the Kaifeng city wall in the distance. We gazed at the imposing structure and were deeply impressed. After crossing the [east-west running] Long-Hai railway, we arrived at the foot of the city wall and entered the city by the south gate. Kaifeng was typical of northern cities, narrow and dirty; the low-ceilinged houses and dilapidated shops completed the scene of devastation. We did not have time to look around, but went straight to the High Court building, where the Political Department was already quartered. The High Court building was voted the best building in town. For the last two months on the road we had always stayed in poor rural cottages, even in Lingyi. The High Court here in Kaifeng was a handsome Western-style building, the interior comfortably furnished with imported Western furniture. After all that we had been through, it was sheer joy to stretch out on a sofa.

Before arriving in Kaifeng, we had done our homework and were looking forward to scenic spots and historic sites, but now that we had arrived, we never had a moment for sightseeing. After all, this was the first appearance of the Revolutionary Army in Kaifeng. One can imagine the work awaiting us.

As we were busy working, we kept wondering when we would take Shunde, when we would take Baoding, provincial capital of Zhili [which was renamed Hebei in 1928], and when, ultimately, we would take Peking. We started wondering: once Peking was taken, what then? Of course we did not forget our rear—Wuhan, but at the moment no one thought about returning to Wuhan. The old saying "Never give up until you see the Yellow River" had been in our minds all the way. And now that we were on the banks of the Yellow River, we would not be satisfied until we had crossed it.

The ways of the world are strange. Just as we were dreaming of taking Peking, who would have thought that orders would come down to return to Wuhan!

On June 12, the third day after our arrival, at about two or three in the afternoon a message came down from General Headquarters ordering us to set out for Xuchang the next morning. Xuchang was a town we would pass on our way back to Wuhan. It was like a clap of thunder. Who would have thought that after barely three days in Kaifeng we'd be heading—not north—but retracing our steps south!

XIV

From where we were in Kaifeng, we could have taken the train to Zhengzhou by the [east-west] Long-Hai line and then transferred to the [north-south] Peking-Wuhan line to reach Xuchang. But because of damage to the Long-Hai railway, we decided to walk. It was a distance of 180 *li* from Kaifeng to Xuchang and we had decided to do it in three days, walking 60 *li* each day. Half the journey was through sandy terrain, making it very difficult to walk. I had been working nonstop for so long that my health was deteriorating, so instead of walking I hired a rickshaw. The rickshaws pullers of Henan, unlike their peers [in other provinces] who usually limit their business to one location, specialize in pulling their clients across provincial borders. For taking me the 180 *li* from Kaifeng to Xuchang, I was charged the pitifully low price of three *yuan!*

We left Kaifeng through the south gate and took a last look at the city walls of this historic city. Outside the gate was a road unevenly paved with pebbles, passing by a little park. The Long-Hai rail tracks were just beyond. Once we crossed the railway track, we were in open country, and the earth under our feet got more and more sandy. By the time we had left Kaifeng behind we found ourselves in a veritable desert. The rickshaw pullers' feet were bogged down in sand with every step as they struggled forward.

It was June, hot and dusty, with sand blowing in our faces, which made the march all the more of a trial. But sitting in a rickshaw was a different story. Unlike rickshaws elsewhere, the rickshaws in Henan were usually owned, not rented, by the pullers. The owners would fit out their rickshaws with bright yellow awnings which shielded customers from the sun and kept away the swirling sand. Looked at from afar, these rickshaws looked like boats sailing on an undulating yellow sea. I sat comfortably in the rickshaw, gazing at the white clouds floating in the clear blue sky, and thoroughly enjoyed myself.

Forty-five *li* into our march, we arrived at the famous Zhuxian Township, one of the best of the four townships collectively known as the "Four greatest townships under heaven," the four being Zhuxian in Henan Province, Xiakou in Hubei Province, Jingde in Jiangxi Province, and Foshan in Guangdong Province. They were designated the best "under heaven" because at the time our ancestors had never conceived of anything beyond China.

Zhuxian of Henan, a transportation hub for the central plains since ancient times, naturally heads the list of the beauties. Due to its position, Zhuxian has even been called the "center" of the world. It is also famous because it was here that the patriotic hero of the Song dynasty Yue Fei[16] fought one of his famous battles, memorialized in Chinese opera as "the battle of the eight flying banners of Zhuxian," where Yue won a decisive victory against the northern Jin invaders. Thanks to a pervasive conservative mentality, Yue Fei has always been worshiped by the masses. There is even a Yue Fei Temple in the township, reportedly the former dwelling of the general.

Zhuxian Township is surrounded by an ancient wall of imposing aspect. But once inside, one is shocked by a scene of utter desolation. The streets were full of rubble, while all the doors were sealed under layers of dust, denoting lack of habitation. After walking around, we did find a couple of ghastly looking old men sitting in a little teashop. Talking to them we learned more about the history of the township, most of which had to do with Yue Fei.

We could also see at a glance why the township was so deserted. The fact was, nowadays the Long-Hai railway runs from east to west, while the Peking-Wuhan railway runs from north to south, leaving Zhuxian in the middle, overlooked, ignored, and forgotten.

Being in Zhuxian Township, however, one cannot afford to miss the Yue Fei Temple. The temple is fairly large, housing many statues. Apart from that of Yue Fei himself, there are statues of his wife and of the

16. Yue Fei (1103–1142), patriotic military commander of the Southern Song dynasty.

stalwart warriors under his leadership, as well as figures of his son and daughter. The kneeling figures of the evil minister Qinhui who had persecuted Yue Fei to death, and that of Qinhui's wife, are down below as was usual wherever Yue Fei is venerated. The only difference is that people at the other famous Yuefei Temple in the West Lake area piss on the figures of the hated couple, while here people limit themselves to hitting them.

There are many tablets in the garden, on which are engraved Yue Fei's poems and paintings. Yue Fei was not only a great leader and military strategist, but he was also well versed in the arts. One must concede that he was indeed an outstanding historical figure worthy of our respect.

At the rear of the Temple complex there is a multi-storied building put up to house people who were passing through. I climbed up and looked southward—is that Guangdong Province beckoning me? Where is my native Zhejiang?

We were supposed to cover sixty *li* every day, but on this the first day, we had only covered forty-five *li*. We spent the night at the multi-storied building behind the Yue Fei Temple. A sandstorm woke us up in the middle of the night, covering us in dust. It was pure misery.

Leaving Zhuxian Township the next day, we covered another forty-five *li* and arrived at Weishi Township. There is a moat circling the township, and a drawbridge across the moat operated by two iron chains, which are pulled up at eight o'clock every evening, thus shutting off the town from the rest of the world. We had only read about such places in adventure novels, never thinking that they still existed in real life. We learned that Weishi dates back to the Warring States period,[17] and is a fine specimen of an ancient citadel. At the time, Weishi had served to protect the feudal fiefdom; but nowadays, looking at things from the standpoint of trade and commerce, shutting down the town at eight o'clock is really a bad idea. The general decline of the economy is not surprising. The streets are paved with pebbles, which felt bumpy under our feet, and the low-ceilinged houses on either side of the narrow streets were mostly built of beaten clay. There are hardly

17. Warring States period, 475–221 BCE.

any shops, but placards and signs announcing this bureau or that association are visible everywhere.

Covering another forty-five *li* heading south after leaving Weishi Township, we arrived at Xiemaying, meaning literally a stopover to rest one's horse. Although not as famous as Zhuxian Township of Yue Fei renown, Xiemaying is a landmark in Chinese history—it is the birthplace of the founder of the Song dynasty, Emperor Zhao Kuangyin.[18] But now what is left of Xiemaying are just a few delapidated hovels, hardly a village any longer. One could not but be struck by the relentless passing of time.

Thirty *li* before we arrived in Xuchang was the little township of Xutian. Xutian, now a dusty little hamlet, is also famous in history. During the Three Kingdoms period, the Han Emperor Xian held a royal hunt in Xutian. During that famous hunt, the young emperor aimed at but missed his target, whereupon his ambitious minister Cao Cao grabbed the royal bow and arrow and killed the deer. The crowd cheered, thinking it was the emperor who had shot it, but Cao Cao stepped forward to receive the cheers. Guan Yunchang, one of the Liu-Guan-Zhang sworn brotherhood, was going to cut down the transgressor, but was stopped by a sign from Liu Bei, the eldest of the three sworn brothers. This episode is graphically described in the novel *Romance of the Three Kingdoms* [San guo yanyi]. When we chatted with the locals, they invariably referred to this episode of the Hunt in Xutian as if it was the only thing the town could be proud of.

Three days after leaving Kaifeng, we arrived at the city of Xuchang.

In our imagination, the famous ancient city of Xuchang, situated on the Peking-Wuhan railway line, was an imposing fortress as well as a flourishing market town, totally unlike the run-down Zhuxian Township that we had just left. It turned out, however, that Xuchang was nothing like what we had imagined. It lags behind Kaifeng, and cannot even compare to Xinyang in size.

We entered Xuchang through the east gate; the city ramparts are not imposing, though there is a lingering air of ancient grandeur, which made one think back to the heyday of the usurper Cao Cao. Where is

18. Zhao Kuangyin (927–976), first emperor of the Song dynasty.

the grandeur of yesteryear?

Following a straight line after entering through the east gate and exiting by the west gate, we had witnessed the best of Xuchang, which was really not much to boast of. The one and only street is narrow, mostly of unpaved beaten earth. Luckily the weather was dry as we passed through; otherwise the muck would have been intolerable. There are hardly any shops along the street, and not a single decent one. Such is Xuchang.

The only two buildings worth looking at were a Catholic church and an Evangelical chapel. Otherwise all the buildings were of beaten clay. The people of Henan have never cared much for housing; this we found out to our cost during this expedition. But there are two imposing European-style buildings outside the city gate, belonging to two tobacco companies.

We of the Political Department were quartered at the Xuchang branch of the Nanyang Brothers' Tobacco Company. We were surprised to find ourselves in such an aristocratic environment: the Western-style building, the interior furnishings, the well-tended garden, the modern office desks and chairs and writing utensils. This was not only a singular sight here in Xuchang, but would even be rare in Kaifeng. Now if the Nanyang Brothers' quarters had surprised us, the opulence of the British-American Tobacco Corporation was simply shocking. As we walked through the garden of the latter, we felt we were being wafted to some retreat in southern Europe; never would we have imagined this grandeur in the barren land of Henan.

XV

We stopped for three days in Xuchang, and ate a lot of apricots which were just then in season. The train arrived on June 17, and we boarded the train that afternoon and headed for Wuhan. The train moved very slowly, and it wasn't until the morning of June 19 that we passed through the Wusheng Pass. Dear people of Henan, we are leaving you for the time being. For the last two months that we have been here, what have we done for you? Forgive us! Forgive us!

CHAPTER FIVE

The Eve of the Split

I

We were brought into Wuhan in freight cars used to transport cattle.

It was midnight by the time we arrived at a stop called Liu Family Temple, and it was raining. There was no way we could continue on our way. We had to pass the night at this stop. All acommodations having been taken, there was barely any standing room on the platform. Why couldn't the train have made it straight to the station, instead of stopping here? Or why couldn't the train have gone faster and arrived at the Liu Family Temple station earlier, in which case we could have made our own arrangements. Or, in the worst case, if we were stuck here but it wasn't raining, we could have made our way back and gotten a good night's sleep. As it was, nothing worked, and we spent a sleepless night in helpless misery.

We had only been away for two months, but the tri-city of Wuhan felt different somehow. Streamers sporting slogans in big square characters were still hanging everywhere, but the contents were unfamiliar. Most notable were the three slogans:

"Down With Traitor Xu Kexiang!"

"Stop Zhu Peide From Eliminating Political Workers!"

"GMD-CCP Cooperation Will Endure!"

These three slogans were put up by the Hubei Workers' Union, but who was Xu Kexiang? If he was in the headlines, he must be somebody; there was no sense in mobilizing people to topple a mere nobody. Who was he anyway? That was my first question on arrival.

My next problem was that I knew nothing about Zhu Peide eliminating political workers. I had been away from Wuhan a mere two months, and now I barely recognized the place!

The next morning, the Political Department left with Army Headquarters, heading for Wuchang, one of the tri-cities of Wuhan. I stayed behind to get together with old friends whom I had not seen for the last two months—Mao Zedong, Luo, Liu, Zeng and company—at the Organization Department of Party Central. There I found the answers to my questions.

Regarding Xu Kexiang betraying the Party, etc., I learned that this Xu was the villain behind the Horse Day Massacre. Xu was a regimental commander under Tang Shengzhi—a mere nobody himself—until he sparked the Horse Day Massacre. At the time [when we left Wuhan on our recent Henan campaign], Changsha [capital of Hunan Province] was in the hands of the XX [Chinese Communist] Party and the mass movement was at high tide. The conservative forces were busy looking for an excuse to bring down the XX Party. They finally found an opening with Xu Kexiang as their tool, setting off the Horse Day Massacre.

The fact was, during this last Henan expedition, our defenses in the rear, including Changsha, were weak. The troops in Wuhan could not be spared, so the Changsha defense was made up of the combined forces of Xu Kexiang's regiment, local public security, and pickets of the General Workers' Union. Xu Kexiang was an old-style military man who obeyed orders and did not have much to say for himself. In the middle of that volatile situation, the unexpected happened.

Xu Kexiang

In fact, Xu Kexiang was a native, and his father a much-hated landlord in the rural areas. Now that the peasant associations and peasant self-defense units were organized, not to mention people arriving from town to cheer them on, the peasants pitted themselves against the landlord-backed so-called "self-defense" bands, and actually got the upper hand. The landlord households and local gentry took French leave, some to the capital city Changsha, some even farther to Wuhan. But his lordship Master Xu did not leave. His own son being a regimental commander of the Revolutionary Army, Master Xu believed that he himself had nothing to fear. He continued to act high and mighty, with the result that one day a large group of bare-foot peasants charged into his home and ransacked the place. Old Master Xu, who was used to having the upper hand, gave them a piece of his mind, with the result that he had to leave in a hurry if he wanted to come out in one piece. Old Master Xu ran all the way to Changsha, where his son was stationed, and gave the latter his own version of the story. To Xu Kexiang, this was powerful provocation, and nothing less than fighting the XX to the death would be adequate revenge. Landlords and members of the gentry, already congregated in Changsha, egged him on. The result was that just as our Wuhan Revolutionary Army was in Henan fighting the northern warlord faction, Regimental Commander Xu Kexiang launched an attack against the XX on the night of May 21, sparking the incident later known as the Horse Day Massacre. After the massacre, Xu became the idol of the exiled gentry, at the same time becoming the target of the XX's hatred, which explained the slogan against Xu Kexiang hanging from streamers in the streets of Wuhan.

Later we learned more details about the Horse Day Massacre. On the night of May 21, Xu Kexiang had led his regiment in an attack on the headquarters on the Hunan General Workers' Union and the Hunan Peasants' Association, disarmed the worker pickets and peasant militia, and arrested almost all of the worker and peasant leaders. More than three hundred people were killed. Apart from the worker and peasant associations, other mass organizations were also destroyed. Overnight Changsha changed from being a center of peasant and worker activities into a world where landlords and capitalists held sway.

In response to the attack, the XX [CCP] Hunan Committee called a meeting and passed a resolution to hit back at Xu Kexiang. It was decided at the meeting to mobilize one hundred thousand people from the city and the countryside and attack Changsha on May 31. But the plan was never put into action. The fact was, when head of the Hunan XX branch Li Weihan reported the plan to Chen Duxiu, then head of the XX Party Central, Chen, being a staunch upholder of the GMD-CCP alliance, vehemently opposed the plan. Li Weihan protested: "So many of our comrades have been killed. Why should we not fight back?" Chen is known to have said: "I would willingly sacrifice ten thousand comrades' lives to keep the GMD-CCP alliance alive. Only through this alliance can the revolution achieve success!" After debating back and forth, Chen Duxiu came out on top and the counterattack was called off at the last minute. The masses, who had already gathered, were dismissed. No wonder they became suspicious, saying: "Is this a joke? Yesterday we were told to rally for the attack on

Changsha, and today we are told to go home! What's going on?"

Chen Duxiu

As for the matter of Zhu Peide, he was made president of the Jiangxi Provincial Government right after Jiangxi was taken by the Revolutionary Army. After the break between Nanjing and Wuhan, Zhu Peide had initially sided with Wuhan. When the Revolutionary Army set out on the recent campaign to Henan, Zhu Peide stayed put, charged with guarding the rear in Jiangxi. Then Xia Douyin mutinied on May 17, Xu Kexiang launched the Horse Day Massacre on May 21, and the warlord Yang Sen seized the opportunity to attack Wuhan. Suddenly Wuhan was in jeopardy. Zhu Peide took advantage of the situation to get rid of many CCP members among his own staff. He sent them off to Wuhan with a big show and rally. In staging that ostentatious "send-off," Zhu Peide in Jiangxi was in line with Xu Kexiang [in Changsha] in undermining the CCP. This explains why the [Leftist] organs in Wuhan branded Xu and Zhu as partners in crime.

II

The Political Department was no longer housed inside the Public Stadium and had moved to Zhonghe Lane, a temporary accommodation.

It was an ordinary residential home but very spacious, and I secured a room for myself. I was exhausted by those two months on the recent Henan campaign; now with this sunny room all to myself, I wanted to settle down and do some reading. I needed to read more if I wished to improve myself. Since leaving Canton for Wuhan, I had barely read anything, and I felt that if I let myself slide down the path of least resistance, it would be very dangerous. New publications were plentiful—if I was not to be left behind, if I wanted to make a contribution to the Revolution, I must read. Of course we should give up reading when the Revolution needs us elsewhere, but the Revolution per se cannot be an excuse to give up reading and improving oneself.

But more often than not, reality does not fit neatly into one's resolutions. I wanted to settle down to reading, but caught up in such an environment, how could one concentrate? When we left Wuhan for Henan, Wuhan had been a hotbed of revolutionary fervor. Now, however, after a mere two months, there were only dying ashes. A mere two months, but all brightness, all hope was fading. The fate of the Wuhan Revolutionary Government was hopelessly handicapped by the prevailing darkness and confusion. What should one do? Seeing no way out, I was sunk in despair and was in no mood for reading.

The third day after our return to Wuhan, Director Liao [Qianwu], after looking in at Army Headquarters, confronted me: "Why did we put out those slogans demanding the overthrow of Xu Kexiang?"

I blurted out: "And why shouldn't we?"

"The commander [meaning Zhang Fakui] has said that those slogans might be offensive to Commander-in-chief Tang [Shengzhi]. Go and tear them down. [Zhou] Enlai has also said that we are the Army—the Party and the mass organizations may put up such slogans, but not us. Enlai asked me to pass this warning along to you."

Warning? Ridiculous! Why should the Party CEC be allowed to put out these slogans and not we at the Political Department? Don't we share the same position? Were we not under the leadership of the GMD Party Central Executive Committee? Should we not have supported those individuals who were being attacked by the Party? Right then, we were following the Party's position and we actually got a warning! Warning for what? I was bursting with indignation!

The very next day, [Zhou] Enlai[1] treated a group of us to dinner in Wuhan. We sat in a circle: Enlai the host; [Director Liao] Qianwu; Li Tao, director of the Political Department of the Twenty-fifth Division; Yu Zengsheng, political director of the Twenty-fifth and Seventy-third divisions; Guan Shun, head of the Organization Section of the General Political Department; Ye Ting, commander of the Twenty-fourth Division, a female guest whom I did not know, and myself.

Ye Ting brought up the subject of Commander Zhang Fakui's disapproval of the posters denouncing Xu Kexiang, and Enlai asked who was responsible for putting up those slogans.

Zhou Enlai

Actually, the first I knew of those slogans denouncing Xu Kexiang had been those put out by the Political Department of the Twenty-fifth Division. The fact was, the Twenty-fifth Division had not stopped in Kaifeng as we had done; therefore they were back in Wuhan several days ahead of us. When we arrived, their posters with those slogans

1. Zhou Enlai (1899–1976), activist during the May Fourth Movement, founder of the CCP European branch in France, one of the most important leaders in CCP history. Zhou served as premier of the PRC starting in 1954 and was influential in foreign policy for three decades. He was one of the most respected CCP leaders.

were already on display for all to see. Seeing their posters, we went ahead and put out some of our own. If those slogans were a mistake, then it was the Political Department of the Twenty-fifth Division which should take the initial blame. Li Tao was the director of the Political Department of the Twenty-fifth Division and he should own up. But he said that it was the *Army* Political Department that had put out such posters first, that he was only copying the posters of the *Army* Political Department. Thus the finger was pointed at *me*. Of course I did not mind admitting that I supported those slogans, but Li Tao's underhandedness was really upsetting. We should take responsibility for our own actions, especially when something goes wrong. How can one try to shift the blame to others? It was no big deal, but such underhandedness was so upsetting. After the dinner, I looked up several friends at the Party CEC and we spent the whole night playing mahjong.

When one is upset over something, it is natural to look for a distraction to dispel the gloom, thus mahjong became my constant occupation after my return to Wuhan. There was not much to do at the Political Department in those days, so after hours I would slip over to Hankou for mahjong. Hankou was incredibly hot, even at night the temperature would remain around a 100 degrees Fahrenheit. Fortunately we had electric fans in the hotel, as well as ice cream. We invariably spent all our nights in a hotel room playing mahjong. When mahjong was not enough of a stimulus, we would turn to drink. Bottles of beer and soda were consumed by the dozen. Thus drinking and chain smoking and mahjong took over my life, wretch that I was.

Sometimes, when we could not find mahjong partners, we would drink. But drinking in a hot hotel room was no fun, so we would go out and take long walks. My friends and I left our footprints everywhere—on the pavement along the river and on the grassy lawn of Victoria Park. We would sit down on the deck chairs in the park, or lie down on the lawn and, looking up at the sky, we would talk for hours. Thus time passed. Sometimes I would ask myself if there was any meaning to this kind of life? But such questions can only bring on gloom. I tried to deaden myself to all thoughts and feelings.

III

Commander Zhang Fakui planned a memorial for the dead and fallen comrades of the First Column. I was put in charge of publicity for the preparatory committee. I drafted the "talking points" for the meeting. Nowadays, you must really watch your step, or before you know it, you will be accused of this or that error. For safety's sake, I consulted [Zhou] Enlai. Zhou looked over my draft and sent it back unchanged, saying that it could be released.

The memorial was held in the Yuemachang. We comrades from the Political Department were here, there, and everywhere, to ensure that things ran smoothly.

That same evening, Director Liao Qianwu paid a call on Commander Zhang Fakui at his residence. Wang Jingwei, member of the standing committee of the Revolutionary Government, was also visiting, as was Deputy Commander Huang Qixiang. During the conversation, Committee member Wang Jingwei asked in all seriousness: "Commander, may I ask who was in charge of the 'talking points' for this memorial?"

"Section chief Zhu of the Political Department," answered Zhang.

"These CCP hotheads, so immature," Wang Jingwei commented, "Note that the 'talking points' never mentioned the *Three Principles*, only talking up a blue streak about the *Three Alliances*![2] They don't even know that without the *Three Principles*, the *Three Alliances* we would not have a leg to stand on. These CCP elements, so immature they forget the basics!!! How can we get anything done with this lot running things . . ." And then he went on to make a litany of complaints. I don't know on what basis he capped the CCP label on my head.

"Although the talking points did not mention the *Three Principles*, it is imbued with the spirit of the *Three Principles* . . ." Director Liao explained mildly.

But Wang Jingwei would not be placated, and he continued severely: "It really is going too far. First the workers' pickets, now the workers'

2. *Three Alliances*, formulated by Sun Yat-sen, namely alliance with the Soviet Union, with the Communist Party, and to support the workers and peasants.

boy scouts—what do boys know? Not content to use the youth, they are using children, and women too! These workers' pickets, these peasants' associations, they are raising hell wherever they go! The government, the GMD are nothing to them—Marx and Lenin and Communism, that's all they know! Did it ever occur to these hotheads they would be nowhere if not for the Government and the GMD!!! . . ."

Wang Jingwei had made a complete about-face! He used to be such a supporter of the CCP! I still remember his famous words when he first arrived in Wuhan: "Revolutionaries, stand to the Left! Nonrevolutionaries, back off!" Another famous saying of his was: "Opposing the CCP is opposing the Revolution!" But now, he was openly attacking the CCP!

The "talking points" I had drafted were indeed imbued with the spirit of the *Three Principles*, but it did not satisfy Wang Jingwei since the *Three Principles* had not been explicitly mentioned. That same evening, he put a copy of the "talking points" in the breast pocket of his Western suit, looked up Zhou Enlai the very next morning, and repeated his harangues against the immaturity of the CCP. Enlai patiently explained that the "talking points" were one hundred percent imbued with the spirit of the *Three Principles* without mentioning them by name, and that it had nothing to do with communism. As an analogy Enlai pointed out that even the publicity leaflets of the Bolsheviks did not necessarily spell out Communism. But Enlai's arguments were not enough for Mr. Wang. He brought out the incriminating copy of the "talking points" at the GMD-CCP Joint Meeting, shoving it in Chen Duxiu's face. I never imagined that the piddling "talking points" for a mass rally would have raised such a storm. A perfect case of you're damned if you do and damned if you don't!

Since Wang Jingwei had raised such a storm over the "talking points," what does Enlai do but turn around and give me a sermon! Times are stressful, he admonished, and we should watch our mouth, and so on and so forth. Good Heavens, this is the limit! I had bent over backward to be careful, revising the thing over and over again, sending a copy to him for approval. If anything goes wrong, it would be his responsibility and not mine! It was really too bad!

Enlai's lecture, however, was not the end of the matter. Commander Zhang Fakui scribbled a memo, which was passed down, laying down the law that from then on, documents drafted by the Political Department must secure his approval before being released. Previous to this, political work within the Army had been independent of the military. But a recent political meeting of the Party CEC had passed a resolution, based on a draft submitted by Wang Jingwei, stipulating that political personnel and political work would be put under the supervision of the military leadership, thus making political work an accessory to the military. This explains Zhang Fakui's order. I was dead set against reducing political work to the position of a concubine. But [CCP head] Chen Duxiu preached restraint; he insisted that for the sake of "consolidating the United Front"—Chen Duxiu's lifeline—even being a concubine was an honor.

As if that weren't enough, Chen Duxiu wrote a long letter to all of us in leadership positions at the political departments of the various Army units. In the letter, Chen exhorted us to uphold the revolutionary United Front and nurture cordial relations with the military leaders at all levels, even piddling regimental/battalion commanders. He added that all propaganda about "class war" should be eliminated in the Army, so as not to offend the sensibilities of the military leaders. Chen went so far as to say that even if a military chief was stealing soldiers' pay or had degenerated into a bandit chieftain, it was not for us to interfere!

Had political work sunk to this? I wanted to chuck it all, but I couldn't. I was caught in a position where I had to keep on performing mindlessly.

The only way to deal with the pain was mahjong and drink. All my friends in Wuchang were in the military and had no family. The Wuchang hotels not being good enough, we would cross over to Hankou to play mahjong in decent hotels. As for drinking, though, Wuchang boasted many good restaurants providing alcohol. My salary from the Political Department was mostly squandered on mahjong and restaurants.

Under these circumstances, I of course was not the only one trying to bury my misery in drink and gambling. All my friends were in the same boat, and we were all going down the primrose path. In Wuhan, we had been the cream of the revolution—pure, brave, progressive—but now even we ourselves had to admit that we were a bad lot. If we, supposedly the cream of the revolution, had sunk to this level, one may imagine the direction in which the Wuhan Revolutionary Government was heading!

IV

"One general's glory and ten thousand dead"[3]—the result of the victory in Henan was promotion for all the commanders.

Tang Shengzhi was promoted to commander-in-chief of the Fourth Group Army.

Zhang Fakui was promoted to general commander of the Second Army Corps, and there were adjustments in his chain of command as follows:

General commander, Zhang Fakui

Chief of staff, Xie Subai,

Director of the Political Department, Guo Moruo,

Secretary general, Gao Yuhan.

Commander of the Fourth Army, Huang Qixiang,

Director of the Political Deparment, Liao Qianwu.

Commander of the Eleventh Army, Zhu Huiri,

Director of the Political Departmen, Xu Minghong.

Commander of the Twentieth Army, He Long,

Director of the Political Department, Zhou Yiqun.

Commander of the Twelfth Division of the Fourth Army, Miao Peinan.

Commander of the Twentieth Division, Fu Shuangying,

Commander of the Twenty-fifth Division, Li Hanhun,

Commander of the Tenth Division of the Eleventh Army, Cai Tingkai,

---

3. Quoted from Tang dynasty poet Cao Song:
Speak not to me of Imperial rewards,
One general's glory and ten thousand dead.

Commander of the Twenty-fourth Division, Ye Ting,

Commander of the Twenty-sixth Division, Duan Qiri,

Commander of the First Division of the Twentieth Army, He Jinzhai,

Commander of the Second Division, Qin Guangyuan.

The headquarters of the Second Army Corps as well as the headquarters of the Fourth Army and the Eleventh Army were all accommodated in the old Military Supervisor's Residence. We people at the Political Department of the Fourth Army were also moved—from Zhonghe Lane (our temporary quarters) to the secluded back garden of the Residence. I secured for my own use a multi-story building in the garden. It was said that when Xiao Yaonan had been military supervisor of Hubei in the old days, this building had housed Xiao's favorite concubine, a beautiful young woman. The story was credible, as the building was exquisitely suited for a lady's retreat. The pity was that the lady had left without a trace, and I was in the empty chambers wondering what had become of her.

When I first transferred to the Fourth Army, I had been favorably impressed with Zhang Fakui, seeing in him not only a brave general but also an astute politician. But the victory in Henan had gone to his head, and I began to have doubts about him. He was swelling with self-importance—apart from Wang Jingwei, he looked down his nose at all the world. Prior to this, he had been all for Deng Yanda, it was Director Deng this and Director Deng that. Now Deng was forgotten. Lost in self-complacency Zhang never saw the writing on the wall as far as the Wuhan government was concerned; all he saw was a glorious future for himself.

At the time Zhang was all aflutter preparing for the ceremony to induct him into his new office as general commander of the Second Army Corps. The ceremony was to be held in Wuchang in the precincts of the old Military Supervisor's Residence. All the commanders from the Fourth Army, the Eleventh Army, the Twentieth Army and officers from the various divisions and departments were in attendance. The cadets from the Wuhan campus of the Central Military Political

Academy were also brought in. The grounds of the Residence were squeezed to bursting; to create space, officers above the rank of lieutenant colonel went and stood on the platform.

Having learned a lesson about "talking points" from that "memorial" meeting, this time I made sure that all references to the *Three Alliances* were eliminated from slogans hanging around the yard, while posters upholding the *Three Principles* met the eye whichever way you turned.

After a quasi-religious ceremony, Wang Jingwei stood up to deliver the eulogy on behalf of the Party Central Executive Committee. He was in a light-colored Western suit and tie, his hair combed back slickly, done up like a professor. Wang's facial expression, however, was lethal, reminding one of the occasion years ago when he had attempted to assassinate the imperial Prince Regent.

Wang Jingwei

He walked to the front of the platform, saluted, and started his speech. Letting his eye sweep across the slogans fluttering around, he began: "I am happy today. Looking around me, I see slogans supporting the Nationalist Party [GMD] and upholding the *Three Principles*. This goes to show that in this time and place, the Nationalist Party continues to prevail. But just a few days ago, during the memorial held by the First Column, it was heartbreaking to see that in their 'talking points'. . ."—saying which he fished out of his pocket a neatly folded copy of that unfortunate "talking points" of mine and started reading it out loud. "Note," he said, "here are only references to the *Three Alliances*, nothing about the *Three Principles*. To those Communist Party people (it used to be "Communist Party comrades" now demoted to "people") obviously the *Three Principles* were dispensable, but they must hold on to the *Three Alliances*, . . ." and so on and so forth.

After working himself into a pitch of fury denouncing the CCP, Wang went on to announce a conspiracy of the Third International.

"Since this past May," he began, "we have been talking to the Communist Party every single day at the Joint Meeting. We are earnest (here he made an expression of intense earnestness) in cooperating with the Communist Party, hoping to solve our differences through the joint meeting. Despite this hot weather, we spent day after day talking with them, hoping to iron out our differences. But they (here Mr. Wang made an expression of extreme distaste) were not sincere. While they kept us talking, they were busy with a conspiracy . . ."

Mr. Wang stopped there, holding us all in suspense. All present, on stage and down on the grounds, were waiting to learn of the conspiracy. I was standing on stage, and looked closely at the other people on stage. Mr. Wang, his face streaming with sweat, worked his face into an expression of extreme indignation, similar to the expression at his welcome meeting three months ago when he had reviled XXX [Chiang Kai-shek]. Sun Fo, representative of the Republican Government, wore a serious expression on his face. Tang Shengzhi, commander-in-chief of the Fourth Group Army, kept pulling casually on his expensive cigarette, looking completely relaxed. Zhang Fakui, his face darkened like a pig's liver, looked severely down at the audience, while the young cadets, one and all, kept up a fiercely determined expression as they looked up at Mr. Wang, not wanting to miss a word of the "CCP plot."

Mr. Wang continued: "One night, the representative of the Third International [M.N.] Roy—he is an Indian national—came to see me and showed me a telegram in Russian. He said that it was an order from the Third International to the Chinese Communist Party. According to Borodin and Chen Duxiu, Roy confided to me, this telegram should be kept secret from the Nationalist Party. But he, Roy, felt duty-bound to show it to me (meaning Wang himself). As for the contents, Roy left it to me to figure it out." Saying which, Mr. Wang paused, like story-telling performers keeping their audience in suspense, and sipped from a glass of lemon juice sitting on the table in front of him. Then he resumed his narrative.

"Now if the telegram were in English, many folks at the Central Executive Committee could read it. If in French, I your humble servant could manage. Even if it were in German, we could find someone to read it. Unfortunately, the thing is in Russian, and we had to look for a translator. Only after reading the translation did we realize how serious the problem was. It turned out that the Third International had given an order to the Communist Party to destroy the Nationalist Party . . ." Mr. Wang, who usually appeared cordial, now assumed an expression of vengeful fury.

The suspense was intense; not a sound was heard from the audience, not even a cough.

"According to this order," Mr. Wang continued, "The Communist Party must lead the revolution and not give up the leadership to the Nationalist Party," Here Sun Fo, who was standing next to Wang, coughed deeply. "Therefore, according to the telegram," Wang continued, "the Communist Party must undertake the following steps:

"One, reorganize the cadre structure of the Nationalist Party Central Executive Committee, get rid of the old conservatives and promote left-leaning newcomers, so as to create a new Nationalist Party Central Executive Committee which can adapt to the leadership of the Chinese Communist Party.

"Two, get rid of the rightist military leaders within the GMD, and thoroughly reform the army units.

"Three, arm twenty thousand (minimum) Communist Pary members, as a basis for reforming the Army.

"Four, select fifty thousand radical members from among workers and peasants to join the Nationalist Army, to change the make-up of the army;

"Five, set up Revolutionary Tribunals to put counterrevolutionary elements on trial, the judges to be chosen from among the Nationalist Party left-leaning leaders . . .

The above is the gist of the order."

Wang paused, and then started indignantly to refute the order point by point.

"Isn't it clear that they are out to destroy the Nationaliat Party? To say that the Nationalist Party is not fit to lead the revolution! And that only they the Communist Party should lead! And how are they to lead? By destroying the Nationalist Party of course!

"They find fault with the Central leadership, they want to eliminate some, to reform others, to mold the Central leadership into an accessory of the Communist Party.

"They find fault with the Army, they want to eliminate some of the military leaders . . ." Here, Sun Fo gave Tang Shengzhi such a look as if to warn him: "The Communist Party is going to eliminate you!" But Tang kept pulling at his expensive cigarette, totally oblivious to Mr. Wang.

"They want to arm twenty thousand Communist Party members," Wang continued, "they want to train fifty thousand worker-peasant activists to reform the Army, to turn the Nationalist army into a Communist army. Thus would the Nationalist Party be destroyed . . .

"In the past, the Communist Party had controlled the mass organizations, trying to keep back the Nationaliat Party. Now they want to keep the Nationalist Party away from the Army, away from the Central leadership! Such are their designs!

"But to cap it all off, they plan to set up revolutionary tribunals to indict counterrevolutionaries, meaning the Nationalist Party of course. They want to assign a Nationalist Party member to preside over the trial, which means to say that they are plotting to make the Nationalist Party destroy the Nationalist Party! "

Mr. Wang was so affected by righteous anger that he had to stop after every paragraph to catch his breath. "We learned of the plot, yet we could not deal with it—we had to put everything aside to go to the front to cheer up our troops. When we returned from Zhengzhou, Roy, the representative of the Third International, had disappeared! We asked around and were told that Roy, by showing us the telegram, had leaked their secret, so the CCP had gotten rid of him. We know that the CCP is not only cruel to the GMD, the CCP is also cruel to their own. They want to destroy the GMD, and Roy, who had given away their secret, should also be gotten rid of. Who knows, he may already be dead . . ." (Later events revealed that Roy had not been killed.)

Mr. Wang kept on in this vein for a while and then ended his speech.

Mr. Wang was supposed to represent the Party CEC at the ceremony of Zhang Fakui's induction to his new position. But his talk became a declaration of war against the CCP. It was totally unexpected. Everyone present, whether for or against the CCP, was tense. The cadets of the Wuhan campus of the Military Political Academy were mostly CCP sympathizers; they were very upset—some of the girls cursed under their breath, some were in tears.

"This is the beginning of the end," was the thought on everyone's mind. A pall was cast over the meeting.

In the past, there were two individuals who never missed a mass rally, one was the corpulent Borodin, the other was the combative Deng Yanda, and both liked to give speeches. Borodin could not speak Chinese, but he was fluent in English, and always won applause for his eloquence. Deng was not as gifted a speaker as Borodin, but he made up for his deficiency in eloquence by his infectious enthusiasm. In the past, those two speakers, never missed a mass rally, but on that day neither showed up.

After Wang Jingwei, it was Sun Fo's turn to speak. Sun had been fidgeting restlessly, impatient to begin. Before the chairman had finished announcing: "Next, the representative of the Republican Government . . ." Mr. Sun was already at the front of the platform bowing to the audience.

Mr. Sun was chubby with a fleshy round head, like all overfed offspring of the rich. Dressed in a Western suit, and almost ten years younger than Mr. Wang, Sun was not as attractive as Wang in the eyes of the opposite sex. Moreover, in eloquence of speech he was no match for Mr. Wang nor for his respected parent Sun Yat-sen. Actually, Sun Fo could not even stand comparison to Deng Yanda. Sun had once been co-named with Deng Yanda as "a genuine revolutionary leader" by no less a person than CCP leader Chen Duxiu himself in the pages of *Weekly Guide*! Today, Sun Fo was representing the government to address the meeting in honor of Zhang Fakui's induction. In reality he, like Mr. Wang, was here to attack the CCP.

Sun Fo began by recalling the origin of the GMD's "toleration" of the CCP. Originally, the GMD's *Three Alliances* had been the alliance with Russia, with the CCP, and with the masses of workers and peasants. Mr. Wang Jingwei later felt that the term "alliance" with the CCP was inappropriate and came up with the term "toleration" [*rong gong*] to define the GMD's policy with reference to the CCP. According to Mr. Wang, "alliance" implied a parallel relationship, which was not acceptable, as it would be giving the CCP undeserved credit. But "toleration" was another matter, implying that the CCP was looking up to the GMD. At one point in his career, Sun Fo himself had pursued a policy of "alliance" with the CCP, but he now concurred with Mr. Wang Jingwei in replacing "alliance" with "toleration." The problem was that the term "alliance" had long been established as the definition of the relationship between the two parties, while the term "toleration" was unfamiliar and quite a mouthful. In his speech, which dealt mostly with the problems of the relationship, Sun kept using the term "alliance" by mistake, and then correcting himself to "toleration," until the air was buzzing with the sounds of the two words.

What was remarkable in Mr. Sun's speech was the fact that he was trying to open up a new path for the GMD—the GMD of Wuhan. He showed them a new path which was neither to the left nor to the right—but a path "forward." Mr. Sun said: "XXX [Chiang Kai-shek] of Nanjing is going right; the CCP is going left, neither is on the right track. Neither of the two is on a truly revolutionary path." According to him, "a truly revolutionary path, a true Nationalist Party path, the path of the "*Three Principles*," was neither right nor left, but Forward." Here Mr. Sun raised his voice for emphasis and paused for applause, but none was forthcoming, neither from onstage nor from the mass audience down below. Mr. Sun obviously felt let down. In the days when he had been named by Chen Duxiu in the *Weekly Guide* as "a true revolutionary leader," every word of his anti-Nanjing [anti-Chiang] speeches had been warmly applauded. Now that Mr. Sun had discovered a new path for the GMD, he was met by a loud silence. "Today," Mr. Sun continued, "we should turn neither left nor right." Here Mr. Sun turned to catch Mr. Wang's eye, perhaps recollecting Mr. Wang's famous dictum, "Revolutionaries, stand to the left, nonrevolutionaries, back off," but Mr. Wang kept his eyes on his drink, totally unresponsive. "We must march *forward!*" (Here Mr. Sun again raised his voice for emphasis, and again was met by silence.)

After Sun Fo's oratory, it was Tang Shengzhi's turn. Tang [commander-in-chief of the Eighth[?] Group Army] was the superior of Zhang Fakui who was being honored that day. We expected him to follow in the footsteps of Wang Jingwei and Sun Fo and go after the CCP, or even exceed them in the severity of his condemnation. Surprisingly, Tang only delivered five minutes of mumbo jumbo about discipline and was done. Our nerves had been stretched to breaking point by Wang Jingwei and Sun Fo's thunder, but now were relaxed by Tang Shengzhi's lullaby.

Zhang Fakui

General Commander of the Army Corps Zhang Fakui, the man being honored that day, rose and gave a formal response. Like

Commander-in-chief Tang Shengzhi, he too never referred to the CCP in his response. Commander of the Twenty-fourth Divison Ye Ting (a CCP member) listened closely to Zhang Fakui's words. Wang Jingwei watched him closely, but Ye Ting ignored him.

As for the commander of the Twentieth Army, the chubby He Long, he stood composedly on stage all through the show. When Wang Jingwei was hysterically announcing the details of the CCP plot, He Long had grimaced, and both Tang Shengzhi and Zhang Fakui had noted his reaction. When Zhang Fakui was giving his response, again Tang Shengzhi had kept his eyes on He Long, checking his reaction.

The face of Secretary-general of the Second Front Army Gao Yuhan turned a dark red, like the Wei Yan[4] character in Chinese opera. From where he stood onstage he stared at the back of Wang Jingwei with barely suppressed anger.

Only Guo Moruo was relaxed, looking idly at the posters hanging on the wall. His eyes moved from one poster to another and then back again, oblivious to the drama going on around him.

After Zhang Fakui's speech, it was Huang Qixiang's[5] turn to give a speech on behalf of the newly appointed Army commanders. Director Liao Qianwu gave him a look as he walked up onto the stage. Huang's speech could not have been more brief, lasting barely three minutes. Predictably, he too did not refer to the CCP.

Political leaders were working themselves into a frenzy of CCP bashing, but military leaders just shrugged it off. This was not what Mr. Wang Jingwei and Mr. Sun Fo had been expecting, and they both seemed disappointed. The meeting dispersed in an atmosphere of

---

4. Wei Yan (? –234), a military leader under Liu Bei during the Three Kingdoms period. "Red-faced" is a stock character in Chinese opera and denotes a headstrong personality.
5. Huang Qixiang (1898–1970), a follower of Sun Yat-sen, a veteran GMD member who had led many successful campaigns during the Northern Expedition, especially in Hunan, Jiangxi, and Henan in 1925–1926, and had briefly worked for the Nanjing Government, notably as military attaché in the diplomatic mission to Berlin in the early 1940s. Later, Huang joined the war effort against Japanese aggression and was firmly opposed to civil war. After 1949, Huang held many honorary positions in the People's Republic of China until his death.

unease. We did some slogan chanting as a matter of routine, but people did not put their hearts into it, and the chanting was feeble.

Back at our office in the Political Department, we all let out a sigh of relief. Someone said, "The bastard!"

V

The situation in Wuhan deteriorated rapidly, sparked by a telegram from the warlord Feng Yuxiang.

[To begin at the beginning,] the main objective of that last Henan campaign had *not* been territory, but to link up with the Northwest Army of Feng Yuxiang, the "Christian general." At the time, we had high hopes for Feng Yuxiang. Telegrams coming from Moscow had praised him in the warmest terms. Judging from accounts of his behavior in Moscow, it seemed that Feng was more radical than Kominsky, more revolutionary than Lenin, more leftist than Trotsky. According to Feng's avowal in Moscow, he upheld Bolshevism as the only truth and asserted that it was Lenin and not Jesus Christ who was the true Saviour. Obviously the folks in Moscow had lapped it all up: they not only provided Feng with arms and plenty of rubles, they also wired the comrades in China singing his praises. Thus the Wuhan leadership placed all their hopes in Feng Yuxiang, thinking that once they had secured Feng to their side, the situation in Wuhan could be turned around.

Our Henan campaign had been successful, and we did achieve the objective of linking up with Feng Yuxiang's Northwestern Army. How we had rejoiced! With Commander-in-chief Feng Yuxiang on our side, we were assured of victory. [Or so we thought.]

In Zhengzhou [the capital of Henan], our Wuhan leaders had taken turns wining and dining Feng. In his many toasts and speeches, Feng had said very deliberately:

"Let me expose a plot. When I was on the point of taking Xi'an, XXX [Chiang Kai-shek] wired asking your humble servant to stay put in the environs of Tongguan Pass and let the Wuhan army and the Northeastern warlords fight it out among themselves. When they had destroyed each other, XXX suggested, then and only then should your humble servant deal the finishing blow to the Northeastern warlords while he, XXX himself, would personally take Wuhan. His objective was clear: it was nothing less than taking over Wuhan. But your humble servant was not to be taken in! XXX wanted me to stand by and watch [as the Wuhan forces were decimated by the Northeastern warlords]. On the contrary, I threw my men into battle and won this victory. Now let me formally expose this plot of XXX. This plot serves to show that XXX is an counterrevolutionary and should be taken down!"

After his high-sounding speech, Feng Yuxiang had suggested to our leaders that they could return to Wuhan with their hearts at ease, that they could carry the campaign farther south, downriver, and leave it to him [Feng] to finish off the mission of this last Henan campaign. A situation was created wherein the Wuhan Army would go south and east [to Jiangxi and Fujian], while Feng's own Northwestern Army would campaign farther north. It is thus that the province of Henan fell securely into the lap of Feng Yuxiang.

We returned to Wuhan with our hearts at ease, leaving Big Brother Feng to finish off what we had left unfinished of the [Second Northern] Expedition in Henan. What more did we have to worry about? But we were in for a surprise.

As we returned to Wuhan, Feng's special rail carriage headed straight for Xuzhou, certainly not to finish off the mission of our Expedition, but to meet with XXX [Chiang] himself, the very person he had reviled two days ago. In Xuzhou, Feng not only did not topple XXX, he actually went through a ceremony with incense and vows and so on, binding himself as blood brother to that very same individual.

His business done in Xuzhou, Feng Yuxiang returned to Kaifeng, and sent a wire to Wuhan demanding that the Wuhan government [meaning the GMD Left] compromise with Nanjing [meaning Chiang Kai-shek], and join hands to destroy the CCP.[6]

6. "In 1927 troops loyal to the Left Wing of the Kuomintang moved north along the railway line from Wuhan and defeated Wu [Peifu]'s forces. The Wuhan leaders then tried to win over Feng [Yuxiang] to their cause. The 'Christian General' promptly demanded—and was given—control over all

It was like a clap of thunder. The situation in Wuhan was going from bad to worse. All my misgivings about the move to Wuhan were being confirmed. The economic blockade downriver had created a shortage of coal, affecting first off the Hanyang Arsenal, which could hardly maintain operations, and then affecting transportation on the Peking-Wuhan railway line and the Wuhan-Changsha line, which were encountering hardships, sometimes replacing coal with diesel oil. Kerosene was in short supply, especially in the interior. The area west of Hunan and Hubei was suffering from a shortage of salt—people had been killed fighting over salt. Rice was also becoming scarce, but most serious was the financial crisis. The shortage of cash had almost paralyzed the economy of Hubei and Hunan provinces. The Wuhan government managed to survive by issuing bonds and printing paper currency (of the Central Bank), thus causing the value of the *yuan* to drop to less than one third of its value. The Wuhan Government's plan to concentrate cash in its own hands did nothing to alleviate the crisis.

On the other hand, the workers and peasants' movement had provoked counterattacks by the landlord and capitalist classes. Landlords from the country now flocked to the city and joined up with the capitalists, forming an counterrevolutionary alliance. Manufacturers and owners in the city had been affected by the workers' movement, just as the landowners had been affected by the peasants' movement. They began deliberately staging slow-downs, cutting back production. This in turn caused panic, but they laid the blame on the workers and peasants' movement. The government agreed that the workers and peasants had indeed gone too far. Wang Jingwei held that if not for CCP provocation, the imperialist powers would not have blockaded Wuhan in the first place.

Just as the public's confusion and panic were reaching a climax and the Wuhan leadership was deeply discouraged, this telegram from Feng Yuxiang was like rubbing salt into a wound. Two hours after the first telegram, the second one arrived, demanding that Borodin and

---

Henan. But in the great struggle within the Nationalist camp over the future of the Revolution, he sided with Chiang Kai-shek in Nanjing rather than the KMT Left in Wuhan. His decision tipped the scales decisively in Chiang's favor." See Graham Hutchings, *Modern China*, p. 191.

all the Russian advisers in the army and government institutions be deported. According to Feng, they had all been dispatched by the Third International to destroy the GMD and turn the country over to the CCP—a complete about-face from Feng's attitude in Moscow, when Feng had praised Borodin as the Grand Old Man of the Chinese Revolution.

Three hours after the arrival of the second telegram, a third arrived. Apart from repeating the contents of the first two telegrams, this third telegram demanded that Borodin leave within forty-eight hours, with the additional demand that Deng Yanda be deported too, since he had turned into a tool of the CCP.

After that, a telegram would arrive every two or three hours, repeating the same requests, demanding Chen Duxiu's or Tan Pingshan's arrest, suggesting that Zhang Fakui leave the country. Thus, with telegrams flowing in day and night, Wang Jingwei hardened his anti-CCP stand, while the Wuhan Government was hounded to its final demise.

At the time when all the above was taking place, The *Repubican Daily* and local papers in Wuhan were still controlled by the CCP, and not a single word of Feng's bombardment of telegrams had appeared in their pages. However, the facts could not be kept hidden for long. Soon, news of the telegrams was all over Wuhan and the townships. There were even rumors that Feng Yuxiang's army had passed through Wusheng Pass and would soon be descending on Wuhan. Actually, people with any sense could see that though Feng Yuxiang might well harbor such ambitions, he did not have the means to carry them out.

VI

The situation took a turn for the worse—Sun Yat-sen's widow Madame Soong Qingling suddenly departed Wuhan, leaving behind a note. I saw that note: it was brief but very moving. Madame Soong pointed out that the GMD in Wuhan had forsaken Sun Yat-sen's dying behest and was now hand-in-glove with the "enemies of the GMD," working against the Revolution. She said that finding herself helpless in such a situation, she had no choice but to leave. From the note, it was apparent that Madame Soong was deeply distressed to see that those very GMD leaders [such as Wang Jingwei] who had formerly declared that "opposing the CCP is opposing the revolution" were now actively opposing the CCP. I also learned from the leadership that apart from this note, Madame Soong had left two other letters, one to the GMD Central Executive Committee, and one personal letter to Wang Jingwei, both steeped in sorrow and indignation.

Soong Qingling

Going over her letter, we were all moved by Madame Soong's faithful devotion to the Revolution. Having always thought of her as a sheltered lady, we were deeply impressed that she could have taken such a forceful step.

Previous to this, in the winter of 1925, when Zou Lu, Xie Chi, and company [from the GMD extreme Right] conspired in the Western Hills [outside of Peking], Madame Soong had sent a wire opposing the Western Hills Meeting.[7] I now finally realized that politically Madame Soong was indeed a fitting consort of Sun Yat-sen

During that last move up north after we had arrived in Nanchang,

7. The Western Hills group, disaffected with the GMD Left, met together in late 1925 in the Western Hills of Peking to form their own faction; its representative figure was Hu Hanmin, one of Sun Yat-sen's close associates.

Madame Soong had also wired us from Wuhan [where she had arrived earlier], opposing the idea of the Party [and the Revolutionary Government settling in Nanchang as Chiang Kai-shek had demanded], advising that we move on to Wuhan as planned. At the time, Madame Soong had been an important member of the Joint Meeting, where her words had carried weight. Obviously, she was already actively involved in politics by then. She had actively participated in the Third Plenum of the Second Central Committee of the GMD that past March. Furthermore, in May, she had stoutly opposed the resolution passed at the meeting of the GMD Second Central Committee regarding the "reshuffling of Party affairs." On the contrary, she had spoken at the meeting, drafting a resolution to strengthen the Party collective against one-man dictatorship. A member of the CEC of the Second Party Congress, she had not been given any post. Later, at the Third Meeting of the GMD CEC, Madame Soong was elected head of the Women's Department. It was not a position from which to launch major initiatives; yet throughout the "Wuhan period" [of the Revolutionary Government], she had consistently sided with the Left.

During the Horse Day Massacre in Hunan, Madame Soong had been even more outraged than the [CCP leaders] Chen Duxiu and Tan Pingshan, and she had insisted that [the main culprit] Xu Kexiang be severely punished. Later, when Wang Jingwei returned from Zhengzhou to Wuhan having become more blatantly anti-communist and having created a depressingly anti-communist atmosphere in Wuhan, Madame Soong had stood up to him in the very GMD headquarters, berating him for betraying the legacy of Sun Yat-sen.

Later, when Feng Yuxiang wired Wuhan demanding the expulsion of the Soviet adviser Borodin, Madame Soong stated that "Borodin was invited by the Party Leader Sun Yat-sen, and Feng Yuxiang is not in a position to expel him." On the contrary, Madame Soong demanded that the Party CEC expose the transgressions of Feng Yuxiang and punish him accordingly.

Considering the situation at the time, Madame Soong's suggestions could not be put into action. Understandably, she was frustrated throughout that last month. And then one night, her residence was searched by soldiers of He Jian's Thirty-fifth Army. It was an absolute outrage that the residence of the late Party leader Sun Yat-sen's widow had been searched; it was an insult to Madame Soong, an insult to the late Sun Yat-sen, as well as an insult to the GMD itself. Madame Soong was very angry of course, but knowing there was more to it than met the eye, she wrote a letter to Wang Jingwei, the top man of the GMD, demanding an explanation. There was no reply. Madame Soong's departure, obviously, was no accident.

Madame Soong's departure made us all the more despondent about the future of the situation in Wuhan. I realized that if things were not desperate, Madame Soong would not have packed up and left.

If Madame Soong's departure had been a blow, what followed was worse—Deng Yanda got up and left too. Considering Deng's position in the Wuhan Government, his departure was a more serious blow than Madame Soong's.

With the exception of the CCP members, Deng Yanda was the most important individual within the Wuhan Revolutionary Government, as far as the GMD was concerned. The relative position of GMD members within the Wuhan government could be ordered thus: Deng Yanda, Wang Jingwei, Sun Fo, Xu Qian, Tan Yankai, Tang Shengzhi, Zhang Fakui, Madame Soong Qingling.

Wang Jingwei had arrived in Wuhan after the government had already been formed. If not for the "Party Power" movement [to combat one-man dictatorship and rein in Chiang Kai-shek, as was obvious in the slogans], the government of Wuhan could not have been formed, and there would not have been the confrontation between Wuhan and Nanjing. Thus the Wuhan government's very existence had been the fruit of the "Party-Power" movement, and one must note that Wang Jingwei was a late arrival and had not been a part of it. In a word, Wang Jingwei, though leader of the Wuhan government from the GMD side, had not struck deep roots within the Wuhan government, his had been a superficial relationship.

Sun Fo had taken an active part in the "Party Power" movement, but his role within the movement was not to be compared with that of Deng Yanda, who had been most forceful and resolute. Besides, after the confrontation between Wuhan and Nanjing, Sun Fo's position within the Wuhan government declined—not to be compared to Deng Yanda's.

Xu Qian's role in the "Party-Power" movement was active, but not to be compared to that of Deng Yanda's either, nor was his position within the Wuhan government to be compared to Deng's. After the victory of the Henan expedition against the Northeastern warlords, Xu Qian had left Wuhan to join up with Feng Yuxiang in Xuzhou to attend meetings with the Nanjing [Chiang] group. In a word, Xu Qian had betrayed the Wuhan government to become a tool of Nanjing.

Tan Yankai was the acting president of the Wuhan government, true, but he had not been part of the "Party-Power" movement either As far as he was concerned, it was "anything for a quiet life." His position within the Wuhan government was more thrust upon him by circumstances than a result of his political stand. Strictly speaking, Tan had only played a supporting role in the Wuhan government.

Tang Shengzhi was the military leader in the Wuhan government, and in this sense, a man of consequence. But he had his own agenda and was not the political lodestar of the Wuhan government.

Politically speaking, Zhang Fakui was more important than Tang Shengzhi, the reason being that he was a follower of Deng Yanda.

So it all comes back to Deng Yanda, the political lodestar of the Wuhan government. His sudden departure, forsaking the Wuhan government, was the catalyst that set off the dismemberment of the Wuhan government.

Like Madame Soong, Deng Yanda also left a letter. Saddened and resigned, Deng bid farewell to the people of Wuhan. Indeed, he had reason to mourn, as he was witnessing the dismemberment of the government which he had personally helped build.

Before his departure, Deng Yanda had had several fierce arguments with Wang Jingwei over the question of the GMD's relationship with the CCP: Wang had turned anti-communist, while Deng Yanda supported cooperation with the CCP. He was disgusted with Wang's sudden turnabout. When Feng Yuxiang wired, demanding that Deng Yanda leave the country, it was Wang Jingwei who personally took the telegram and thrust it upon Deng. At the time, Deng had not given up hope for the Wuhan government and did not resign. But later on, things got worse, and he had no choice but to leave.

Deng Yanda was the initiator of the "Party-Power" movement and the lodestar of the Wuhan government—with him gone, what hope was there for Wuhan?

VII

The political and economic situation in Wuhan was worsening by the day. It was obvious to all that a major crisis was brewing.

Borodin had left, and except for a handful who were still hanging on, so had most of the Russian advisers in Wuhan.

CCP leaflets announcing their break with the Wuhan government were distributed in the streets. Tan Pingshan of the Peasant Affairs Department and Su Zhaozheng of the Labor Affairs Department had both resigned. The Communist Youth Central Committee's leaflets denouncing the GMD for destroying the peasants and workers' movement were also strewn around Wuhan.

However, the CCP had announced that it was *only leaving the Wuhan government, not the GMD*. CCP leader Chen Duxiu was still clinging to his dream of a GMD-CCP alliance. Although the situation in Wuhan was already a shambles, Chen Duxiu ordered his disciples to put up posters around town, declaring that "The CCP-GMD Alliance Will Endure."

Chen Duxiu spared no pains to maintain the alliance.

Wang Jingwei complained that the apprentices' union in Wuhan was going too far—Chen immediately broke up the apprentices' union.

Wang Jingwei complained that the workers' pickets exacerbated the volatile situation—Chen immediately dissolved the workers' pickets and turned their arms over to the Wuhan garrison commander, Li Pingxian of the Eighth Army under Tang Shengzhi.

Wang Jingwei complained that the peasants' associations in the various counties were getting out of control—Chen immediately asked the CCP leaders of the peasants' movement to rein in the peasants.

Wang Jingwei pointed out that the peasants' armed self-defense brigades were alarming the locals—Chen immediately dissolved the peasants' self-defense brigades and turned their arms over to the local military.

Wang Jingwei complained that the CCP political cadres within the army were preaching class struggle to the rank and file, to the disgust of their commanding officers—Chen immediately notified Zhou Enlai that CCP cadres within the army were forbidden to advocate class struggle.

In a word, Chen Duxiu carried out Wang Jingwei's orders to the letter, but that did not ameliorate the situation. On the contrary, the situation was getting more explosive by the minute.

By then, the die was cast: Wang Jingwei, Sun Fo, Tang Shengzhi, and company had chosen to take an anti-communist stand. That they had not yet started killing the Communists, as Chiang was already doing in Nanjing, was only because Zhang Fakui was still undecided.

It had been more than three months since I had been appointed to the Fourth Army, and I had a pretty good idea of what Zhang was like. He was brave in battle, a man of mettle, but a shallow political thinker. It is true that he had sympathy for the working masses, but only to the extent that it did not interfere with his own career. Compared to his peers, Zhang Fakui could be considered a man of reason, but he was not completely free of the traditional values of the old-style military man. In a word, Zhang was mildly progressive, but not a sophisticated thinker, having a very dim idea of communist theory. He simply admired the fighting spirit of the CCP members in his army and often held up Ye Ting or Jiang Xianyun as examples for his own men to emulate. Because of his appreciation of the CCP in the military, there were more such in his army than in any other. And precisely because of their sizable presence, Zhang Fakui's attitude to the CCP in his army was more tolerant than that of Tang Shengzhi to the CCP members in his. This was the reason that Zhang Fakui did not want to see a split with the CCP—his own force would be cut down in size. Besides, he did not personally feel threatened by CCP policies. But, as I mentioned, being an unsophisticated army man, he looked to Wang Jingwei for direction. Wang Jingwei being dead set against the CCP, Zhang found himself in a dilemma.

Should he continue to work together with the CCP? Wang Jingwei would not allow it, and how could he flout Wang's wishes? Kick out the CCP members in his force? These included division commander Ye Ting; regimental commanders Lu Mingde, Zhou Shidi, Xu Jishen, Fan Jing, Liu Mingxia and Zhou Yiqun; and Liang Bingshu, regimental political director of the Twentieth Army. Moreover, there was He Long, commander of the Twentieth Army, who was decidedly sympathetic to the CCP. As for CCP members below the regimental level, their numbers were legion. Should he turn against the CCP? His army would be depleted by half! How could Zhang Fakui let that happen!

The situation had deteriorated beyond repair, but Chen Duxiu still nursed his dream of an enduring "GMD-CCP alliance." He pampered Wang Jingwei, bowing to his every request. At the same time, he tried to win Zhang Fakui to his side. Meanwhile Wang Jingwei also needed Zhang Fakui's military might if he wanted to split with the CCP.

Thus Zhang Fakui found his left hand held by Chen Duxiu and Zhou Enlai dragging him left, and his right hand held by Wang Jingwei and Sun Fo dragging him right. Which way should he go? Before coming to a decision, Zhang Fakui became two-faced, vowing tearfully to Zhou Enlai, Gao Yuhan, Liao Qianwu, Ye Ting, and company that he would never turn against the CCP, would never purge his Second Army Corps of CCP members. To Wang Jingwei, Tang Shengzhi, Sun Fo, and company he solemnly pledged himself to their anti-CCP stand. Although two-faced, Zhang Fakui was actually leaning toward the anti-communist side.

But Chen Duxiu, getting positive reports from Zhou Enlai, Gao Yuhan, Liao Qianwu, Ye Ting and company, and unaware of the direction in which things were moving, never doubted Zhang Fakui's sincerity.

Chen Duxiu did have a plan, though. He thought that once he had Zhang Fakui on his side, he would take Zhang's army and other forces in Wuhan sympathetic to the CCP, bring them to Canton, and build another revolutionary base.

During the month of July, Chen Duxiu and Zhou Enlai threw themselves into this project. At the time, apart from Zhang Fakui's army, the Government's Independent Division (actually the cadets of the Central Military Political Academy) was completely under CCP control. There had been a plan to move the cadets, fully armed, out of Wuhan on the pretext of military exercises and take them away. In addition, two military police regiments of the Hubei provincial government were also available to the CCP.

But Chen Duxiu was not decisive, deluding himself that Wang Jingwei might still join up with him. The cadets were taken out of Wuhan as planned, but then taken back again!

Wang Jingwei, on the other hand, wanted to take Zhang Fakui's army east, to move against [Chiang Kai-shek] in Nanjing.

Should he return to Canton [with the CCP]? Or should he go east [with the GMD Left wing] to take down [Chiang Kai-shek] in Nanjing? Zhang Fakui could not make up his mind. Meanwhile his forces were moving toward Jiangxi Province.

VIII

The summer heat of Wuhan was deadly. Between the desperate situation and the stifling heat, life had become intolerable. It was not the kind of life that I had committed myself to. Should I hang on? Was it worthwhile? Political work in the army was virtually abolished. My job as the head of the Propaganda Section was an empty title, although my salary continued to be paid. But what was I living for?

I had to leave Wuhan, I said to myself, but where should I go?

Nanjing? Never!

Shanghai? Hangzhou? All impossible. Not to mention the fact I do not want to go!

Back to Canton! Although Canton had changed, it still had its charms for me. The scenes of Dongshan must be still there. My beautiful young lady continued to pull at my heartstrings—was she still in Dongshan? Thinking of her, I wanted to fly back to Canton, to my old home in Dongshan. Within the army, there was a prevailing urge to return to Canton. Therein lay the reason why I had not left the army. If the army was going to return to Canton, I would be better off returning to Canton in their company rather than going on my own.

Generally speaking, here in the Second Corps we were better off than anywhere else. Although feeling depressed at the prevailing political situation, our personal circumstances were not straitened. But it was a different story with the men under Tang Shengzhi. All the political workers in the Eighth Army, the Thirty-fifth Army, the Thirty-sixth Army and other armies under Tang had lost their jobs. They flocked to us here in the Second Corps. Some applied to me personally, asking me to fit them in somewhere. But what could I do? Being unable to help made me miserable and guilty, not only my old comrades who had moved together with me into Wuhan now looked me up—complete strangers from as far away as Zhejiang sought me out, asking me to help them find a means of livelihood. And that made me even more depressed.

The Wuhan campus of the Military Political Academy had always been considered a stronghold of CCP influence. Under the deteriorating situation, the fate of the Academy was truly in jeopardy. The cadets there were now scrambling in all directions, looking for a means of livelihood. The men were better off: if bad came to worse, they could always enlist in the army. But for the young women cadets, it was another story. These well-bred young ladies had arrived there as rebels fleeing the oppressive feudal tradition. In the eyes of their families, their clans, and their neighborhoods, they were depraved, doomed to a fate worse than death. With a few exceptions, none of them could return home. Even if their families should take them back, their presence would not be tolerated in the larger conservative environment. On the other hand, they could not join the army. They did undergo some training, but the Women's Corps had not yet been formed, so there was nowhere for them to enlist.

Over the past couple of days, many women comrades had stopped by to talk about their hopeless predicament. This plunged me into a dark melancholy.

One Sunday, to lift myself from depression, I went with a group to the Yellow Crane Tower off the Hanyang Gate. There were six of us: four young women from the Academy, myself, and Zhang from the

General Political Department. We climbed up the tower, planning to drink ourselves into a stupor.

The Yellow Crane Tower was the most famous attraction in Wuchang. I had enjoyed myself there on first arriving in Wuhan. Now, after just a few short months, the scene remained as it had always been, and the Yangtze River below kept flowing quietly onward. But how the world had changed!

The tea and dining space at the top of the Tower was overflowing with customers; after much searching we found a table next to a window with an unobstructed view of the river. We ordered two catties of heated Shaoxing wine with some dishes on the side.

"Let's enjoy ourselves today and drink to our hearts' content!" exclaimed Miss Chen, "We will part in a few hours, and who can tell when we will meet again!"

"Drink and make merry while we can . . ." murmured Miss Zhang as she sipped her wine.

"Is Miss Chen planning to return home?" I wanted to say something to cheer her up but could not find the words.

"No," she replied, "I am homeless . . ." Miss Chen's eyes welled up with tears as she replied.

"What about you, Miss Zhang?" I could not bear to look at Miss Chen, and turned to Miss Zhang.

"Me? I do have a home, but I can't go back . . ." said Miss Zhang, trying to keep a stiff upper lip.

Silently we continued to sip our wine.

Two women comrades from the Wuhan Campus showed up. Miss Liu, who was in our company, spotted them looking for seats. We invited them to our table, and now we became eight. Miss Chen started to make the introductions, but Miss Liu quoted the lines from Bai Juyi's "Song of the Pipa":

> Drifting alike through the edge of existence,
> Let us meet when we meet, and part when we part[8]

The newcomers did not help enliven the mood. Actually, the addition

8. Bai Juyi (772–846), poet of the Tang dynasty.

of two more people somehow only deepened our despondency. Trying to drown our sadness with wine did not help, it only made us more sad. Miss Zhang stood up and leaning against the window frame, started to sing "The Internationale" in English. The solemn strains swept away our petty-bourgeois self-pity.

We paid the bill and left the Tower. But no one was ready to leave. There was a photo shop nearby, so we went in and took a group picture. Then we strolled into Shouyi Park. The wall on the west side of the park was heavily scratched with visitors' inscriptions. We went up and added some of our own. I wrote: "Look around you and take note: who is holding sway in this city?!" I signed myself "Ya Lin." By the time we were done, the sun was setting in the western skies. We shook hands sadly and parted.

Alone, I went back to my place in the old Military Supervisor's Residence where I was quartered. My room looked charming, having been scrupulously tidied up by my orderly. Unfortunately, like the erstwhile supervisor's concubine, I must soon leave this space. I wondered who would be the next occupant. I looked around nonchalantly, and for the first time noticed a line of writing on one side of the beautifully papered wall. The writing was blurred, but I was able to make out lines from *Dream of the Red Chamber* [Honglo meng]:

> This spring, the heartless swallow built his nest,
> Beneath the eaves of mud with flowers compressed,
> Next year the flowers will bloom as before,
> But swallow, nest and Maid will be no more![9]

It was taken from Daiyu's verse when she was burying the fallen flower petals.

I'd been living here for a month. How come I had not seen the inscription? The discovery just added to my gloom. It was obviously in a woman's hand; I wonder if it was the hand of Xiao Yaonan's concubine. When I first took possession of this room, I had felt pity for the young woman, wondering where she had drifted to. Now it is my turn to wonder who would be the next occupant and whether he or

9. *The Story of the Stone*, translated by David Hawkes (Hammersmith: Penguin, 1977), Vol. II, p. 38.

she would wonder about my whereabouts, and think of me with pity. Burdened with these thoughts, I took a pencil and scribbled four lines of poetry by Cui Lu.[10]

> Wild grass overruns the stone steps,
> Muted now the bells of the royal entourage.
> The moon waxes and the moon wanes,
> But the jade balcony is deserted.

I realized that I had changed. I was no more the revolutionary soldier fired by the spirit of self-sacrifice. I had now become a sentimental pale-faced scholar! This must not be allowed to go on! I was afraid I would *not* be able to sleep that night. Off to Hankou for mahjong!

IX

Finally it was time to leave Wuhan.

The night that I crossed the river to Hankou, I had stayed up all night playing mahjong until nine o'clock the next morning. I was exhausted and not in any condition to cross the river to find my way to my office in Wuchang. Not bothering to ask for leave, I stayed in the hotel and slept till four in the afternoon. Hankou was livelier than Wuchang. Perhaps it was just my mood, but I felt that Wuchang was haunted. If not for my charming room in the erstwhile Military Supervisor's Residence, I would have stayed away from Wuchang and spent all my nights in lively Hankou.

When I finally staggered into my office in the Political Department, a secret directive from Liao Qianwu was awaiting me:

"Tomorrow evening at nine, Army Commander Huang Qixiang is leaving for Jiujiang. I am going with him, and so are you. Notify staff members Mao and Luo to get ready to leave with us. *Confidential.* Qianwu."

So, after two months in Wuchang, I was about to leave.

Now about this trip to Jiujiang: who knew what it had in store? Heaven knows why the Army commander was leaving in secrecy. Damn it, as far as I was concerned, it is just one life after all! No big deal! Let

10. "Hua Qing Palace," by Cui Lu.

whatever was coming, come!

As I would be leaving the next day, I decided to skip over to Hankou for one last night of mahjong. Just as I was about to cross the river, Liao Qianwu sent for me—*again—to join him immediately!* There went my plan for one last night in Hankou.

It turned out that Huang Qixiang, our Army commander, was about to leave, but not with his entire Army Headquarters, not with the full staff of the Political Department either. We met up at Pinghu Gate at seven o'clock in the evening, and they all boarded the boat. But I had to stay outside the Gate to wait for Yun Daiying. He was supposed to leave with us, but he did not know the way and I had to wait for him.

There was a little steamship, which did not dock. We were rowed out to it and scrambled up onto the ship in the dark. Huang Qixiang, the commander, had not arrived yet. So I and Yun Daiying and Liao Qianwu loitered in the dining area. Things had come to such a pass [that we had to leave]. What more is there to say? We avoided talking about politics. The dining area was very hot, so we went on deck and looked across the river at the sparkling lights of the Hankou marketplace. We all felt drained.

"Damn it," said Liao in his Northwestern twang, "the Wuhan that we built up is now over and done with."

"Why is it so hot?" said Yun Daiying, trying to change the subject, "Westward lies Xiakou, eastward lies Wuchang" Yun Daiying was quoting from Cao Cao's Ode at Chibi.[11] True, talking about politics only made us more depressed—might as well change the subject.

"Shouldn't it be *northward* lies Xiaokou, and *southward* lies Wuchang? Why do we say 'westward lies Xiakou, eastward lies Wuchang'?" Liao Qianwu pointed with his finger to Hankou (Xiakou) on one side and

---

11. *Romance of the Three Kingdoms* (San guo yanyi), chapter 48, Cao Cao's Ode at Chibi:

> To the east he could see the boundary of Chai Sang (Wuchang),
> West, he contemplated the stretch of the Yangtse (Xiakou).

See *The Three Kingdoms*, Moss Roberts, trans. (New York: Pantheon, 1976), p. 183. In the novel, Cao Cao had used the ancient terms for Xiakou and Wuchang.

Wuchang on the other.

"The *Wuchang* mentioned in Cao Cao's ode is not *this* Wuchang, but the city of E'cheng," I explained to Liao.

"When I first arrived in Wuhan [two months ago], Wuhan was like a volcano [burning with revolutionary fire]. And now all the fire has turned to ashes . . . Wuchang, Hanyang and Hankou, they are all steeped in darkness." And I could not help letting out a deep sigh.

A new moon peeped out from among the clouds, its light quivered in the center of the river and it made me think back to Gao Yuhan's poem about crossing the Whampoa River at night:

> Reading the Lamentations and listening to the plaintive reed pipe,
> Gazing at the ripples entangled like silver snakes,
> I have lived here through three moons,
> And now a strip of water cuts me off, exiling me to the ends of the earth.

I recited the lines to Liao Qianwu and Hui Daiying, and they too were infected with the pain of parting that the poem conveyed.

The ship got under way at midnight.

Farewell, Wuhan! Farewell good people of Wuhan!

CHAPTER SIX

Jiujiang and Nanchang

I

We arrived in Jiujiang on July 23 [1927] and were greeted at the docks by a security detail of Army Headquarters' Secret Service. We went to a girls' missionary school, the Ruli School, but our Army Headquarters could not be accommodated there, so the staff went off looking for other accommodations, while we waited under the shade of some trees. Jiujiang was even hotter than Wuhan.

It was the summer holidays, so there were no students around, and all the doors were locked. Seen from the outside, the building was excellent, even superior to the Baoling Girls' School in Nanchang [where I had had a row with the female principal].

Ye Ting,[1] a CCP member and commander of the Twenty-fourth Division, came to call on Army Commander Huang Qixiang. Ye Ting had arrived in Jiujiang two days earlier and his troops were already on their way to Nanchang, the capital.

1. Ye Ting (1896–1946), commander of the Revolutionary Army from 1919 onward, joined the CCP in 1924. He was one of the leading figures in the August First Uprising and one of the founders of the People's Liberation Army.

Ye Ting, his head completely shaved, dressed in gabardine uniform with his legs bound in dark yellow leather leggings, paced up and down the yard of the Ruli Girls' School as he chatted with Huang Qixiang. Huang was slightly older than Ye, and taller. The two men were both from Canton and chatted in Mandarin with a Cantonese accent.

Ye Ting

A staff officer returned to report that suitable quarters had been found in the Jiujiang Chamber of Commerce. The last time I passed through Jiujiang on my way from Nanchang to Wuhan, I had been with Mao[2] and had visited the Jiujiang Chamber of Commerce. It was situated on a beautiful scenic spot, facing Gantang Lake. Army Headquarters could do worse than be set up there. But after he had seen the Chamber of Commerce, Commander Huang Qixiang decided that he wanted to set up his personal residence at the Misty Lake Pavilion in the middle of the lake. Thus we in his retinue were also quartered in the Pavilion complex, which I had visited the last time I was here.

The story goes that Zhou Yu [of the Three Kingdoms period] had trained his navy on the lake here and that the Pavilion complex had

2. Probably Mao Zedong, as Zhu Qihua is reminiscing about the time when they arrived in Jiujiang and Nanchang on the way to Wuhan.

been his personal residence. The story is corroborated in the Jiujiang gazeteer. Huang Qixiang took the main rooms; Liao Qianwu, Yun Daiying, and I took the side rooms on the right wing. Ours was the best spot in the Pavilion complex, with a little garden and a minature pavilion. Qianwu and Daiying took the two rooms within the little pavilion. As for me, having gotten used to camping in the open during our Henan expedition, I took out my folding bed and slept in the beautiful little garden. The weather was hot, but we were pleasantly secluded in this little spot.

Misty Lake Pavilion is a famous scenic spot of Jiujiang, a popular tourist destination in summer. Predictably, the walls had been profusely inscribed by visitors. There were couple of verses worth looking at, but most of them were pure doggerel.

I had always loved reading classical poetry. Since the downturn in the political situation in Wuhan, I had turned to reading poetry in my depression and also liked to inscribe it where I could, to give vent to my own feelings. So one day I inscribed Du Mu's[3] famous poem on one side of the little pavilion, the poem commemorating the battle of Chibi, with a comment on the famous young general Zhou Yu.

It goes like this:

> The broken halberd in the sand has not decayed,
> Restored, it tells the story of Red Cliff.
> If the East Wind had not helped Zhou to victory,
> The two Qiao beauties would have been borne to the Bronze
> Crane Tower!

While reading *Romance of the Three Kingdoms* in my youth, I had always admired Zhou Yu: his brilliance, his achievements, his good fortune in love had all inspired in me an envious admiration. He died an early death, but he had lived life to the full.

Previous to this, I had been busily occupied wherever I was—this was the first time in my life that I idled my time away. Now I could enjoy myself, strolling along the streets with staff members Mao and Luo. As noted above, Misty Lake Pavilion, where I had staying, was on an island in the middle of Gantang Lake. We had to be ferried to and

3. Late Tang poet Du Mu (803–852), on the battle of Chibi.

fro to get into town.

Once across the Lake into town, the first thing to get was a cool drink to beat the heat. Luckily there was a cold drink stand right across the street, run by a Cantonese. How expensive things were in Jiujiang! Soda water was only thirteen *fen* a bottle back in Wuhan, while here the same thing costs over seventy *fen*. But a silver *yuan* could fetch four bottles. The fact was, tradesmen in those days did not trust the cash issued by the Wuhan government but dared not reject it, so they raised prices to offset their possible loss. The three of us each drank three bottles of soda and were out of pocket by over two *yuan* each. It was outrageous! Restaurants, too, were much more expensive compared to the last time we passed through. The weather being so hot, there was nothing to do except stay indoors to sleep or read.

In those two years past, as I passed through Canton, Nanchang, Shanghai and Wuhan, I had bought quite a few books, eight boxes altogether. Drifting here and there, I had not accumulated anything else: these eight boxes of books could be considered my life savings, but they were too bulky to move. When last in Hankou, as we were about to leave on this last trip, I had left them with Du Xiangshu, a colleague at the Political Department. Du's home was quite close, in Huangpi of Hubei Province. But having left them, it was hard to say when I might be able to retrieve them. Who can foretell the vagaries of fortune? Those books were my only possessions, but I could not keep them with me—such is the life of a revolutionary. This explains that though I had the time for reading, I did not have my books with me. Mao Jiayi, having some books in his pack, lent me a popular novel, Zhang Ziping's *Drifting Catkins,* and I found the love story very moving.

During the days in Henan and after our return to Wuhan, I had read a novel by Turgenev, translated by Guo Moruo as *Xin shidai* [The new age],[4] but had not been able to finish it. Now I went to the Commercial Press bookstore for a copy, which I read through in one breath. I felt that I myself was Nezhdanov.

4. Nezhdanov, an idealist young man, is the protagonist of the novel *Virgin Soil,* by Ivan Turgenev. In the story, Nezhdanov tries to go down among the common people but they rejected him and he ultimately committed suicide.

In his preface to this translation, Guo Moruo said that he had managed to kill the Nezhdanov in himself. That was Guo Moruo. As for myself, I do not know when I will ever kill the Nezhdanov in me.

II

Gao Yuhan had arrived in Jiujiang, and he shared our quarters at the Misty Lake Pavilion. I have nothing against this [eccentric] old fellow; sometimes it was fun chatting with him. He gave me a book, *Citizens' Handbook,* a recent publication of his. Gao had seen my orderly reading one of these cheap kungfu thrillers. He forthwith advised the young fellow to give up reading trash and read his book instead, to learn something about the basic rights and duties of a citizen.

CCP notables kept arriving in Jiujiang. In addition to Gao Yuhan sharing our quarters, Tan Pingshan, Wu Yuzhang, Lin Zuhan, Li Lisan, Zhang Guotao, Peng Pai, and others did too. With the arrival of so many CCP leaders, the atmosphere in Jiujiang grew tense.

A new paper appeared in the streets of Jiujiang, the *Gongmin bao* [Citizens' News], which carried articles denouncing Wang Jingwei. The paper sold very well. Gao Yuhan was one of the contributors.

The day after we arrived in Jiujiang, Huang Qixiang gave a welcome dinner in honor of Zhu Peide, commander-in-chief of the Fifth Column, and Jin Handing, commander of the Ninth Army. A huge retinue of security men followed Zhu Peide wherever he went. Misty Lake Pavilion, where the banquet was held, could hardly hold them all.

That same night [after dinner], Liao Qianwu, Gao Yuhan, and Yun Daiying were chatting in the garden of the Pavilion when someone mentioned that He Yaozu was showing signs of turning against Nanjing [Chiang Kai-shek]. Huang Qixiang pricked up his ears and said that they should send someone over immediately to find out, but there was no one available for the job.

The past couple of days had been very boring for me, so when I heard of the affair, I jumped at the chance and volunteered to sneak into Anqing to do the spying. Gao Yuhan agreed that I was the best choice, as I was from the South [with a Southern accent], and I could easily be disguised as a student. The next day, Gao Yuhan reported my offer to Huang Qixiang, and Huang immediately approved, handing me 300 *yuan* for expenses. There were no suitable Western outfits available in Jiujiang, so I decided to go back to Wuhan, which I had just left, to buy some clothes and leave for Anqing by way of Wuhan. This plan carried the added advantage of allowing me to see my old friends at the Political Department who should still be in Hankou. Liao Qianwu and Gao Yuhan approved of my plan, and I left Jiujiang for Hankou on July 26, just three days after I had left that city not knowing when I would ever be back.

The minute I arrived in the tri-city of Wuhan, I sensed a change. All the CCP notables had left. The Hubei Provincial Workers' Union and the Hubei Provincial Peasants' Association had been virtually dissolved. All government employees with any CCP sympathies had made themselves scarce. Sun Fo, Tang Shengzhi, and company were in the act of launching a massive anti-Communist campaign.

The minute I went ashore at Hankou, I headed for the Party CEC office, where I met an old friend, Wu Wenqi, who told me that he was heading for Zhejiang. Many friends had left, leaving no trace of their whereabouts. I suppose they had all gone underground. I went to the Ningbo Guild to look up Kong Lingjun, but he too had disappeared.

That same night, I went to Wuchang, assuming that the Political Department where I had served was still there, but I was told that they had all left for Jiujiang that very morning! That was a blow indeed, especially as I had hoped to draw some cash. Who would have thought that they would be gone!

My Western suit was easily acquired, but the situation looked ominous. The talk was that the Second Army [now in Jiujiang] was going to move from Jiujiang to Canton! Under such circumstances, if I ventured alone into Anqing, wouldn't I risk being left behind on my own? I had to stop and think it through and find out more about the true situation. I decided to stay one more day—if the situation took a turn for the worse, I would return to Jiujiang. If it was imperative for me to discharge my assignment in Anqing, I could easily leave from there.

From Wuchang, I made my way to Hankou and went to a restaurant for a late night snack in the company of a few friends. Waiting for the dishes to arrive, I leaned against the railing, looking idly at the people passing by in the streets below. It was stifling hot, with not a hint of a breeze. Suddenly I saw an old acquaintance sitting in a rickshaw. It was my former colleague at the Military Affairs Department Tian Ruqin. There he was sitting in the rickshaw in a soldier's uniform. I called out to him and he joined me in the restaurant. His story was that with the dissolution of the Military Affairs Department, he had gone to work at the Political Department of the Wuhan campus of the Military Political Academy. There he found the Academy in a shambles. He promptly took off his officer's leather belt and enlisted in the Training Brigade of the General Political Department.

Tian Ruqin gave me a detailed report on the situation at the Wuhan campus. According to him, the Wuhan campus was crumbling by the minute. The trio of Deng Yanda, Hou Lianhu and Yun Daiying, who had been the backbone of the Academy, were now all gone. As for second-tier leaders such as Yang Shusong and Shi Cuntong, the former was muddle-headed, while the latter had not shown up for a long time. All those on campus who had shown any radical leanings had fled.

According to Tian, the female cadets were the most to be pitied. They had been rebels against the traditional family system. Now, they either had no homes to go to, or had been rejected by their families. With the disintegration of the Wuhan campus, these young women cadets were like birds driven out of the woods . I couldn't help thinking back to the six young ladies who had shared a drink with me at the Yellow Crane Tower. I wondered where they had drifted to.

Revolution, Revolution, and this is what it has led to!

III

I decided to abandon the trip to Anqing. I now had reliable information that Wang Jingwei, Sun Fo, and Tang Shengzhi were scheduled to leave Wuhan for Jiujiang that very day! What were they up to?

I decided to return to Jiujiang to find out. I started off from Hankou on July 29 and arrived in Jiujing the next day.

Once back in Jiujiang I discovered that my former group of colleagues at the Political Department had arrived and were installed in an abandoned public bathhouse. The rooms were small and the people crowded inside were like buns in a steamer. I stood around for a minute, my sweaty shirt stuck to my back. Since Director Liao was still quartered at the Misty Lake Pavilion, as was Gao Yuhan, I felt justified in remaining there with them.

Yun Daiying, meanwhile, had gone off to Nanchang. Actually, many CCP notables have left Jiujiang for Nanchang already: Li Lisan, Zhang Guotao,[5] Peng Pai, Lin Zuhan, Wu Yuzhang, Tan Pingshan, and others had all left for Nanchang, the capital of Jiangxi Province.

According to Director Liao Qianwu, since we would soon be heading for Canton I might as well forget about that clandestine mission to Anqing. As for the 300-*yuan* business expense, it had already been spent, but everything had been open and aboveboard.

Now that my clandestine mission to Anqing had been officially canceled, and our move to Canton not yet scheduled, again I found myself with nothing to do. In Wuhan, one could at least play mahjong. In Jiujiang, even that was not possible. There were no sizable hotels except for one, the Dadong Hotel, where mahjong was prohibited. Moreover, no one among us had a home where we could get together. It was so boring. I decided to climb Lushan.

The Dadong Hotel situated across from the railway station on Nanxun Road was one of the most respectable hotels in Jiujiang. Many of my friends were settled there. Since I had already made an appearance at the public bathhouse, [I felt justified in following my own inclinations] and headed for the Dadong Hotel to look up friends. Jing Dakang, one of the activists at the Wuhan campus [of the Military

5. Zhang Guotao (1897–1979) was an early member of the CCP. He had been elected to leading positions through the 1920s. Zhang had opposed the August First Uprising in Nanchang. He was the CCP 's representative to the Comintern in 1928 and returned to China in 1931. In 1935 Zhang had led the Fourth Army on the Long March, and in 1938 he left the CCP base and joined the GMD. Zhang left for Hong Kong in 1949 and emigrated to Canada in 1968.

Political Academy], had brought over some female comrades from the campus and installed them at the hotel. Jing himself was about to leave for Nanchang to join the Political Department of the Twenty-fourth Division.

Shen Yanbing[6] was staying in the Dadong Hotel, and also planning to climb Lushan. Shen Yanbing had been my colleague in Canton at the Propaganda Department under the GMD CEC. He was secretary of the Propaganda Department at the time, and had left for Shanghai after the Zhongshan Gunboat Incident.[7]

I had run into Shen Yanbing when I first arrived in Wuhan. At the time, the Military Affairs Department had not yet been dissolved. I was quartered at the Provincial Assembly, while Shen Yanbing was somewhere near the Yuemachang, where he had shared rooms with [the historian] Li Da. One evening in March, I had gone to visit him in the company of Kong Lingjun, his brother-in-law, and we engaged in an animated chat for a full two hours. Our paths never crossed again after that evening, although we were both in Wuhan. Shen knew how to make the best of life. During the high tide of the revolution, he had received a lot of publicity as a famous revolutionary figure. Now that the Revolution was at low ebb, Shen was going to climb Lushan. His wife and child had already returned to Shanghai.

Song Yunbin, Shen Yanbing's colleague at the *Republican Daily* in Wuhan, had left Wuhan and arrived in Jiujiang in Shen's company, and they were going to climb Lushan together. Song Yunbin was also a friend of mine. Actually he was the reason that had brought me to the Dadong Hotel that day and I had stopped by and chatted with Song before he left in Shen Yanbin's company. Their trip gave me the idea of spending a few days on the mountain myself. What a lucky

---

6. Shen Yanbing (1896–1981), whose pen name was Mao Dun, was one of modern China's most important writers and an influential cultural figure. Shen was in the vanguard of the May Fourth Movement in his youth, and had always taken part in leftist politics. He has many major works to his credit and is best known for the novel *Midnight*, an exposé of Shanghai society in the 1930s.

7. Zhongshan Gunboat Incident, see Chapter One, note 20.

coincidence! I ran into Li Shuoxun (with his wife Zhao Junyue) and Ouyang Jixiu (with his wife Tang Dihua), all friends of mine now staying at the Dadong Hotel. They were all leaving for Nanchang.

I had decided to climb Lushan, but it was no fun going alone. There were no female comrades available, so I had to make do with two men: Luo Yonglie of the editorial group at the Political Department, and Mei Dianlong, director of the Political Department of the Twelfth Division. We three decided to go up the mountain the next day. In preparation for our trip, we went to bed earlier than usual.

But as the saying goes, man proposes and God disposes. Around midnight, someone shook me awake. I rubbed my eyes and saw Liao Qianwu and Gao Yuhan.

"Shhh, don't make a sound. Get up quickly"—it was Liao Qianwu. Something had happened.

I got up quietly and followed Liao and Gao to a back room. Guo Moruo was fast asleep, lying on two tables pushed together.

"We must leave immediately," Liao Qianwu whispered.

"What happened?" I was finally shocked out of my sleepiness.

"Wang Jingwei, Tang Shengzhi and the others have decided at a meeting on Lushan to secretly arrest the four of us: you, me, Daiying, and Yuhan. We must leave immediately," Liao Qianwu whispered.

"How do you know?" I asked.

"Chief-of-Staff Ye Jianying[8] sent someone down the mountain with the information."

"They want to arrest you three because of your positions, but why me?" It was beyond my understanding. My connection with the Second Army Corps had been brief, and my position was pitifully low, the mere propaganda chief for the Army Political Department. They wanted the

8. Ye Jianying (1897–1986), follower of Sun Yat-sen since early youth, had helped thwart the warlord Chen Jiongming's plot to kidnap Sun. Ye had joined the staff of the Whampoa Military Academy at the invitation of Liao Zhongkai, and later joined the CCP. One of the top military leaders of the CCP, Ye held important military and Party posts in the People's Republic of China, and was influential in bringing down the "Gang of Four" and setting China on a new course.

big shots. Why drag me into it? I had no seniority, no position. What's more, I was known as an ineffective, romantic dreamer. Why come after me?! I was not worth their attention! More fools, they!

"Who knows why," said Liao. Actually we are not the only ones . . ."

"Who else is on their list?"

"Leaders at the Jiujiang GMD Committee, staff at the *Citizens' News*, and the Jiujiang Bookstore people—orders for their secret arrest has been passed down to Jin Dinghan, chief of the Jiujiang police. They will act tomorrow, so we must leave tonight."

"Where to?"

"Nanchang is our only choice."

"What's there for me in Nanchang? I am not going!" I said.

"Where else, if not Nanchang? Why not just get there and look around?" urged Liao.

Where else indeed! I, too, was now a homeless drifter. What could I do except follow them to Nanchang!

We discussed ways of getting to Nanchang. Yun Daiying was there already. The three of us must leave together. It was too dangerous to stay on at the Misty Lake Pavilion. We must leave immediately for the Dadong Hotel across the street from the railway station and catch the first train out of Jiujiang.

When leaving Wuchang a couple of days before on July 23, I had taken twenty-six rifles from the stock of the General Political Department. At the time, the General Political Department was about to be dissolved, and Commander Zhang Fakui had given us permission to share a stock of over fifty rifles with the Political Department of the Eleventh Army. Now that we were about to leave, I could not bear to leave those twenty-six rifles behind. I told my orderly to pack them into two suitcases and take them to the Dadong Hotel along with my other things.

We took two rooms at the Dadong Hotel. I shared one room with Liao Qianwu, the same room that Shen Yanbing and Song Yunbin had given up that very same morning. Now they must be safely asleep up on Lushan, while here I was hiding out. How ironic!

IV

We boarded the train in the morning and headed for Nanchang, not knowing what dangers were lying in store. *Rush on, oh train!* I thought to myself. Take me to the ends of the earth, take me to where human feet have never tread, let me live the life of Robinson Crusoe. I let my imagination run riot as the train rumbled on.

I caught a glimpse of Lushan; then the train moved on and Lushan was lost to view. Shen Yanbing and Song Yunbin must still have been asleep. If not for this mishap, I myself should have been halfway up the mountain by now. As my imagination wandered, I fell into a deep sleep. When I awoke, we were already at the Yellow Gate Railway Station.

Once at the Yellow Gate station, we were beyond the reach of our pursuers. This was because the Seventy-third regiment of the Twenty-fifth Division was stationed here. They were technically under the command of Zhang Fakui, but the Seventy-third Regiment was formerly a part of Ye Ting's Independent Regiment, and the regimental commander, Zhou Shidi, was a buddy of Liao Qianwu and Gao Yuhan.

Before reaching the Yellow Gate Railway Station, we were exiles fleeing arrest, but once there, we felt completely at home. We had not only shaken ourselves free of our pursuers, we ourselves started ordering people around. For instance, the train was supposed to stop for five minutes only, but relying on the authority of our rifles, we ordered the station master to hold the train while Liao Qianwu and Gao Yuhan went to the command post of the Seventy-third Regiment for a get-together with their old comrade Regimental Commander Zhou Shidi.

We were treated to a generous dinner at the Seventy-third Regiment. Having missed breakfast, we ate with hearty appetites and rounded off the meal with a watermelon. It was already one o'clock by the time the train resumed its journey southward.

We made a brief stop at the Mahuiling station; some of He Long's men were stationed here, though they too were ready to leave for Nanchang. We had another stop at De'an. Then, at the Tu Family station, we had trouble with the engine and had to wait for it to be repaired. Thus by the time we reached Buffalo Market station in Nanchang, it was already nine o'clock at night.

The Gan River lay between the railway station and Nanchang City proper. There was a regular ferry service to make the crossing. But due to our delays on route, by the time we arrived, the ferry service was already closed. Liao Qianwu and Gao Yuhan had never been to Nanchang; they did not even know that a river lay beween us and the town. They became alarmed. Besides, we were hungry, as we had had nothing to eat since that lavish meal at Yellow Gate station. So there we were, hungry, frustrated, and totally helpless.

Finally I managed, at a ruinous price, to coax a boatman to take us across the river. We got off the boat at Zhang River Gate, and found ourselves in Nanchang at around ten. Then a new problem popped up: there were neither rickshaws nor porters to be hired, and we had more than ten pieces of luggage, including two suitcases holding those twenty-six rifles. We finally did get hold of a few porters, but then another problem came up—all the hotels were full-up. We first went to the Jiangxi Hotel, but it had been taken over by He Long's Twentieth Army. It was the same story at other hotels, as many parts of the army [in Wuhan] were arriving here. After dragging ourselves and our luggage hither and thither, we finally found a place to put down our heads. By then it was already half-past eleven. We took three rooms and then found ourselves ravenously hungry. We immediately ordered food—meat, chicken, everything. At one o'clock, after having eaten a good meal, we put our heads down and immediately fell asleep.

We hadn't slept for long, however, before we were awakened by the sound of heavy gunfire, which sounded like street fighting. What was going on? Those past couple of days, I had been hopping from Hankou to Jiujiang [in the retinue of Commander-in-chief Huang Qixiang], and from Jiujiang back to Wuhan [to prepare for that clandestine trip to Anqing], then back to Jiujiang [when I decided to give up the trip], and now from Jiujiang to Nanchang [to escape arrest]. I had no clue about the changing situation, and did not understand what the fighting was about. Lost in perplexity, how I wished for a quiet life away from the fray.

I decided to ask Liao Qianwu and Gao Yuhan for information, but they were not in their rooms!

I had left my windows open due to the heat, and now I could see shadows of men moving on the rooftops. By the ghostly light of the street lamps, I could make out that they were fully armed soldiers and they could see me as I lay in bed. I had no clue as to which part of the army they were from, so I lay there unmoving, frozen with fear.

The street fighting lasted about half-an-hour and stopped when bugles sounded a reprieve. I crept out, but there were still no signs of Liao or Gao. I asked the owner of the hotel for information; the man said that the Fourth Army had mutinied and disarmed the forces of Zhu Peide, meaning Wang Jun's forces from the Third Army and part of Jin Handing's forces from the Ninth Army. According to my informant, Zhu Peide had been beaten and the Fourth Army had achieved a complete victory.

But I knew better: the Fourth Army was not in Nanchang at the time. The hotel owner must have meant He Long's Twentieth Army and Ye Ting's Twenty-fourth Division under the Eleventh Army. They had always been considered as belonging to the Fourth Army. When the man said the Fourth Army, he was actually talking about He Long's and Ye Ting's forces.

At the time I was still in uniform, wearing the insignia of head of propaganda for the Political Department of the Fourth Army and the badge "4A." The hotel owner looked at me in amazement, put his two hands together in a gesture of respect, and said: "Congratulations, your side has won!" I could only look at him in perplexity, not knowing what to say.

By then it was dawn, August 1.

V

Liao Qianwu showed up at nine the next morning. "A Paris Commune kind of government has been born. We have set up a Revolutionary Committee!" he announced.

Then he sat down and told me about this coup. He Long's army and

Ye Ting's army had reached Nanchang a few days earlier. He Long was all for the coup, saying: "Damn it! If the Wuhan government is going to surrender to the imperialists, we can take them down. I have twenty thousand men under me!"

The fact was, having lost their toehold in Wuhan, the revolutionary figures Tan Pingshan, Lin Zuhan, Wu Yuzhang, Zhang Guotao, Peng Pai, Han Linfu, Yun Daiying, and Zhou Enlai had congregated in Nanchang over the past couple of days.

On the morning of July 31, as we were starting out from Jiujiang, He Long and Ye Ting had received peremptory orders from Zhang Fakui to immediately leave Nanchang and return to Jiujiang for an eastward expedition [ostensibly toward Chiang Kai-shek in Nanjing]. He Long and Ye Ting realized [it was a trap]. The die was cast. After consulting with Tan Pingshan and others, they decided to disarm the forces of Zhu Peide. Zhu Peide did not have a strong force in Nanchang at the time. Moreover, because Zhu De, second in command of the Ninth Army, was hand in glove with He Long and Ye Ting, Zhu Peide's forces were disarmed in a matter of half-an-hour.

When morning dawned on August 1, the Wuhan Revolutionary Government was replaced by a new organ of power—the Revolutionary Committee.

The members of the new Revolutionary Committee were legion, and all were familiar names to me.

The CCP side included Tan Pingshan, Zhang Guotao, Li Lisan, Peng Pai, Yun Daiying, Ye Ting, Han Linfu, Wu Yuzhang, Gao Yuhan, Lin Zuhan, Zhou Enlai, Fang Weixia, and Xu Teli, altogether several dozen people.

On the "loyal" GMD side [the GMD Left] were Soong Qingling, Deng Yanda, He Long,[9] Guo Moruo (He and Guo were not CCP

9. He Long (1896–1969), commander of the Revolutionary Army since the 1920s, a leading figure in the August First Uprising in 1927, one of the founders of the People's Liberation Army, and head of the national sports commission in the People's Republic of China. He Long was persecuted to death during the Cultural Revolution, and posthumously rehabilitated in 1982.

members at the time), and Zhang Shushi. Even the names of Zhang Fakui, Huang Qixiang, and Cai Tingkai had been included.

The members of the Presidium of the Revolutionary Committee were: He Long, Tan Pingshan, Yun Daiying, Guo Moruo, Zhang Fakui, Soong Qingling, and Deng Yanda. Several organs were set up under the Revolutionary Committee:

Wu Yuzhang, secretary-general,

Zhang Guotao, president of the Workers and Peasants' Committee,

Lin Zuhan, president of the Finance Committee,

Guo Moruo, president of the Propaganda Committee,

Guo Moruo, doubling as director of the General Political Department,

Zhang Shushi, head of the Committee of Party Affairs,

Li Lisan, head of the Political Security Department,

Liu Bocheng, head of General Staff,

Liao Qianwu, member of the Propaganda Committee and the General Political Department.

The Revolutionary Committee still operated in the name of the GMD, and stranger still, even flaunted the names of Zhang Fakui and Huang Qixiang.

I was very doubtful about the significance of this coup. What purpose could it serve? It existed in name and titles only, there was no substance. Liao, Gao, and I left the hotel and moved in with the Twenty-fourth Division, which was quartered in Xinyuan University where we had stayed on a previous stop. I disliked Ye Ting and felt uncomfortable staying with the Twenty-fourth Division.

I had now become a homeless orphan.

The Revolutionary Committee still flaunted the name of Zhang Fakui, but in fact he was openly opposed to them, thus my title as head of the Propaganda Department under the Political Department of the Fourth Army (under commander Zhang Fakui) was null and void.

I was bored and listless. I decided to go out and have some fun.

I was visiting Nanchang for a second time now. My friend Mao [Jiayi?] had just arrived from Wuhan. I looked him up and we chatted about this and that. He told me that his pursuit of a young lady in the

Baoling Girls' Academy was being rewarded with success.

Nanchang had changed since the coup. Stores were mostly closed on August 1, the day of the coup. He Long and Ye Ting's men were posted in the streets for security checks. The former Military Supervisors' Residence, which had served as Headquarters, has now become the address of the Revolutionary Committee.

Cai Tingkai,[10] commander of the Tenth Division of the Eleventh Army, had brought his Division over to Nanchang. He had arrived on the night of July 31, two hours ahead of us. By then He Long had already decided to hold the coup, and had informed Cai to get his reaction. "*Good for you! Exactly what I had in mind!*" Thus Cai Tingkai was included as a member of the Revolutionary Committee and as a member of the General Staff, which consisted of Liu Bocheng (president), Zhou Enlai, Ye Ting, Zhu De, and now Cai Tingkai.

Cai Tingkai

On the afternoon of August 1, as I parted from my friend Mao, Zhou Enlai sent for me. He was staying at the quarters of the Artillery

10. Cai Tingkai (1892–1968) was an early follower of Sun Yat-sen, and a commander in the Revolutionary Army. Cai led the Nineteenth Army, which had put up a spirited resistance against the invading Japanese Army in Shanghai in 1932. He had opposed Chiang Kai-shek's civil war and later held honorary positions in the People's Republic of China.

Battalion. He said that he wanted me to be the political director for the Tenth Division. After thinking over the offer for five minutes, I refused. I had been suffering from depression and did not trust myself to take on such a responsibility. And I was not really qualified, even though it just entailed working at an army division. Besides, I knew that the Division commander, Cai Tingkai, was difficult to get along with. His previous political directors had all clashed with him and left. I knew myself to be headstrong—I was sure I could never get along with Cai. So I refused no matter how much Zhou Enlai tried to talk me into it.

After two years, I was now sick of being an officer in the Revolutionary Army. I wanted to quit and return to Shanghai and go back to my life as a drifter.

I returned to the Twenty-fourth Division where we were staying, and Liao Qianwu immediately asked me about the result of my conversation with Zhou. Liao said that I should not have refused. But, Liao suggested that since I had refused Zhou, why didn't I go and work for him, Liao, at the General Political Department.

I evaded the question and went back to my friend Mao Jiayi. Mao himself wanted to return to Wuhan, but tried to persuade me to take up the job at the Tenth Division. Returning to Wuhan was out of the question for me. I knew my own mind: I definitely wanted to return to Shanghai.

My spirits were very low all night long: what was I going to do with myself?

VI

I was finally appointed head of the Propaganda Division of the General Political Department. I had also tried to turn down this offer, but Enlai would not hear of it. "You used to be critical of the political work at General," he said, "Now we have upgraded it to *Division* level with a larger range of operations. This is your chance to make something of it." I ended up accepting.

Guo Moruo was head of the General Political Department. He was still in Jiujiang, and I was not sure when he would show up.

Zhou Enlai summoned me again. He was still residing at the headquarters of the artillery battalion. When I arrived, he was upstairs, and there were a lot of people going in and out, young and arrogant, just the sort that I found intolerable, Nie Rongzhen being one of them.

I had no idea why Zhou wanted to see me, but I had no choice but to go, and once there, no choice but to wait.

Someone from the Jiangxi Provincial Committee of the XX [CCP] was also waiting. He too had come at Zhou's request. He had been waiting, he said, for the last two hours.

"Hey, when will you be free? I can't wait any longer!" the fellow shouted into the room. Enlai, who was talking to someone else, shouted back: "Just a minute!"

"Just a minute." To me it sounded more like an order. The fellow from the Jiangxi branch muttered: "Official airs!"

A quarter of an hour passed, but Enlai was still busy. A few more people joined the group in the anteroom.

The fellow from Jiangxi couldn't contain himself any longer. "What's going on?" Then he shouted in a loud voice, "I'm leaving!"

Enlai appeared in the doorway, saying sternly: "What's wrong with you! Can't you see people are busy!" and returned inside. "Official airs!" the man snorted, loud enough to be heard inside the room.

"Official airs! Go back and ask your own Provincial Committee about official airs!" Zhou replied as he stepped back into the room. "I said official airs," retorted the man, spoiling for a fight, "and I mean you. Now what are you going to do about it?!" "This is not going to work," said Zhou angrily. "Go back to your own Provincial Committee!"

The situation was getting explosive, and people in the room tried to calm them down. The man from Jiangxi left, without being able to settle matters with Zhou, who muttered angrily: "This is not going to work."

Personally, I agreed with the man from Jiangxi: Zhou Enlai did have official airs. But in justice, I must say this for Zhou Enlai: he is very responsible in his work.

I finally got my interview with Zhou. It turned out that he wanted me to draft a publicity piece about the coup. Being head of the Propaganda Division of the General Political Department, it was within the scope of my duties, so I could not refuse.

So I sat down and took down from dictation the main points that had to be included:

After the death of Sun Yat-sen, Liao Zhongkai[11] *inherited the mantle of the GMD of China; after the death of Liao Zhongkai, the GMD lost its bearings, thus the Purge in Nanjing, followed by the anti-Communist wave in Wuhan. All the above are departures from the GMD. The present Revolutionary Committee has inherited the mantle of the GMD.*

I followed Zhou's instructions and drafted the Outline for the Declaration of the August First Uprising then and there. Zhou expressed his satisfaction, but not I. I had my own interpretation of this recent coup and was not happy with the draft, but I had no say in the matter. Besides, I knew that it was not Zhou's own idea either; he was only relaying the decisions of Tan Pingshan and company.

By the time I had done with the draft Outline, it was late evening. Bored as I was, I hired a rowboat and drifted about on Donghu Lake, then went over to the Political Department of the Twenty-fourth Division to kill time. The director, Chen Xinglin, was an old friend from Wuhan days. He was in his office with a young woman, both flirting as they shared a watermelon. I tried a slice and then left to look up other friends. I saw Jing Dakang, who was heading the Organization Section under the Political Department of the Twenty-fourth Division. Another old friend, Cai Renguan, was also around; our acquaintance dated back to my time in the Military Affairs Department.

By normal standards, such an uprising should have caused a lot excitement. On the contrary, things were very quiet in Nanchang: there were no mass rallies, no spark of revolutionary fervor in the air. With the uprising, all newspapers had stopped publication. There was talk

11. Liao Zhongkai (1878–1925), American born, Japanese educated, a close associate of Sun Yat-sen. Liao was a major figure in the GMD Left and managed GMD finances from 1914 until his assassination in 1925, possibly by the GMD right wing.

of the *Republican Daily* resuming publication, but nothing happened, so my Draft was never published. All stores were boarded up. Except for men in uniform, hardly anyone was in the streets.

Rather than having gone through a revolutionary coup, Nanchang looked as if it had suffered a bandit rampage.

Thus the August First Uprising! I let out a deep sigh.

VII

By August 3, the situation was clear: hopes that Zhang Fakui and Huang Qixiang might join the Revolutionary Committee were completely dashed. On the contrary, their attitude was one of total enmity. Both Zhang and Huang had been named members of the Revolutionary Committee—Zhang as a member of the Presidium and commander-in-chief of the Second Corps, and Huang as front line commander-in-chief. Now their names had to be deleted. So that left six members for the Presidium: Soong Qingling, Deng Yanda, Tan Pingshan, He Long, Yun Daiying, and Guo Moruo.

He Long took over as commander-in-chief of the Second Corps, while Ye Ting took over as frontline commander-in-chief. By then, Ye Ting had already been promoted to commander of the Eleventh Army, while Zhu De had been promoted from deputy to commander of the Ninth Army, though there were only two regiments under the Ninth Army.

The Revolutionary Committee decided to move to Canton. The route, roughly speaking, was to move from east of Jiangxi through Fujian to Chaomei [the Chozhou-Meizhou area], and from there to arrive in Canton by way of Hai-Lu-Feng.

Ye Ting led the Eleventh Army (including the Twenty-fourth Division under a newly promoted former regimental commander named Gu) and the Twenty-fifth Division (under the newly promoted regimental commander Zhou Shidi) and started out for the little town of Fuzhou.[12]

We at the Political Division traveled together with the Revolutionary

12. Not to be confused with Fuzhou, the capital city of Fujian Province.

Committee, in the retinue of General Headquarters, and started out on August 5, one day later than the Eleventh Army.

We all moved into the former Military Supervisor's Residence in preparation for leaving the next day.

Guo Moruo unexpectedly turned up at nine o'clock that evening, looking a total wreck. With him were Mei Dianlong, Li Minzhi, and Ouyang Jixiu. It turned out that Zhang Fakui had that very morning put the four of them on a train under escort, banishing them to Nanchang. But as they reached De'an, they ran into the remnants of the disintegrated Third Army, who highjacked their train and relieved them of all their cash. Guo Moruo, moreover, had been roughed up, and his orderly taken away. Finally they were able to talk themselves aboard another train leaving from De'an station, and arrived in Nanchang in the nick of time. One day later and we would have already left.

Mei Dianlong looked at me and sighed. We were supposed to climb Lushan on my return from Wuhan. When I had left precipitately in the middle of the night, there was no way to let him know. And now here he was, much the worse for wear. We looked at each other and sighed. What could we say?

Guo Moruo was the director of the General Political Department, and I was supposed to work under him. That made me very uncomfortable. I began to regret having turned down that earlier offer from the Tenth Division.

The three men in Guo Moruo's company were assigned jobs: Ouyang Jixiu, secretary at the Political Department of the Twenty-fourth Division; Li Minzhi, managing director for the General Political Department; Mei Dianlong, political director for the Seventy-first Regiment.

We all spent a restless night at the former Military Supervisor's Residence.

We left Nanchang on the morning of August 5, heading for the main road to Fuzhou. I had stayed but four days in Nanchang, and barely a week in Jiujiang. Rushing about to and fro, and to what purpose? I found myself quite ridiculous. But returning to Canton was always welcome to me. I wondered what changes there were in Canton since I had left. The young lady in the secluded street in Dongshan—I wondered if she was still there.[13]

Farewell, Nanchang! My two trips to Nanchang, though under different circumstances, had been very different experiences, but both depressing. Now that I was leaving again, I hoped that my next trip to Nanchang would be more pleasant.

Farewell, Nanchang! Farewell, all my friends in Nanchang!

---

13 Zhu first mentions the young lady as corresponding with her. There is no mention of meeting until Zhu is in Hongkong and reminisces about a clandestine meeting and dinner "a year ago." At some point in time, deleted from these chapters, Zhu must have returned south. See Translator's Note.

CHAPTER SEVEN

On the March South

I

As we were about to leave Nanchang [for Canton], a friend was there to see me off. I took a photo of the two of us and inscribed it with Wang Han's poem.[1]

> The glittering cup, the sparkling wine
> At my lips—a pipa sounds the call to arms.
> Judge not the drunken warrior lying on the ground,
> How many come back from war since time immemorial?

My friend walked with me for several *li* before turning back.

It was early August. The temperature was over ninety degrees Fahrenheit when one was sitting quietly in a room. On the march, however, in straw sandals with a gun strapped on one's back, the sun overhead enclosed us in a fiery embrace.

I thought with envy of Shen Yanbing and Song Yunbin enjoying the cool breeze on Lushan, but then thought of other people languishing in prison—I was lucky to be where I was. Leaders such as He Long,

1. Wang Han (687–726), a Tang dynasty poet.

Guo Moruo, Yun Daiying, Zhang Guotao, Zhou Enlai, Li Lisan, Gao Yuhan, Wu Yuzhang, Lin Zuhan, and company were all walking together with us.

Li Lisan[2] was a nuisance. He was merely head of the Political Security Department, but strutted about in uniform, leggings and all, as if he were an officer. I had never worked with him before; it was only on this march that I discovered what a toady he was. After exiting through the city gate, we sat down for a break waiting for Tan Pingshan to catch up with us. "Salute!" Li Lisan shouted, giving a lopsided salute. I couldn't help spitting out "Fawning dog!"

Li Lisan

At noon, we stopped for a meal, but there was not enough food to go around. We waited a while, and some of us became restless.

"Hey! What's going on? We're just on the first day of our march, and already out of food? Somebody is not doing his job!" I remarked .

Tan Pingshan gave me a dirty look. Taking his cue from Tan, Li Lisan jumped up and shouted at me as if I were an underling:

"You'll get your meal! What's the fuss!"

2. Li Lisan (1900–1967) was an early CCP member and labor organizer. He had been selected in 1928 to replace Qu Qiubai as leader of the Communist Party, and was removed in 1930.

"And who are you to say so?!" I shot back.

The silence was deafening as everybody waited for what was coming next.

"Who the hell are you? Troublemaker!" He glared at me as if he could kill me with a look.

"Troublemaker yourself! You better put away your damned airs. So what if you are a department head, I'm every inch as good as you are!"

At this point, Tan Pingshan, Lin Zuhan, Wu Yuzhang, Han Linfu, and others present stepped in and tried to make peace.

So this is what he was like! I would keep it in mind.

Thus passed the first day of our march south. Our goal was only sixty *li* for the first day, but with the debilitating heat, it was tough going, especially for the older folks in our ranks. Peng Zemin,[3] head of the Overseas Department for the Revolutionary Committee, was barely sixty, but he struggled on pitifully with a wife the same age as himself. Born and bred overseas, I doubt they had ever undergone such hardships. There were neither horses nor sedan chairs; the old couple had to share our lot, scrambling up hill and down dale.

Another elder was Jiang Jihuan, head of the Jiangxi Provincial Government. He was about the same age as Peng Zemin, but in contrast to Peng's rickety frame, Jiang—even worse—was overweight. One can imagine his suffering as he labored forward in the sweltering heat.

Lin Zuhan, head of the Finance Committee, was also elderly with a head of white hair. However, he was in good spirits.

Zhang Guotao, head of the Workers and Peasants' Committee, was weak and broken down, and he staggered painfully along like an opium

3. Peng Zemin (1877–1956) was one of the early followers of Sun Yat-sen. Peng spent his early years in Malaya and later in Hong Kong, carrying on revolutionary activities abroad. In 1924, Peng joined the GMD-CCP Allied Revolutionary Government, first in Canton and later in Wuhan. After the break-up of the alliance, Peng followed the CCP on their march south. He ended up in Hong Kong where he spent twenty years campaigning against Chiang Kai-shek and later against Japanese aggression, and he was one of the founders of the Peasant-Worker Democratic Party. After 1949, Peng held many honorary positions in the People's Republic of China, and was a practicing doctor.

addict. Happily, he stuck to Peng Pai, who was his exact opposite. Peng Pai sang and danced and indulged in antics all the way. He sang the "The Internationale," then shifted to Cantonese local opera, making us all laugh. "What a kid!" Gao Yuhan remarked with a smile.

Yun Daiying was also in good spirits. He was in a coarse homespun short-sleeved jacket and skimpy shorts, so skimpy in fact, that his private parts sometimes peeped out.

Zhou Enlai looked like a wandering quack as he plodded on with a box of documents on his back.

The elderly Xu Teli was in the best of spirits. He would call out when he caught us youngsters taking a break. "Come on," he would say laughing, "Show us your mettle! Get going!"

Chief-of-staff Liu Bocheng, with a patch over one eye looking like a pirate, was always upbeat. It is said that he had been an old warrior from Sichuan, and had lost one eye in battle

Secretary General Wu Yuzhang, weak and elderly and suffering from a hernia, was carried in a sedan chair, as a special dispensation. He sat in the sedan chair borne by two able-bodied porters, like the legendary Zhuge Liang of the Three Kingdoms period.

Head of the Revolutionary Committee Tan Pingshan, dressed in a Sun Yat-sun suit with a straw hat to match, sat on a black horse, himself looking as sooty as the horse. He was a nuisance like Li Lisan!

Guo Moruo had been mistreated by renegade soldiers of the disintegrating Third Army on the road from Nanxun, and was slightly wounded. But he was cheerful, reciting his own verses as he limped along.

Han Linfu, tall and muscular, was a typical northerner, striding up and down uneven ground without batting an eyelid. With him was his beautiful young wife, who spoke perfect Mandarin.

As for Gao Yuhan, with his big lumbering frame, he ambled along sometimes singing, sometimes reciting poetry.

These were the people in my company as we left Nanchang and marched south [seeking to set up a new base in Canton].

II

We may have taken too many breaks along the way because by the time we reached camp, it was already dusk, and we never got to figure out the name of the place. It may have been called Longevity Palace or something. Whatever the name, our scouts had not done their job in looking for somewhere to camp. Now, at the very start of our march, we had to spend the night in the open!

We put our heads down in the fields by a river under a starry sky. Fortunately it didn't rain. Even so, we found ourselves thoroughly drenched when we woke up at dawn, our clothes and thin bedspreads dank with dewdrops still clinging to our clothes.

Someone mumbled, "What fools we are, to leave home and find ourselves here shivering in misery!" Nevertheless, we got up, shook off the dewdrops, and started off on the second day of our march.

That Tan Pingshan was certainly a nuisance, no doubt about it! He got himself to be addressed as *Chairman* Tan. Actually "Chairman" was the title we had originally reserved for Tan Yankai [previously acting president of the Revolutionary Government]. Four leaders from the army were currently members of the Presidium, namely, Tan Pingshan, Guo Moruo, Yun Daiying, and He Long, but somehow Tan Pingshan had maneuvered to make himself the one and only leader to be addressed as *Chairman*. He is a downright good-for-nothing, I said to myself. With such a bumpkin at the helm, where was the Revolution heading? The thought was depressing.

However, the first day's march had not been too bumpy. On the second day, unfortunately, we encountered hillocks the whole way, and under a burning sun, too! One may imagine the misery! The only alleviating factor, one might say, was that unlike the expedition in Henan where we had worked so hard, now we did nothing but march. I did not lift a finger to make propaganda along the way, and I was not alone in idleness. No one did any work. The folks at the Workers and Peasants' Committee did put up a couple of posters, and that was all there was to it—a couple of posters.

And what did the posters say? "Farm Land Over 200 *Mou* Will Be

Confiscated!" "Carry Out the Land Revolution!" "Set Up the Rule of the Peasants!"

And how were we to go about confiscating "land over 200 hundred *mou*"? And how were we going to carry out the "land revolution" according to Tan Pingshan's "personal decoding" of Sun Yat-sen's legacy? These leaders of the revolution here never bothered their heads about practical details. They throw out a few slogans and their job is done. As for the General Political Department, it never even bothered to put up a poster.

The second night on our march, we put up at a family ancestral temple. It was deserted and dirty, with several coffins lying inside. But at least we had a roof over our heads to keep off the dew. It was too early to sleep, and five or six of us who had made our beds on the floor lay around chatting. Our orderlies, however, were not idle; they had managed to get hold of five chickens. A most valuable find indeed! For the past two days, not only were we exhausted, we were also starving. Without asking any inconvenient questions, we ordered the men to kill and cook the chickens without delay, and that same night we had a most satisfying meal. This bandit-like existence had its charms, we discovered. I remember how, during that expedition into Henan, we had reviled the northern warlords for pillaging the villagers! Now we were doing the same ourselves and enjoying it!

[Steadily moving southward] on August 8 we arrived at Fuzhou, a little town under the jurisdiction of Linchuan Prefecture [still in Jiangxi Province]. Fuzhou used to be a lively little town, but when we arrived, all doors were shut, all shops closed, the streets deserted. We flaunt the flag of fighting on behalf of the masses, but obviously the masses are not appreciative.

We were housed in a school which was closed for the summer holidays.

Fuzhou is famous for its watermelons. My own hometown in Zhejiang has its own variety of watermelons, too. But over the last year or two, being in Canton and Wuhan where there were no watermelons worthy of the name, I had pined for one of my favorite fruits. At last here in Fuzhou I had a chance to eat my fill of watermelons.

The second day of our arrival in Fuzhou, there was a serious incident—the Tenth Division under Cai Tingkai had disappeared! During the August First coup, Cai Tingkai had been resolutely supportive and was known to have said to Ye Ting, "*Good for you! Exactly what I had in mind!*" Thus the Revolutionary Committee had trusted him. But where had he, with the men under him, wandered off to? Zhou Enlai would not consider the possibility that he had deserted. Zhou was concerned that Cai Tingkai may have been surrounded by Zhang Fakui's army, now hot on our trail. But Cai's men had been in the *middle* of our army on the move. Ye Ting was in front of him, and He Long brought up the rear. Zhang Fakui's pursuit would have caught up with He Long first. In the event of any ambush at the front, Ye Ting would have borne the brunt of it. There was no explanation for Cai Tingkai's disappearance. Tan Pingshan came up with the idea that he had lost his way, which was complete nonsense! How could one division lose itself in the middle of a moving army of tens of thousands?

Six hours later, the situation was cleared up. Deserters from the Tenth Division reported that after starting off from Nanchang, Cai Tingkai had immediately arrested all the CCP officers in his army, including Fan Jin, commander of the Thirtieth Regiment, and led his men eastward into Fujian Province, seeking out [the local strongman] Chen Mingshu, under whom he had previously served.

The loss of one whole Division was a blow indeed, and it hit us hard. I thought to myself how lucky I had refused the job of Political Director of the Tenth Division. If I had accepted the job, I would have been arrested and forcibly taken to Fujian![4]

We stopped in Fuzhou, waiting to be joined by more men taking the Nanxun route. We had hopes of the regimental guard of Zhang Fakui's Headquarters joining us, as prearranged with the regimental commander Lu Deming. Likewise, we had an understanding with Xu Jizeng of the Seventy-seventh Regiment under the Twenty-sixth Division. Moreover, the Military Police Battalion and the Artillery Battalion had been under Headquarters, the Thirty-fifth Regiment

4. This statement erases all doubt that Zhu Qihua was a member of the CCP.

under the Twelfth Division, the political directors group under the General Political Department . . . We had cherished hopes of these forces joining us, but we were disappointed. The Seventy-seventh Regiment under Xu Jisheng, for which we had high hopes, was reassigned the minute they arrived in Jiujiang. Likewise Lu Deming's regimental guard had been disbanded on arrival.

To our happy surprise, however, Luo Maoqi, Propaganda Section chief of the Political Department of the Eleventh Army, brought a handful of people and caught up with us as we were resting in Fuzhou. In the midst of our disappointment over the nonappearance of the other groups with which we had *had* prearrangements, the unexpected appearance of this little group of die-hards was a boost to our spirits. With only twenty rifles between them, they could not risk taking the main road from Nanxun to Nanchang. Starting off from Jiujiang, they crossed the Lushan area, zigzagging over back roads to avoid the vast number of enemy troops, and finally caught up with us in Fuzhou.

Seeing these people from the Political Department of the Eleventh Army, I could not help but wonder where my colleagues at the Political Department of the Fourth Army were. Director Liao Qianwu and I had left Jiujiang precipitately on the eve of the August First coup, and Ouyang Jixiu had been left in charge. But Ouyang had joined up with Guo Moruo on August 4, also heading for Nanchang. Thus the remnants of the Political Department were left behind to disintegrate. Seeing how Luo Maoqi had tried to save the Political Department of the Eleventh Army, I was very ashamed of myself. But at the time, Liao Qianwu and I had to leave Jiujing on the eve of the August First coup. There was no way we could foresee the future and what it held.

Many young women from the Eleventh Army had now joined us. They had been cadets at the Wuhan campus of the Military Political Academy. When the Revolutionary Army arrived in Jiujiang, these young women, uprooted from Wuhan, had gone and joined the Fourth Army and the Eleventh Army as nurses. But shortly after their arrival in Jiujiang, the August First coup took place in Nanchang. Not wishing to follow Zhang Fakui, they had stuck with the Political Department of the Eleventh Army and managed to catch up with us here in

Fuzhou. These young women from well-to-do families had given up everything to join the Revolution, fearing neither hardship nor danger. They deserved our respect; compared to them, I couldn't help but be ashamed.

We stopped for three days in Fuzhou without doing a spot of work, but I got a promotion: apart from the title of head of the Propaganda Division, I was now concurrently head of Organization, under the General Political Department, which existed in name only.

On the afternoon of August 11, we were still in Fuzhou, and I was standing in the yard of the school where we were staying, chatting with someone. Tan Pingshan's orderly was cleaning his gun for him when suddenly there was a shot and a bullet landed two feet from where I was standing and made a hole in the ground. I would have lost a leg if the bullet had been any closer. I gave the fellow a good round scolding, as may be imagined. That was a close shot indeed!

III

[not included in original Chinese edition]

IV

The morning of August 12, we left Fuzhou in a drizzle, continuing south toward Yihuang. Marching in the rain was unpleasant, our wet shirts sticking to our backs. On the other hand, the temperature had dropped so we did not sweat as much.

On the march, we behaved like bandits. Walking through the fields, we dug up melons and ate to our hearts' content. If a villager's chicken were sighted, it would end up as soup at our table. Chicken soup became a fixture of our mess; we could not bear being cheated out of our daily chicken soup. We'd had chickens in Henan, too, but those had been bought from the locals. Now, the locals disappeared before we showed up; there was no way we could buy anything even if we had the money. All we had was printed paper money from the Jiangxi Provincial Bank or the local Wuhan bank. That kind of money was as good as wastepaper in the cities, to say nothing of the countryside, where people rarely saw cash anyway. We had no choice but to catch our own chickens. Fortunately for us, the place was deserted, so we had a free hand.

The Peasants and Workers' Committee was still making posters flaunting the slogans "Land Over 200 Mou Will Be Confiscated!" "Carry On the Land Revolution!" and so on. But now, on this march, we had requisitioned grain from the locals and had raided the villagers' chickens, all without paying a cent. Was that what we meant by "land revolution"? It was nothing short of ridiculous.

As for that nuisance Li Lisan, he was head of the Political Security Department, and there was a lot going on in that department of his! Their job was to punish local despots and counterrevolutionary elements, and to requisition grain—in a word, their job was extortion pure and simple.

We arrived at Yihuang on the afternoon of the same day. As we approached, we saw that the earth was yellow and the water flowing in the river was yellow. Yun Daiying pointed out, in the comic tones of a pedant, "Ah, thus is *yi huang*, the essence of yellow," *huang* meaning yellow.

The General Political Department was housed in a cottage outside the town itself. The scenery was stunningly beautiful, with Phoenix Mountain in the background and Phoenix Temple crowning the mountain. Regrettably there was no time for sightseeing.

Yihuang had become a ghost town, having been deserted by almost all its inhabitants. A handful of old or dying residents was all that remained. The people clearly regarded us as bandits. Now here we were, flying the flag of the working class, and there they were, running for their lives at the news of our coming! Such a "reception" was depressing indeed. But we must remember that all this was Wang Jingwei's doing. The fact was that after the August First coup, Wang had sent out telegraph messages far and wide to denounce us as a bunch of bandits. Who could blame the people for running away? But this did not change the fact that people had turned away from us. Under these circumstances, what did the future hold for us? I could not help pondering this problem.

That night of our arrival, [Zhou] Enlai had a job for me. He asked me to draft a "Propaganda Outline for the Land Revolution"! I thought it preposterous, but he insisted. Goodness, I had not picked up a pen since the start of our march, and now he expected me to turn out a major declaration at the drop of a hat!

Enlai gave me some tips about the policy of confiscating land exceeding 200 mou. I knew that the idea was completely impractical. Supposing a man had 300 mou of land, but insisted that it was only 190 mou, what were we going to do about it? Without practical measures, we were just kidding ourselves. But I did as I was told and drafted an outline for propaganda purposes, and it was even mimeographed. But it served no purpose. We were not doing any real propaganda work at the time.

We decided to leave the town of Yihuang. There was no point in staying, there being only twenty-one people in the whole town, all of them old, sick, or dying.

We started out from Yihuang on August 15. The weather had turned even hotter and the road ahead was rocky. To beat the heat, we adjusted our timetable. We would get up at midnight, have breakfast, and start marching until close to noon, when we would stop and rest. Thus we could avoid the heat of the afternoon, but marching in the dark over rocky terrain was no picnic either.

One day at noon we stopped at a little village at the foot of a mountain. I was feeling sick from heat and fatigue; all I wanted was some nice chicken soup. To my disappointment, the combined efforts of all our orderlies could not come up with a single chicken, not even an egg. In other places, we could make do with pumpkins, but there were no pumpkins around there. Plain rice with nothing to go with it is really hard to swallow. One fellow finally discovered two piglets. Having no choice, they killed and boiled them. I remembered that in Canton, a piglet was a very expensive item on gourmet menus, but those two boiled piglets were tasteless.

Since setting out on our march southward, we had been totally cut off from news about Wuhan or Nanchang. Now finally we got some news.

First, we learned that Zhang Fakui had returned to Canton. He had placed his wife with the [warlord] Li Jishen as a hostage, pledging allegiance to Li. He had arrived in Canton by a shorter route, cutting directly through south Jiangxi, while we were traveling the longer route via east Jiangxi, more or less along the north-south border between Jiangxi and Fujian provinces.

Second, we learned that Shi Cuntong [formerly of the Political Military Academy] had published a declaration in the pages of the *Republican Daily* in Wuhan, titled "Confession in Sorrow." In his "confession," he not only declared his withdrawal from the CCP, he also roundly abused the CCP.

Last but not least, Wang Jingwei has decided to go to Nanjing [to join Chiang Kai-shek]!

I was most interested in the latest move of Shi Cuntong. He used to be such a staunch supporter of the CCP and would go to such extremes to uphold Marxism, as if nothing less than Marxism could save China. Why go to the other extreme now?

V

We arrived at the town of Guangchang on August 17, and put up at a Catholic Church. The situation seemed better than what we had seen in Yihuang—at least there were more than just twenty-one people left. Some shops were even open, although in such a period of turmoil, a pervasive sense of depression was to be expected.

We were all dirt poor, and my thoughts went back to the hodgepodge provisional divisions in Henan, which had never received any payment. Our own Finance Committee had totally run out of money.

It was almost half a month since we had left Nanchang, and surprisingly we had not yet encountered the enemy, nor had we fought a single battle.

We were getting closer and closer to Canton. To Canton! To Canton! That was our only hope of survival. There was no way out for us here in Jiangxi Province. "Get to Canton in time for the mid-Autumn Festival!" That was the slogan urging us onward.

After one day in Guangchang, we moved on. It was August 19.

The heat lingered with no signs of abatement, while the road ahead was stubbornly rocky.

When we started off from Nanchang, we had brought along many horses to be used as pack animals. These horses bred in the plains of the north were now dying of the heat and the struggle with the tortuous mountain roads. By the time we started off from Guangchang, eighty percent of our horses had died, and many of the hired porters had run away. We had a transportation problem on our hands. There were no waterways, or main roads, the only mode of transportation being horses or the backs of porters. Under the circumstances, we had no choice but to conscript new carriers.

Struggling with the heat, the mountainous road, and the transportation problem, our men were disheartened. After trying this and that, it seemed that the only effective way of boosting morale was to hold out the prospect of being in Canton. Once in Canton, all our problems would be over.

Ye Ting's Eleventh Army was uniformly Cantonese. It was more than a year since they had started out on the Northern Expedition. So the prospect of returning home was a strong enticement.

He Long's Twentieth Army was mostly drawn from Hunan and Hubei, so to them Canton was not such a strong attraction. But being such a rich and famous city, Canton was still something to look forward to. Back in their native Hunan, they had never received regular pay, so for them the current situation was not intolerable, not worse than what they had been used to. But discipline among the Twentieth Army was down the drain: opium smoking, invasion of civilian households, pilfering civilian property, conscription of carriers and like offenses were prevalent. But who were we to complain?—We were all doing the same thing. The Revolutionary Committee had to look the other way, just to keep everyone in tow.

In Guangchang, we did get something done, however: He Long, Guo Moruo, and Peng Zemin formally joined the CCP.

During the Nanchang August First Uprising, He Long was not yet a CCP member. Zhang Fakui did not get his facts right when he accused

He Long of being a Communist. Guo Moruo had applied to join the Party back when he was in Nanchang, working for the General Political Department's branch office. But it was only now in Guangchang that his application was approved. As for Peng Zemin, he had chosen to side with the CCP after the GMD Second Congress, but he had never formally joined the CCP. Thus by now there were very few non-CCP members within the leadership of the Revolutionary Committee, the two singular exceptions being Zhang Shushi of the Party Affairs Committee and Jiang Jihuan, head of the Jiangxi Provincial Government, those two being true-blue GMD members. However, most of the middle or lower ranking officers of the Revolutionary Committee were non-CCP.

[Zhou] Enlai fell ill. He was a member of the General Staff Advisory Committee, but his powers were considerable, actually exceeding those of Tan Pingshan. Everything had to go through him. Among the men surrounding Zhou, I simply could not stand Nie Rongzhen, good for nothing except as an ass-kisser. He revered Zhou as he would his own ancestor, but to those beneath him, his arrogance made one's blood boil. Sometimes I had a mind to give him a good thrashing. Back in Wuhan, Nie had been quite powerful, especially in the appointment of political workers within the Army. Nie's standard for promotion or demotion of political workers was clear-cut—his own personal preference. Nie Rongzhen would promote a buddy, be the man a good-for-nothing fool, to be the director of a department. For someone not personally related in any way, be the man a genius, Nie would consign him to some obscure corner to waste his life away. Thus it was that in Wuhan talent had not been appreciated, while people who got the top jobs were often good-for-nothing fools. I personally think that the future of the Party will be bleak if brutes like Nie Rongzhen have their run of things.

Yun Daiying was very short-sighted, like me, and could not survive without glasses. Unfortunately, he broke one arm of his spectacles while in Guangchang, and there was no shop to fix it for him. In a predicament, Daiying got a length of twine and tied his glasses to his ear, presenting a very comic appearance. There had always been something of the clown in Daiying, and now he was really in character.

Since joining the CCP, Guo Moruo appeared to be in high spirits. He even got himself a paramour en route. It happened this way. Gao Yuhan had brought along a mistress by the name of Peng when we had first set out from Nanchang on this current march. This Peng had first worked in Canton, later in Wuhan at the Wuhan campus of the Military Political Academy, and had always enjoyed the reputation of being a romantic Communist. Now, unfortunately for Gao, Guo Moruo caught the Peng woman's eye. Guo was not only younger than Gao, he was more famous, with a higher position to boot. Position and prestige, that's what the bitch was after, and she could sniff them out miles away. Guo Moruo fitted her requirements to a "T". As for Guo himself, he had always prided himself on being a ladykiller; now that a woman had offered herself, how could he say no, especially on this boring march. Miss Peng and Guo hit it off right away. They had hopped into bed way back in Fuzhou, surreptitiously at the beginning, but later out in the open, and had sex in broad daylight heaving and shoving, even with people standing by and cheering them on! These woman warriors were really something! I simply could not stomach it.

As for poor Gao Yuhan, not only his hair but all the strands of his beard shot up in outrage.

VI

"Gradual Entry into the Land of Delight"—those were the words carved into a stone archway as we approached Shicheng—literally Stone City [the next town on our trail south, still sticking to the route running north to south along the Jiangxi-Fujian border]. The words sent a thrill of delight through us: for the past two weeks or so, we had felt like Zhuge Liang when he found himself among savage-like creatures in the riverlands of western China. We had suffered in body and mind, and now there was something to look forward to. We entered Shicheng through the south gate on the afternoon of August 20. The gate was right by the river, and the wall of the city paralleled the main street, which was rare in any town that we had passed through. The situation in Shicheng was much better than that obtaining in Guangchang, which we had just left. The local residents did not leave, and the shops were open as usual. The problem was that we had no money.

The day of our arrival fell on the second anniversary of the assassination of Liao Zhongkai. Owing to the circumstances of our march, there was not even the formality of a memorial.

We stopped for one night at Shicheng and resumed our march on August 22. Up to that point, since leaving Nanchang, we had marched on unchallenged. But now for the first time on our march, we learned that there were enemy forces seventy or eighty *li* farther down, in a place called Rentian Township. Suddenly energized, we made ourselves ready.

On the morning of August 24, our advance forces had a skirmish with the enemy in Rentian, the first battle on this march. The enemy was quickly routed, and we entered the township of Rentian at one o'clock in the afternoon. The township had not been disrupted by the skirmish, people went about [their daily lives] as usual, and the shops were open. Rentian was under the jurisdiction of Ruijin County, the county seat situated some twenty or thirty *li* away.

Although the skirmish in Rentian had been brief, we suffered casualties. Taking part in the action were Ye Ting's Eleventh Army, Zhu De's Ninth Army (actually consisting of only one regiment by now!), and Qin Guanyuan's Second Division (under He Long). The enemy was led by Qian Dajun, who had been forced out of Guangdong Province. Zhu De's one-regiment Ninth Army was brave in battle; so was Ye Ting's Eleventh Army, which was called the Iron Warriors. Qin Guangyuan's Second Division also performed well. However, the deputy commander of the Second Division doubling as head of the Fourth regiment, a certain Commander He, died on the battlefield. He was of He Long's clan and was known for bravery in the field, always positioning himself at the front lines. Unfortunately, he was an opium addict. After that victory at Rentian, he ordered a pursuit of the fleeing enemy, while he himself lay down on a mat and started to enjoy a smoke, right on the battlefield! I happened to be at the front myself and was witness to that incongruous sight. As I was looking at him, an enemy shot flashed by and hit him in the head, killing him instantly. I was standing about thirty steps from where he was killed.

The main body of the army did not linger in Rentian, but moved on to Ruijin proper some twenty or thirty *li* away as more of the enemy had been spotted there. As for us noncombatants, we stayed the night in Rentian and celebrated. We had won a battle, and we were close to Canton; we were heartened and drank a lot of wine.

We learned that our troops had arrived in Ruijin on August 24, that they had exchanged fire with the enemy in a brief skirmish, and that the enemy had retreated. So we sallied forth and arrived at Ruijin on the afternoon of August 25. Ruijin was an important urban center in the eastern part of Jiangxi Province, close to the border with Fujian, and our troops had actually taken it after a brief skirmish! The enemy had retreated to Huichang [farther south], with Ye Ting's and Zhu De's troops in hot pursuit. There, the enemy was again disposed of in a matter of hours, we were told, and our troops occupied Huichang.

As for us noncombatants, we stayed on in Ruijin for the night and were put up in a local middle school. From the top floor, there was a distant view of an imposing mountain range dotted with ancient pagodas. The local people did not leave, and it was business as usual in the town itself. Ruijin was the best place we had passed through since leaving Nanchang on this march

The Revolutionary Committee held a celebratory rally in Ruijin, which ended with a lantern show that night, the first time we have rallied the masses since our march began. It was not a great crowd, barely one thousand people. Tan Pingshan gave a speech and we passed resolutions and sent telegrams to the world at large, all of which I drafted. But I had to laugh at the whole thing—how were we going to send out those telegrams and resolutions?

We stopped for a couple of days in Ruijin. I really liked the place; we were told that in his time Sun Yat-sen himself had stopped here for a whole month on his way north.

Since Ye Ting and Zhu De had defeated the enemy in Huichang, a couple of us, representing the Revolutionary Committee, went over to honor them and to thank the troops. Huichang was only eighty *li* away from where we were in Ruijin, but it was no comparison to Ruijin.

When we returned from Huichang, we found that there was some unrest among the ranks of He Long's Twentieth Army. There was a rumor afloat that in taking Huichang, Ye Ting had pocketed 700,000 yuan and the men in He Long's Twentieth Army felt cheated of their share. This was obviously a rumor spread by spies to sow division among us. Nothing of the sort had happened. He Long and the commanders of the Twentieth Army all had confidence in Ye Ting. Tan Pingshan, Zhou Enlai, and He Long gave detailed explanations, vouching for Ye's honesty, and thus the matter was put to rest.

VII

We left Ruijin on September 1. This would be our last day in Jiangxi territory; that same night we were supposed to be in Gucheng, under the jurisdiction of Changding County in Fujian Province.

The days were getting colder, especially in the morning. We sallied forth from Ruijin in high spirits. The scenery was beautiful and we were getting closer to Canton, which put us in a good mood. The dejection of the last couple of weeks had vanished.

The border between the two provinces of Jiangxi and Fujian is mountainous, much higher than Dayu Mountain which we had encountered on the Jiangxi-Guangdong border.

We reached Dingzhou on September 3. Though small in size, Dingzhou was really not bad, with several paved roads and modern buildings. Probably due to its proximity to Guangdong Province, there was a Western air about it. And luckily for me, it had one of my favorite fruits, the star fruit. It was like meeting an old friend in a foreign land, and I ate to my heart's content.

We bivouacked in a pharmacy and, as always, experienced a period of idleness. Little did I know that it was not to last. The morning after our arrival, Enlai called me over. He decided to transfer me to the Twentieth Army. He said that the political work there was in shambles, and he needed someone to take charge and clean up the mess. I learned that Liao Qianwu [my old boss] had just been appointed head of the Political Department of the Twentieth Army, and Enlai wanted me to be the secretary.

I knew something about the situation at the Twentieth Army: because of special circumstances, the head of the Political Department was always at the side of the commander, like a political adviser, while the secretary was de facto head of the department, shouldering all the work. It was common knowledge that the secretary of the Political Department of the Twentieth Army had a much heavier workload than the secretary at any other political department. As I had said, there were special circumstances at the Twentieth Army, and the troops had not been professionally trained, all of which added together meant a heavy workload and weighty responsibilities for the secretary. Enlai wanted me for the job, and would not take no for an answer.

Having idled away a month without doing anything as the head of the two departments of Propaganda and Organization under the General Political Department, I was ready to take up some real work, so long as I could handle it.

He Long, the commander-in-chief, doubled as commander of the Twentieth Army.

The head of the Political Department had originally been Zhou Yiqun, who was now assigned to be commander of the Third Division. (The Twentieth Army originally comprised two divisions and one Training Regiment, e.g., He Jinzhai heading the First Division and Qin Guangyuan heading the Second Division. Now the former Training Regiment had been expanded and converted into the Third Division, and Zhou Yiqun was appointed its commander.)

Liao Qianwu was now appointed head of the Political Department. Since starting out from Nanchang, Liao had always been in He Long's company; the two seemed to hit it off, so Liao was a good choice. But Liao then insisted on having me as secretary. As he was being supported by Enlai, I had no choice, and thus the matter was settled.

Even so, because of internal matters of the Twentieth Army and the business of finding replacements for my two departmental positions, I did not join the Twentieth Army right away when we were in Dingzhou. This had to wait until we arrived in Shanghang.

We started out from Dingzhou on September 6.

It was getting colder by the day. We did not suffer from the summer heat anymore when marching, but the cold at night was something. When we started out from Nanchang, we had only brought summer clothes and very thin matting, which was not enough protection against the cold. The stores in Dingzhou did sell warm clothes and thick matting, but we had no money. In a word, the heat of summer was now replaced by the equally painful chill of fall.

The second day after we started out from Dingzhou fell on the Mid-Autumn Festival. We stopped at a little village located in a deep valley, as if at the bottom of a well. "The moon shines brightly on mid-autumn" goes the saying, and indeed it did not shine the less brightly on our ragtag band. To pass the Mid-Autumn Festival in a little valley, closed in by high cliffs, with the moon gazing down at us, what could be more romantic! It was an once-in-a-lifetime experience!

The orderlies found a jug of wine in a villager's home—what a catch, perfect for Mid-Autumn! Pity though, there was nothing to go with the wine. The orderlies looked far and wide, but came up with nothing, not even a pumpkin or a bunch of vegetables, not to mention chickens or ducks. How could we enjoy wine without a dish? It put a damper on things. My young orderly, it turned out, was the smartest of them all. He came back with a family dog, and asked for my permission to kill it for a dish to go with the wine. I said yes, by all means. We were getting tired of chicken and pork. Dog meat was the ideal dish to go with wine, not to mention the fact that I had never tried this delicacy before. When the cooked dog meat was brought up, its aroma bowled me over. The 300-*yuan* "Dragon versus Tiger [snake and cat]" dish at the prestigious Southern Garden Restaurant in Canton paled beside it. That evening was the best Mid-Autumn Festival I had ever enjoyed! Who could have imagined that we would spend a Mid-Autumn Festival in a deserted valley in Fujian territory!

In my wandering life, I had spent the Mid-Autumn of 1926 in Canton, dined at a top restaurant and spent the whole night playing mahjong.

The Mid-Autumn of 1925 I was at the Whampoa Military Academy. By the Western calendar it fell on October 2, the day that Wang Jingwei was to take office as the GMD representative to the

Academy. Dinner was served in the dining hall of the Academy, and I remember we had our dinner standing, due to the great number of people. The ceremony to initiate Wang Jingwei into office took place after dinner; both Wang Jingwei and Chiang Kai-shek gave long speeches.

The Mid-Autumn of 1924 I had spent in Shanghai.

The Mid-Autumn of 1923 I had spent at West Lake in Hangzhou.

Who knows where I will be spending the Mid-Autumn next year? As a poem says:

> This life, as this night, will not stand still,
> Where will I see the moon next year?

VIII

We arrived in Shanghang on September 8 [dipping into the southwestern corner of Fujian Province]. The town of Shanghang was even livelier than Dingzhou, with more Western-style buildings. It was closer to Guangdong Province, thus more stylish, with a Cantonese flavor.

On September 9, the day after our arrival, we called a meeting at the headquarters of the Ninth Army to discuss political work. Present were Zhou Enlai, Guo Moruo, Yun Daiying, Gao Yuhan, Liao Qianwu, Nie Rongzhen, He Chang, Li Mingzhi, Li Shuoxun, Ouyang Jixiu, Fang Weixia, Xu Teli, Zhang Bojun, Luo Maoqi, and me. There were three or four others whose names now escape me.

The Ninth Army was quartered in a Christian church, and we held our meeting on the second floor of that spacious modern building. Before the meeting started, the Ninth Army commander Zhu De made us welcome, pouring out tea and opening packets of biscuits. I had met this old soldier before, in the Nanchang office of the General Political Department.

After going over some problems of style and method, we went on to the division of labor. Guo Moruo was head of the General Political Department, but he had no say whatever—it was all up to Zhou Enlai. By then it was already decided that I would move to the Twentieth Army. After a lengthy discussion, Zhou Enlai picked He

Chang to replace me as head of Propaganda for the General Political Department. He Chang was reluctant, but finally had to accede. Luo Maoqi was picked to replace me as head of Organization.

After the meeting, Zhu De played host and threw a dinner. Over our meal we talked about our plan of action. Enlai said that after reaching Shantou we would change the name and insignia of our army. We would drop the name of the National Revolutionary Army and rename it the China Revolutionary Army, and the commander-in-chief would remain General He Long.

The existing Twentieth Army would be the new First Army with He Long doubling as commander.

The existing Eleventh Army would be the new Second Army, commanded by Ye Ting.

A part of the existing Twentieth Army would be incorporated into the existing Ninth Army to form the new Third Army, to be commanded by Zhu De.

The new Fourth Army was to be made up of the existing militia joining forces with troops in Guangdong Province, which we hoped to acquire, to be commanded by Liu Bocheng.

After disposing of army affairs, Yun Daiying reported on plans to convene the GMD Third National Convention after our arrival in Canton.

On the morning of September 10, Chen Gong, then secretary of the Political Department of the Twentieth Army, whose job I was supposed to take, showed up and wanted us to get started on the hand-over. First he took me to the General Political Department, where I met He Long and my old boss Liao Qianwu. He Long was pleasant and expressed his welcome. I was meeting He Long for the first time, and was very favorably impressed. Only thirty-one years old, he had been a bandit in the old days, but now actually looked gentle and scholarly, with a hint of the Japanese in his deportment. He offered milk, but I never drink milk, so I picked up a biscuit instead. Once the formalities were over, I left with Chen Gong for the business of the day. Chen took me to the Political Department of the Twentieth Army and introduced me to the staff. That done, Chen got up and left to join the Second Division as director of the Political Department, while I was on my own, as secretary for the Political Department of the Twentieth Army.

Liao Qianwu was the director, but in name only, as he was always at the side of Commander [He Long] and so far had not showed his face at the Political Department. Everything was left to me to handle, and I must say that the Political Department there at the Twentieth Army was a mess, not to be mentioned in the same breath as ours back at the Fourth Army. I had to start from scratch, but being on the march, I was sorely limited by time and resources, and as much as I struggled to put the department on its feet, there was not much that I could do.

In Shanghang, we made some changes in our political slogans; for instance "Land over 200 hundred mou will be confiscated" was changed to "Land over 50 mou will be confiscated." I found both equally impractical.

On the military side, our Russian adviser suggested that our armies stop in the Dingzhou-Shanghang-Yongding area [in southwestern Fujian Province bordering Jiangxi to the west and Guangdong to the south], where according to him, the land was rich and we could take a break and replenish our supplies. Moreover, according to him, we could recruit enough hands to form three new divisions, while also helping arm the local militia. He said that after we boosted our strength, there would be time enough to enter Canton. But this suggestion was not acceptable to the majority. "Back to Canton" had been our rallying cry since starting out from Nanchang. He Long, Tan Pingshan, Zhou Enlai, Ye Ting, Liu Bocheng, Zhu De, and the rest were all for marching on to Guangdong Province. According to the calculation of the chief of staff, we would have no problem taking Canton, the capital.

Since the leadership was dead set on taking Canton right away, the Russian adviser's advice was rejected. We stopped in Shanghang for three days and then marched southwestward toward Guangdong Province on the morning of September 12.

We reached Dapu County on the border of Guangdong Province on September 14.

After that last parting [in late 1926, when we had moved to Wuhan], we were now back on Guangdong soil! How could we not be elated!

We did not stop at Dapu, however, but pushed deeper westward, the only difference being that now, starting from Dapu, we have changed to sailboats— much nicer than marching over mountains. The added advantage was that having everybody on the boat, we could put our heads together and plan the political work ahead.

Following the river route, we encountered the enemy at the upper reaches of the Han River. We noncombatant personnel traveled closely behind the troops for safety.

At Sanheba, Songkou, and Liuhuang, we continued to have skirmishes with small groups of the enemy. They would quit as soon as they caught sight of us, so we had no problem taking over these three military outposts.

Back in Jiangxi, the masses had not been welcoming, taking us for bandits. But now in Guangdong, the masses were totally on our side. Actually when we were still on the Fujian border and technically not quite in Guangdong territory, the people of Dapu had sent over representatives to welcome us. Once in Dapu, people there volunteered to stake out the enemy and report their movements to us. At the news of our coming, the students of a high school in Sanheba went ahead and disarmed the local military, all on their own initiative! There was just no comparison between the people of Guangdong and those of Jiangxi!

Thanks to the support of the people, we entered Chaozhou without opposition on September 19.

IX

Chaozhou was an affluent center in eastern Guangdong. Now that we had taken Chaozhou, we could stock up on provisions. More important, our presence in Chaozhou would be felt in the capital, Canton. Before arriving in Chaozhou we had been scurrying around in the barren regions of Jiangxi, ignored by the world. Now that we were masters of the foremost city of eastern Guangdong, we had become a force to be reckoned with.

Personally, I was happy to be in Chaozhou. The neatly laid out paved roads, the picturesque Western-style houses on either side . . . I had never imagined Chaozhou to be such a lovely place.

Headquarters was set up in a Western-style building in the vicinity of West Lake,[5] and the Political Department of the Twentieth Army, where I was now positioned, was put up in a large housing complex known as Kaiyuan Temple. The Chaozhou Trade and Civic Association, along with several other associations, used to be housed there. It goes without saying that they had swiftly disappeared at the news of our approach. We took over most of the rooms, which were all in good condition.

Now that we were settled for the time being, I decided to put the affairs of my Department in order, and for a while I was very busy. Chaozhou was beautiful, with the lake and a fountain nearby, but I was too busy to go sightseeing.

The park near West Lake was the best part of town, and we held a mass rally there. As usual, I drafted the resolutions and the telegrams for the world at large—more or less a repeat of what I'd done back in Ruijin.

Now that we were in control, Chen Xinglin, political director of the Twenty-fourth Division, was appointed mayor of Chaozhou.

In Chaozhou I met up with Ye Guyi, head of logistics for the Fourth Army [where I had previously served], and we talked over the circumstances of the disintegration of the Political Department back in Jiujiang. Ye Guyi then met up with Liao Qianwu who gave him an assignment in Shantou [and thus we lost touch again].

The people of Chaozhou were very supportive of us. On the eve of our arrival, the enemy in Shantou had wanted to move their troops into Chaozhou and then to Sanheba, which we had taken, but the railway workers went on strike, and the locals destroyed some of the tracks. Thus the enemy's plan was foiled, and we entered Chaozhou without firing a shot.

Destroying the railway tracks had repulsed the enemy, it was true, but just then the interrupted rail transport had become a problem for us. Since the enemy had retreated from Shantou, which was our next destination southward, our troops could easily have moved into

5. Not to be confused with the famous West Lake in Hangzhou.

Shantou by rail. But now there was no transport. When the railway workers learned that the enemy had retreated and that we were in control in Chaozhou, they worked overnight and repaired the tracks within twelve hours! Thanks to the support of the workers, our troops moved swiftly into Shantou, the next destination being Canton.

[But coming back to Chaozhou for the moment,] Commander-in-chief He Long had me over for dinner; in fact, I had not had a decent meal since starting off from Nanchang—this shark fin banquet was the first I had enjoyed since then. He Long was very particular about his food: his aides were mostly occupied in keeping him well-fed. In his own defense, He Long claimed that he was afflicted with a strange complaint: if his food did not satisfy him, he would lose his appetite, break into a cold sweat, and his mind would stop working, and therefore, according to him, his daily menu was an important part of his working life. Guo Moruo mentioned that Chiang Kai-shek was not particular about his food, while Gao Yuhan talked about what he knew of the eating habits of Lenin [and thus went the conversation over dinner].

Then Enlai got me over and told me to organize a special party cell of the GMD within the Twentieth Army, because the minute we arrived in Canton, we would convene the GMD Third National Congress. There was a Party Affairs Committee in place under the Revolutionary Committee headed by Zhang Shushi, Han Linfu, Peng Zemin, and others. Each province had a Party representative within the Party Affairs Committee, although many of them were purely nominal. Since there was no representative from my native Zhejiang Province, Han Linfu suggested that I represent Zhejiang, though I had left Zhejiang three years before and had never been back. I thought it all quite ridiculous.

I had a long conversation with Peng Pai in a teahouse near West Lake. He was the noted " Peasant Leader" in Hai-Feng and Lu-Feng [usually referred to as Hai-Lu-Feng]. He gave me a detailed description of the situation in Hai-Lu-Feng and was very optimistic about the future.

On arrival in Chaozhou, our people had taken it for granted that we would march on and take Canton, but I had my doubts. Our army was but thirty thousand strong. Now, with such an insignificant force, how could we expect to overcome the warlord Li Jishen, now in control of Canton? Besides, on our arrival in Chaozhou, it was confirmed that Zhang Fakui had arrived in Canton ahead of us. Now, unless Zhang Fakui colluded with us from within, I could see no way we could go in and take over the city of Canton, the capital of Guangdong Province. We were short on ammunition, and we could not restock until we got to Canton. On the other hand, the Guangdong warlord Li Jishen had two artillery regiments and a navy. Besides, Li was hand-in-glove with the Guangxi warlords Li Zongren, Bai Chongxi, and Huang Shaoxiong. The combined forces of these warlords of Guangxi and Guangdong amounted to no fewer than a hundred thousand men who could be called up at a moment's notice, not to mention their artillery and navy and unlimited ammunition. They could also rely on support from the Western imperialists coming from Hong Kong. Taking all the above into consideration, I simply could not believe that we could take Canton.

[As mentioned above], our advance troops had entered the port city of Shantou on September 20.

Our arrival had alerted the imperial powers stationed there: the gunboats of the British, the Japanese, the Americans, and the French showed their flags in port, and British soldiers actually strutted about onshore.

The situation was serious.

Our army had remained inland and never had any truck with foreign powers; we never imagined that we would ever have a "diplomatic" problem on our hands. The Revolutionary Committee had always been plagued by a dearth of professionals—as for diplomatic professionals, they were totally unheard of. Now the Revolutionary Committee was caught unprepared. But the problem must be dealt with. Whom should we send? The mission fell on the shoulders of Guo Moruo, who had started his career in medicine, moved on to literature, and now was engaged in revolution. Guo was given his credentials, which comically anointed him "Negotiator for Shantou and Overseer of Shantou Customs Affairs." Luckily for us, the presence of foreign ships in port and soldiers onshore in Shantou did not balloon into a major problem. If the imperialists had called our bluff, we would have been quite helpless.

Back to Chaozhou [where we at the Political Department were comfortably housed in Kaiyuan Temple buildings]: we discovered a library which had been set up by the Chaozhou Youth Club. It must have been stocked by the CCP before the "purge" in Canton, as the holdings included complete sets of the magazines *La Jeunesse* [Xin qingnian/New youth], *Weekly Guide,* and *China Youth.* I was also surprised to encounter my own writings in a complete set of *Military Affairs Weekly,* which I had edited when I was working at the Military Affairs Department of the GMD CEC.

With our advance troops in Shantou, we lingered for a few more days in Chaozhou, giving me a chance to see old friends.

Li Shaotang, an old friend from my Canton days, was actually with the Twentieth Army at the time, though I only learned of it now after my own arrival in Chaozhou. Li had been a student of the Canton Political Institute while I was on the staff of the Propaganda Department of the Party CEC. At the time we had both been housed in the CEC quarters and met each other every day. Other acquaintances of mine at the Canton Political Institute had been Zhang Wentian, Han Yangchu, Xu De, and Duan Dechang.

There used to be a little coffee house near the reception area of the GMD CEC where we young people would hang out. Apart from us young men at the CEC and the Military Political Academy, there were the young women from the Women's Movement Training Institute, and their presence had cast a special charm over the place. [Over coffee] we would debate the relationship between love and revolution, thrashing out all aspects of the problem. Later, they had all marched off each their separate ways while I too left the CEC for other posts. Later I was reassigned to the Party CEC to work at the Military Affairs Department. But by then the little coffee house was gone.

I remember that on the eve of his departure Li Shaotang and I had spent most of the night walking on Dongchuan Road under the moonlight, trying to say goodbye. We could not bear to part and walked back and forth into the wee hours. He gave me a photo as a souvenir and signed it "Let us meet in Peking." Who would have thought that we would meet again in Guangdong territory! Shocked at how things had turned out I said to him, "Not only did we not take Peking, but now even Canton is not in our hands!"

Zhang Qiudi was also an old acquaintance. He used to be the record-keeper for the Whampoa Alumni Association. We had parted in Nanchang the previous spring, and here we met again. Zhang was currently a regimental leader under the Twentieth Army, but wished to return to political work. I tried to have him transferred to my own Political Department as editor and record-keeper, but things had not worked out.

Fan Delie also showed up there in Chaozhou. He used to be head of training at the Political Department of the Fourth Army, and was now with the Twentieth Army as a battalion leader. He was only eighteen, very slight of build. But he would hop on a horse three times his size and canter about in the streets, looking like a monkey in a circus parade.

Another old acquaintance from my Whampoa days, Cao Sumin, was now a regimental commander in the Twentieth Army. I hadn't seen him for six months; he was almost black from sunburn and still sticking to his native Shaoxing accent.

I had a most remarkable reunion with Luo Feilie. We had been very close in Canton. He had stayed behind when I left for Wuhan, and I heard that he had died. I had shed tears for him when alone at night, and now to see him there in Chaozhou! But even more remarkable was the fact that he had taken me for dead, too. After I had left [on the Henan Expedition], he heard that a department head surnamed Zhu had died on the battlefield, and he had assumed that it was me! We were both overjoyed to find each other alive, and went out to celebrate over drinks. I was to start out the next day for Shantou [to join our advance troops] while Luo was staying on in Chaozhou. More's the pity it was such a brief meeting after so long an absence of mourning each other! I gave him a photo of myself which I had taken in Chaozhou and inscribed it with four lines from Wen Tingjun's[6] "To a Young Friend":

6. Wen Tingyun (812? –866?), a Tang dynasty poet.

Afloat in a drifting world, too late we meet,
Falling leaves on the chilling lake, bespeak my heart.
Wine seals our parting in Huaiyin town,
In a pavilion soaked in moonlight, we raise our voices in song.

X

We had stopped in Chaozhou for a total of five days, and now we were about to leave for Shantou [veering slightly southwest of Chaozhou]. I would miss this beautiful town of Chaozhou, yet I was happy, since we were getting closer and closer to Canton. My dear young lady was waiting for me in Canton. In a little while she and I would be strolling side by side on Dongshan Street.

General Headquarters had set off one day ahead of us. We at the Political Department got hold of a railway carriage all to ourselves and started out on September 24, heading for Shantou. Too bad there was nothing interesting to see on either side of the tracks as we chugged along.

We arrived in Shantou at one o'clock in the afternoon, and were installed in that city's only girls' school. The building was excellent, and I secured a sunny room to myself. School had opened. To make sure that we did not disrupt classes, I directed the management to spare the classrooms, and requisition only a minimum amount of space for our needs.

Since leaving Nanchang, I have had no contact with members of the other sex. Now suddenly to be in the proximity of so many young women was a great distraction. As luck would have it, there was an old copy of *Romance of the Western Bower* in my room, and flipping through some of the sensuous passages had completely destroyed my peace of mind. I must confess that I fervently wished for female companionship. *Young lady in Canton, how I wish you were here with me.*

After disposing of some work, I strolled to the seaside and saw many ships coming from Canton, or about to depart. It was merely thirty hours by sea from Shantou to Canton. If I had not been saddled with this position, I could go aboard and reach Canton in two days. I could hold my young lady to my breast and forget everything. Thinking thus,

I really wanted to take off my uniform and jump onto one of those outgoing ships. What happiness that would be, but I could not do it.

I went to Headquarters, which had taken up residence in a very good building on the site of the Townsmen's Association. The commander-in-chief, Director Liao, and a Russian adviser were in a room upstairs. There were three folding beds, so I assumed that they shared the bedroom. There was a string of visitors in the wake of my arrival: Gao Yuhan, Guo Moruo, Wu Yuzhang, Lin Zuhan, Zhou Enlai. We shared an excellent meal. I got into the habit of dining at Headquarters, the food there being so much better than what we were getting at the Political Department.

Being in Shantou put us in a good mood. Over the meal the commander-in-chief talked about the situation facing us. It seemed that there was still a possibility that Zhang Fakui would work with us, in which case taking Canton would not be a problem. We hoped that as soon as our troops reached Huizhou [which was very close to Canton], Zhang Fakui in Canton would take action, or at least some of his men would take action to coordinate with our move on Canton. We knew that his chief-of-staff, Ye Jianying, was staunchly on our side; we had heard that Ye had joined the CCP, and was now doubling as a political instructor. Liang Bingshu, now promoted to regimental commander of the Presidential Guards, was also staunchly on our side. Taking Canton would not be a problem, *or so we thought.*

In order to get into touch with Zhang Fakui and his deputy Huang Qixiang, the Revolutionary Committee sent Gao Yuhan to travel by way of Hong Kong on a secret mission to contact those two men.

After dinner, the commander-in-chief gave me 10,000 *yuan* in cash for expenses and salaries for my staff. As I was also instructed not to pay out salaries while we were still in Shantou, I turned the money over to our head of finance.

Shantou was bustling with life, and was much more developed than such inland cities as Jiujiang, Wuhu, and Chongqing.

I must add that the recently appointed "Negotiator" and "Customs Supervisor" Guo Moruo was now endowed with yet another title: editor of the *Revolution Daily* [Geming ribao]. The *Revolution Daily* was the official paper of the Revolutionary Committee, newly launched in Shantou. And thus was Guo Moruo's star steadily rising under the patronage of the Revolutionary Committee. What had he done to deserve it? It did not make sense at all.

The people of Shantou were not encouraging. Neither students nor workers had been mobilized, not to mention tradesmen. They kept their distance, casting icy glances our way, with not a whit of empathy. It was a totally different world compared to Chaozhou, where we had been received so warmly. But preoccupied with our march on Canton, we had neither the time nor the inclination to do any rally work among them. Shantou was merely a stop on our way.

The Revolutionary Committee had set up office and opened for business in the quarters of the previous Chamber of Commerce, the main business, of course, having to do with finances. Lin Zuhan, head of the Finance Committee took out 10,000 in the worthless paper money printed in Jiangxi and Wuhan and demanded that the local Chamber of Commerce help convert it into *yuan*. They dodged around a bit, but pushed into a corner, they did come up with the 10,000 *yuan*. How can merchants prevail against the military?

Liao Qianwu, head of the Political Department, finally made an appearance at the Political Department, his first and only appearance since his appointment. He informed us that the Chief of Staff Advisory Board [of the Revolutionary Committee] was to be renamed the Military Committee, the members being He Long, Ye Ting, Zhu De, Liu Bocheng, Zhou Enlai, Zhou Shidi, Yun Daiying, and Zhou Yiqun. The chairman of the Military Committee had yet to be decided between Zhou Enlai and Liu Bocheng, while Nie Rongzhen was designated secretary-general. Nie Rongzhen again! This useless baggage always at the top while talented people were kept down! If this trend continued, there would be little hope for the Revolutionary Committee.

Liao Qianwu also dropped a hint that the Political Department might undergo some changes: the director might be renamed Party representative, and the secretary renamed secretary-general. He further mentioned that once in Canton, we would set up military academies to turn out much needed military and political cadres. Meanwhile, he added, once we established a footing in Canton, the Revolutionary Committee might set itself up as a government, the name of which to be decided later.

After Liao left, I stayed in the room thinking over what he had said, and saw the future as being enveloped in darkness. We were in Shantou, but whether we could make it to Canton seemed problematic to me. And if we could not take Canton, what other option was there for us? Thinking thus, I began to question whether the last two months of marching had been worth it. I had been so positive while in Chaozhou. But now that I was in Shantou, a wave of doubt swept over me.

We stayed in Shantou for five days only, before heading for Jieyang, the next stop on our route.

CHAPTER EIGHT

Notes on a Retreat

We started off from Shantou on the afternoon of September 29, and arrived in Jieyang by chartered boat that same night. It was a tiny vessel, with no dining area. We were all squeezed together in the hold. The din of the engine was deafening, and the smoke suffocating. I felt nauseous all the way and was half-dead by the time we went ashore.

There were no streetlights, so we saw nothing of Jieyang. The Political Department had arranged for us to stop for the night at the local Businessmen's Association. Headquarters had arrived earlier and was stationed in the county government building. I had wanted to go over and look up my boss, Director Liao Qianwu, to find out our marching plans—we had left Shantou so precipitately as if fleeing for our lives. By the time we were settled in, I was completely exhausted; all I could do was send a messenger to inform Director Liao of my arrival.

The Businessmen's Association building was in shambles and completely deserted, with not even an errand boy around. I found two rooms, which were locked. My orderly managed to open them for me, but they were as dirty as the rest of the building. I pushed two tables together and stretched out on them.

I had barely fallen asleep before my boss, Liao, sent for me, asking me to join him immediately as we were to leave early the next morning. What could I do but drag myself over! I felt sorry for myself. People not in positions of responsibility have no idea of the burdens of office. If I were home, wouldn't I be comfortably in bed? And now, with a splitting headache, I have no choice but to dance to my boss's summons.

I arrived at Headquarters in a foul mood. The commander-in-chief [He Long] himself was still up, chatting with my boss. The fact was, when we first set out for Jieyang, only Headquarters and staff members had left together with us. The rest of the leadership—Tan Pingshan, Guo Moruo, Yun Daiying, Wu Yuzhang, Lin Zuhan, and company—had stayed put in Shantou.

Liao told me that we were heading for Tangkeng the very next morning.

More to the point, Liao gave me particulars about the military deployment and the direction of our march:

Zhou Yiqun, commander of the Third Division, was named head of the Shantou garrison, and would stay put in Shantou;

Zhou Shidi, commander of the Twenty-fifth Division, along with Zhu De, commander of the Ninth Army, would jointly garrison the Songkou-Liuhuang-Sanheba area, and would also stay put.

The fact remained that apart from the Ninth Army [under Zhu De], which actually consisted of only two regiments, with the addition of the "rifle brigade" attached to the general staff under Li Minghe, our whole force consisted of five divisions only, namely:

the First Division under He Jinzhai,
the Second Division under Qin Guangyuan,
the Third Divison under Zhou Yiqun,
(the above three Divisions under the Twentieth Army),
the Twenty-fourth Division under Commander Gu,
the Twenty-fifth Division under Zhou Shidi,
(the above two Divisions under the Eleventh Army).

Now that it was decided to keep the Third and the Twenty-fifth divisions in place to garrison the Shantou and the Sanheba areas, respectively, it meant that we now had only three divisions at the front lines.

According to what Liao Qianwu had told me, Headquarters planned to rely on these three Divisions to take Canton. The first step was to get to Fengshun, from there to take the town of Meixian, from Meixian to take the "tri-township" of Hai-Lu-Feng, from Hai-Lu-Feng to move westward to take Huizhou, and from Huizhou to move on Canton.

We had a mere five divisions at our disposal, and now to divide them into three parts—one to garrison Shantou, another to garrison the Sanheba area, leaving only three divisions to take Canton—I wondered if we had underestimated the task we had set for ourselves. Moreover, the combat effectiveness of the First and Second divisions was questionable. I was very skeptical of this deployment and plan of action.

True, Shantou had been taken hands down, but I suspect that it had been a trap to set us up. If we expected to take Canton as easily as we took Shantou, we were obviously in for a disappointment.

"With only three divisions, can we take Canton?" I couldn't help asking.

"Certainly," answered the commander-in-chief offhandedly. What more could I say?

Still woozy from lack of sleep, I left Headquarters and returned to my two tables to resume my interrupted sleep. But I still could not help wondering about the magnitude of the task of taking Canton with a mere three divisions.

We got up early the next morning, September 30, and made ready to start off right after breakfast.

We were supposed to stop in Tangkeng, which was only fifty *li* away from where we were in Jieyang. Fifty *li* was child's play; all I wanted was to get there and get some sleep.

Since entering Guangdong territory, we had always traveled by sailboat—this was the first time that we were marching. It was smooth going, unlike the mountainous terrain of Jiangxi and Fujian we had passed through. Along the way, we could see that the land here in Guangdong Province was more prosperous.

By half-past-two in the afternoon, we had covered forty *li.* Only ten *li* more to Tangkeng! When on a march, one is most cheerful when the end is in sight. As I just mentioned, we had been traveling by boat after entering Guangdong territory, add to that our two days' stop in Shantou, and we were out of practice, and this current march on foot had felt unusually exhausting. But now the end was in sight—only ten more *li*! We would be there in an hour.

But it was not to be. The enemy was ahead, and our Twenty-fourth Division had exchanged fire with them. Running into the enemy was a frequent occurrence on this march, so we were not overly worried. We just stayed in a village nearby, waiting for the end of the skirmish. True, the delay was a nuisance; on the other hand, it was exhilarating to hear gunshots at close range.

The enemy looked down on us from a hilltop and was first discovered by the Twenty-fourth Division. More numerous than had been assumed, the enemy controlled the hills both left and right. The Twenty-fourth Division could not beat them back; the First Division was called in, and then the Second Division. The fighting was becoming desperate on both sides.

Headquarters was stationed about three *li* behind the lines, and we at the Political Department settled nearby, mainly to take care of the wounded. The locals, taken in by enemy propaganda, had fled at our approach. We had a hard time caring for the wounded, who were being brought back in increasing numbers. At this juncture, the young women from the Wuhan campus of the Military Political Academy, truly models of courage and dedication, rushed up to help bring back the wounded from the front.

Accompanied by my orderly, I went to the front lines to take a look. Bullets whistled past my ears; to this day I have never stopped wondering why I was not hit. I dropped down and crept forward. Ye Ting, commander of the Eleventh Army, personally directed the battle. Surprisingly, the usually gruff Ye was now as gentle as a woman.

[As I said] the enemy, in overwhelming numbers, had the strategic advantage of overlooking us from the hilltops, and our troops had no opportunity to launch a counterattack.

The chief-of-staff of the Second Division was wounded, so were many company and battalion commanders.

Commander-in-chief He Long, along with Chief-of-staff Liu Bocheng, and Director of the Political Department Liao Qianwu, went personally to inspect the front lines.

It was getting dark, but the battle still raged on, with no end in sight. If not for this damnable surprise attack, we would be having dinner in Tangkeng!

The worst of it was the hunger. We were out of food. Who would have thought that the enemy would spring its trap on us in Tangkeng! Our supplies had been taken to Tangkeng ahead of us—obviously everything had fallen into enemy hands. We just had to tough it out on empty bellies. Foraging in peasants' homes had only produced a sprinkling of rice, barely enough to make thin porridge.

Night soon descended, enveloping us in complete darkness, and the wounded continued to be brought down from the hills in an endless stream. We had to take care of the wounded, as well as deal with the growing pile of discarded weapons. It being fall, I sent the orderlies to scavenge in the fields for yams and to boil them with whatever rice we could get hold of, to make porridge for the wounded. We ourselves gnawed on raw yams. Meanwhile the battle in the hills raged on, with no decisive victory on either side.

By midnight, when there was still no let up in the fighting, I made my way to Headquarters.

The commander-in-chief himself [He Long], Zhou Enlai, Liu Bocheng, Liao Qianwu, and the [unnamed] Russian adviser—they were all there. One of the staff from the Eleventh Army rushed over to report that the enemy had a massive presence in Tangkeng and that it was personally led by Li Jishen (who, it was later confirmed, was actually in Canton). The atmosphere became ever more tense as Liu Bocheng, with a patch over one eye, pored over a military map spread on the table. "Damn it!" the staff member of the Eleventh Army added, after making his report, "The bullets hitting us were made in the Soviet Union!"

Whereupon Enlai commented: "Who would have thought that

bullets made in a proletarian country would be used to kill proletarian comrades." When the Russian adviser was informed of the matter by his interpreter, he took a look at the shells. "It's true," he sighed, "they were made in Russia. They were brought over to help your Revolutionary Army. Who would have thought they would be helping your enemy . . ."

Commander Ye Ting came back from the front lines optimistic, saying that at most it would take three or four hours to dispose of the enemy. That cheered everybody up.

I followed Ye Ting as he went back to the front. A bullet flashed past me, tearing my sleeve and grazing my skin. I dropped down from the shock wave, and rolled down into the field below. Fortunately, the field was dry, and I got up unharmed.

"Coming through a catastrophe unhurt, one is destined for future good fortune." With that popular saying in mind, I walked on. Bullets are not going to stop me, I thought grimly, as I made my way into the trenches [dug into the hillside]. I ran into Zhu Minggao, an old friend.

"Are you scared" said Zhu, patting me on the shoulder.

"You insult me," I countered, as we shook hands. At that very instant, a bullet hit him in the chest. He fell down, blood flowing from a hole in his chest. He died instantly.

"My friend, go in peace," I said. We had been friends. I looked at his corpse with composure. I was completely calm. Death has become an everyday occurrence. We had just been shaking hands, and before our hands separated, he had departed this life. Is this something to be upset about? No. Is it something for regret? No again. The glory [of the Revolution] is colored by blood! I myself could be lying in my own blood any day, any time.

Night had turned into day, but Ye Ting's prediction did not come true. The enemy was far from retreating. None of us had slept a wink all night.

It was October 1, two whole months since the August First Uprising.

At eight o'clock in the morning, the commander of the Second Regiment of the Third Division was brought down, dead from multiple wounds to his head. Now there were fewer wounded and more dead being brought down from the front.

Weak from hunger and exhaustion, we did not make any headway that morning. By now, we had thrown all our forces into battle, including the Headquarters guards.

Afternoon overtook morning, but there was still no let up at the front. The commander of the Third Regiment was wounded.

By the night of October 1, we were still stuck. The discarded weapons of the dead and dying were piling up higher and higher.

The commander-in-chief kept going to the front, but we could not break through. Even Ye Ting's men, known as the Iron Warriors, could not turn the situation around. The enemy numbers were overwhelming, and they had the strategic advantage of the high ground.

Close to dawn, I went to Headquarters again. They were sipping milk and nibbling biscuits. They had gone without sleep and without any proper food, either, for two nights. Enlai was still looking like a quack as he hovered over his box of documents. Liu Bocheng, with a patch over one eye, paced the room anxiously. Having gone without food for two days, I also nibbled a few biscuits.

The situation at the front suddenly became even more tense. Reports came in that the enemy was preparing to sweep down in a frontal assault. We went out to take a look, but bullets were flying everywhere, and we had to duck for cover.

After a brief consultation, we decided to retreat. Headquarters would go first, then we people at the Political Department, and last the various divisions. We would retreat to Jieyang, whence we had come.

Retreating, we at the Political Department had the difficult job of dealing with baggage, documents, and above all, discarded weapons, which were more than the hired carriers could handle. My boss Liao was not around, so I took charge. We discarded unessential baggage and documents. I took the lead in shouldering an extra burden of two rifles. The others seeing me do this, followed suit.

It was dawn by the time we were ready to go.

It was forty *li* back to Jieyang. After two nights without sleep and two days without food, we were carrying arms, documents, canteens and other paraphernalia, and we had to run, with the enemy in hot pursuit.

Two flags flapped forlornly ahead of us as Headquarters led the retreat.

"Damn it!" an old soldier from the Twenty-fourth Division spat out.

"I have never retreated since I first picked up a gun. This is my first!"

"Do we really have to retreat? Why can't we fight to the finish?"

"Think of the reputation of the Revolutionary Army!" another added.

With soldiers like these, we will prevail, I thought to myself.

We had three Divisions behind us to cover our retreat. For the moment, the enemy did not seem to be pressing hard, so we gave ourselves some breathing space.

After we had covered twenty *li,* Headquarters ahead stopped to rest in a wooded area, and we followed suit. I put down the two rifles I had been shouldering—what a relief!

I saluted the commander-in-chief [He Long]. His face turned scarlet[1] like the Guan Yu figure in Chinese opera. He said, "Take a break!" and I sat down among them.

Peng Pai popped up from nowhere. He has seen us people at the Political Department each carrying two extra rifles over and above our regular load, and he commended us loudly. "Once we reach Hai-Lu-Feng," he said, "we will be all right; the peasants there are wildly supportive of us." I knew of course that he was trying to cheer us up.

After a twenty-minute break, we resumed our retreat back to Jieyang.

The day before yesterday as we left Jieyang, we had kept asking how much distance we had covered? Five *li*? Seven *li*? Ten *li*?—we had been frustrated by the fact that we were making such slow progress, that we had not left Jieyang firmly behind us. Now we were frustrated that Jieyang was so far ahead.

We finally reached Jieyang at ten o'clock in the morning and bivouacked in the quarters of the Businessmen's Association as we had

1. Presumably from embarrassment, not belligerency. Zhu was making a snide insinuation against He Long because he (Zhu) had earlier questioned the feasibility of this campaign and was now proved right.

done before.

Orders came down that we must eat a meal immediately and start off for Chaozhou [which we had taken and which was now being garrisoned by the Third Division under Zhou Yiqun]. Having gone two days without food, we needed to eat. But as I mentioned earlier, our supplies had been taken ahead to Tangkeng. The staff foraged for food and did the best they could, but before we could eat, orders came down that the enemy was on our heels in the outskirts of Jieyang and we had to leave immediately. Helpless, we stuffed half-cooked mush into our bags and were on the run again. Forgetting about food and sleep, we ran for our lives.

A river ran immediately outside the gates of the town of Jieyang. There were five or six ferries there. How long would it take them to ferry us, an army of over ten thousand, across the river?[2]

Headquarters decided that an armed escort should lead the way, followed by us at the Political Department, then in turn followed by Headquarters, and finally followed by the bulk of the troops, bringing up the rear.

It occurred to me that being at the front of a retreating army had its advantages. Now that we had left the extra weapons with Headquarters, our burden was much lighter.

After some waiting, we were ferried across the river. It was raining, and many people fell into the water, only to be dragged up like chickens plucked out of soup. Helped over by two porters and two orderlies, I was lucky not fall into the river, though I was covered in mud by the time I got ashore.

We finished crossing by midnight.

Orders came down: no stopping day or night until we reached Chaozhou.

"How far are we from Chaozhou?" I asked the hired guide. "A hundred and twenty *li* by the main road, and a 150 *li* by back roads. But

2. Zhu earlier put the number at thirty thousand (page 247) and again at "over ten thousand" (page 162). Some were kept back for garrison duty, and there were some depletions along the way.

the condition of the back roads is terrible, worse than walking 200 *li*!"

Good heavens, two days and two nights without food or sleep, and now to walk 150 *li* in the rain, and no stopping along the way!

It was October 2. In our homeland south of the Yangtze, it would be the beginning of fall.

But we were still wearing the summer uniforms we had marched out of Nanchang wearing, and we were shivering with cold. Heaven itself seemed set against us, with nonstop rain and dropping temperatures. I wished I had bought a sweater earlier on.

As I mentioned, it was past midnight by the time we were all ferried across the river. Although I could hardly lift my feet, I had to keep marching forward—no, I should say, marching *back* to Chaozhou.

I chatted with Chen Zhangpu as we walked. He was head of Propaganda. Back when we were in Chaozhou, there had been a plan to move him to the Sixth Regiment as Political director and for me to replace him as head of Propaganda. But nothing had come of it. "If I had been moved to the Sixth Regiment, I would have been spared all this . . ." he said ruefully. Indeed, the Sixth regiment, under the Third Division, had been left behind in Chaozhou. "Well, if I had been moved to the General Political Department, I would be sitting comfortably in Shantou right now," I remarked uselessly.

Chen Zhangpu was from Changsha in Hunan Province and had served as head of the political department of the First Division of the Thirty-fifth Army. Though handicapped with a lingering Hunan accent, Chen was a first-rate orator with a resounding voice, unlike the shrill tones of Mao Zedong [who was also from Hunan]. Chen had been Mao Zedong's classmate and told me many anecdotes about the latter. When Mao was on the wanted list of the warlord Zhao Hengti, he had taken refuge in Chen's home for two months.

We chatted as we marched, struggling to lift our feet with every step.

By two in the afternoon, the rain had stopped. Whenever we passed through a village, the locals made thin porridge. I had always disliked porridge, but now I lapped up three bowlsful as if it was the best shark fin soup. With something in our bellies, we continued our retreat.

Back in the days when we were marching in Jiangxi, I remember seeing Liao Qianwu move slowly forward with the help of a walking stick while keeping his eyes closed. I had wondered how he managed to sleep while walking. But now I understood, as we ourselves now walked in a kind of semi-stupor. Due to our numbers, there was no danger of falling down.

Soon it was dark. We passed another village and again got some porridge. We asked the way to Chaozhou. "A full 100 *li!*" we were told. Well, it meant that we had at least covered one third of our route by the back roads. There were another 100 *li,* true, but at least we had covered fifty *li.*

We could not stop for a break—Headquarters had strict orders. Besides, if we did take a break, everybody would have fallen into a deep sleep, and we would not have been able to continue on. So we stayed on our feet and moved on, buoyed by the strength of our convictions. But for the hired porters, it was a different matter. Unlike us, they had no convictions to support them. In this sense, they suffered more than we did. They needed rest. Overtired, they would throw down their packs and refuse to move. When nothing else worked, we had to use whips to urge them on. We had no other resources. Under our whips, the porters struggled on painfully, but our hearts were aching even more.

We kept moving in the dark. It was our third day without proper food or sleep, but we were not cast down in spirit. Secretary Yang lifted his voice in a marching song. Chen Zhangpu started to sing the Young Vanguards' song:

> Advance! Dawn is beckoning! Comrades, fight on . . .

The sounds were uplifting, and we moved on.

> Su Wu[3] in the barbarian wilds, his honor unstained;
> In ice and snow he held out for nineteen years . . .

A woman's voice broke out in song.

"Who is the female comrade singing? . . ." There were no female

3. Su Wu (140–60 BCE), minister at court of the Western Han dynasty, sent on a mission to the "barbarian" Xiongnu tribes and held captive for nearly twenty years.

comrades in our ranks.

> The north wind rises, the cranes arrive from the Han pass;
> The white-haired mother, missing her son; the bride in an empty chamber;
> Asleep in the wee hours, who is dreaming of whom? . . .

"Oh, it's you, Miss Hong!"

"How are you, Comrade Ya Lin,"[4] we shook hands warmly.

Miss Hong had been marching ahead of us with the officers of Army Command, but having fallen asleep on the way (like us she had gone three days and nights without sleep) she lost touch with her group and—luckily for us—she now joined our group.

With a pretty young woman in our midst, we became energized.

> The first moon of the New Year, every family lights red lanterns,
> Other families are happily united,
> Mengjiang buries her husband under the Great Wall . . .

"And what about your husband . . . ?"

Hong ignored the question and continued to sing:

> In the second moon, it is getting warmer,
> swallows are flying south in pairs . . .

The presence of a woman was stimulating. Since Hong joined us, our feet felt lighter and we moved faster.

"Damn it! I haven't touched a woman in five months. When we get to Chaozhou, I've gotta find a broad and make it up to myself . . ." The man spoke in a Sichuan accent. He was also, like Hong, with General Headquarters and had lagged behind. His words were coarse and offensive, especially with a woman present.

But Hong didn't seem bothered and continued to sing:

> Pitter-patter goes the rain . . .

though it was not raining, and the moon peeped out now and then from behind the dark clouds.

"Come on, another one! . . ." someone shouted.

---

4. Ya Lin, one of Zhu Qihua's pseudonyms. not to be confused with Ya Ling, another pseudonym, which appears in the Whampoa record.

"Come on! . . ." others joined in, with sounds of clapping.

Hong said: "Give me a Peking opera aria, and I will sing some more . . ."

> Under the moonlight, the hero had a fright . . .

someone ventured a line, and then stopped.

"Go on!" a voice piped up, but there was no response. Then someone else started to sing a line from *The Empty City Trap*:

> I was just enjoying the view from atop the city wall,
> When there was a commotion. Asking what it is about,
> I am told it is an army led by Sima . . .

"Damn it! When are we getting to Chaozhou? I can't move my feet anymore . . ."

> . . . every happening, every event, tell your loved one, without fail . . .

Someone started to imitate a shrill female voice.

> Workers, Peasants, Soldiers, let us unite, let us march on, ten thousand hearts as one.
> We march forward, we fight on,
> We hold uprisings, we make sacrifices.
> We smash the stronghold of international imperialism . . .

"Heavens, my stomach is growling!"

In this melee of sound, we managed to drag ourselves forward. Looking back, I cannot imagine how we could have advanced otherwise.

Suddenly someone up ahead shouted: "Comrades, we're in Chaozhou!"

"You're dreaming! Chaozhou is dozens of *li* away!"

"If we are not in Chaozhou, how do you explain this paved road?" the first speaker retorted. Indeed, we found ourselves on a smooth paved road.

"Oh no, we must have lost our way. This is not Chaozhou, this is Shantou, look at the buildings ahead!"

"Impossible! Shantou is on the other side!"

"Have we reached Canton? Isn't that the Yellow Sand Railway Station?"

"You are out of your mind!"

"Guide! What is that place ahead?" I thought it must be a county town, but couldn't identify which.

"Guide! Where is the guide?" Everybody started shouting for the guides, but there was no response. We realized that the guides had slipped away.

"It's Fengshun, and Li Jishen is waiting for us, ready to snap us up in his jaws. We have slipped into the lion's mouth. How did we manage to get lost?"

"It's that singing that got us addled . . ." someone grumbled.

"Comrades, keep calm, let's not lose our heads. This is not Fengshun, and we are not lost. Our second-in-command had just passed through this area."

We walked along the smooth paved road, wondering at a paved road in the middle of nowhere.

By the light of the moon, we saw that we were approaching, not a city, but a building.

"What a huge mansion!"

"More like a minister's residence!"

It was a vast edifice, obviously with hundreds of rooms inside. By the dim light of the moon, we could also see gardens laid out. We ultimately made our way to the front. The massive iron gates were more imposing than those of the Bank of Hong Kong on the Bund in Shanghai. The perimeter of the wall must have been many *li,* broken here and there by side gates. The main gate opened to the paved road. Running parallel to the road was a river. Two sturdy cement bridges guarded the main gate on each side, like the stone lions in front of the Bank of Hong Kong. The entrance was lit on each side by gas lamps, by the light of which we could make out the contours of the building.

"What is this place anyway? It is like an emperor's palace!"

"Look, comrades, there is even electric lighting." Indeed there were electric light bulbs, though there was no electricity—only the gas lamps were working.

"Could it be Chen Jiongming's residence?"

"Nonsense, General Chen's residence is in Haifeng."

"How can there be such a grand building and such a nicely paved road out in the countryside?" I couldn't figure it out.

The huge edifice lay in complete silence, with no sign of life inside.

"Oh no, we must be mesmerized by the fox spirit. Haven't you read *Strange Tales from a Chinese Studio*?[5] This whole thing is conjured up by fox spirits to confuse us."

"Comrade, please do not speak such nonsense."

"Report! I suggest that we go in and take a look," a comrade from the Propaganda Section suggested. I agreed, but knock on the gate as hard as we could, there was no response.

"We can climb over the wall and take a look inside," someone suggested.

"No," I said, "let us make haste to reach Chaozhou. Once there, we'll get some rest . . ."

The prospect of an actual place was a stronger attraction than the baffling building, so we resumed our march.

By the time we had all crossed the exquisitely designed concrete bridge, it was close to four in the morning. Once across the bridge, we were surrounded by fields, but the paved road was still there, cutting through the fields.

We started out with renewed determination, but whichever way we went, we still found ourselves back on the paved road, close to the grand mansion.

"How strange, no matter which way we walk, we are always end up back here."

"We've been bewitched by the headless ghost. We're on the road to death."

"I told you so. We're under the spell of fox spirits. No matter which way we go, we cannot escape her spell. We can keep walking till next year, and we'll still be here." The fellow found satisfaction in the fact that his theory of fox spirits had been validated.

Everybody had a theory. Amid a babble of voices, we kept milling

5. By Qing dynasy writer Pu Songling (1649–1715).

around that edifice in spite of ourselves. Having dragged ourselves through three days and three nights without proper food and rest, it was true that we were lightheaded, as if under a spell.

"Comrades, let's stop here and have a good rest. It will soon be daybreak, and our Headquarters is still behind us." My words worked. Soon everybody had settled down on the clean pavement and dropped off to sleep.

I have always been a light sleeper; the slightest noise will wake me up: if there's an appointment for a certain hour, I wake up at the exact time right on the dot. But now I'd lost the knack—the minute I lay down I fell into a deep sleep and was only wakened up by a string of sharp reports of gunfire. I sat up and looked around me. The sun was shining down on our group—all in deep slumber. By my watch, it was nine in the morning. Under the steady glare of the morning sun, the building seemed all the more imposing.

I wondered from which direction the gunshots had come as I shook my comrades awake. The minute I dragged one up, another would flop down drowsily. Finally when I managed to get everybody up, I told them about the gunshots.

"Impossible," said Head of Propaganda Chen, "you're mistaken . . ."

Just then gunshots rang out sharply, followed by a deep silence.

After four hours' sleep, everybody was in better shape, and started to investigate the source of the gunfire.

"First of all, we must figure out the distance to Chaozhou, and the way to get there. We must get hold of some locals to help." I sent a few comrades out to look for some locals.

After a while, some locals showed up. We learned that we were in countryside which was within Chaozhou County jurisdiction, and that Chaozhou proper was another forty-eight *li* away. Obviously we had not lost our way: only yesterday, according to the locals, our second-in-command had passed through. After spending the night in a local household, he had just left, at dawn that very morning.

As to the grand edifice, we learned that it was the villa of a landowner/businessman from Southeast Asia who owned homes in Chaozhou, Shantou, Canton, Hong Kong, Macau, as well as Singapore.

All the land in the area belonged to him, added our informant.

As to the mystery of why we could not leave the paved road behind us after all that walking, it turned out that the road was circular by design—if you didn't take a side road, you would never leave the [main] road! The locals also explained that every household here owned guns and that gunshots were commonplace.

After answering all our questions, the locals offered to guide us to Chaozhou. Forty-eight *li* was no big deal after all that we had been through, but we were hungry. I asked staff to take some money and ask the locals to make porridge. We stayed put and waited for our porridge outside the gate of the grand building. Some comrades tried to climb over the walls, but the top of the wall was studded with jagged pieces of glass.

The sun shone down, warming us up. Hong snuggled next to me. I tensed up at the contact. I yearned to hold her and join our two bodies, then blushed at the thought.

After some porridge, we were ready to set out with the locals as our guides. There were still no news from Headquarters, which should have been behind us [according to the formation of the retreat from Jieyang].

After we had covered twenty *li* toward Chaozhou, we got the most alarming news: *Chaozhou has been taken by the enemy!* These locals were part of the Peasants' Association and were on our side and completely reliable. They gave us detailed information about how the enemy had encircled Chaozhou and how our troops had made their escape.

It was like a clap of thunder. We had toughed it out through three days virtually without food and sleep—the only thing that kept us going was the hope of Chaozhou! If Chaozhou was lost, not only would we have no haven, no refuge, it meant that all was lost. I could not bear to face the reality of the loss of Chaozhou; I couldn't imagine how it could happen. We had a whole division, the Third Division under Zhou Yiqun, stationed there. Even if the enemy had attacked, wouldn't there be fierce combat? The Third Division could not have given up without a fight! And if so, why did we not hear of it? And if the Third Division had been beaten, where could the men have retreated except in our direction to join the main body of our forces [retreating from Jiechang]. And if so, why was it that we had not seen a single soldier in retreat from Chaozhou? It did not make any sense at all.

On the other hand, we could not dismiss what the locals were saying.

We were now faced with the question: if Chaozhou was indeed taken by the enemy, what should we do? Of course we could simply retrace our steps. But where to? The point was, if Chaozhou [garrisoned by the Third Division] was taken, it meant that Shantou was lost, and if Sanheba was lost, it meant that all was lost! The news was like a bucket of ice water poured over our heads. Hong held my hand and asked, "What shall we do, Ya Lin?"

"I think we should go farther down the road and wait for more information. I still doubt that Chaozhou is lost. Even if we didn't run into retreating soldiers of the Third Division, our second-in-command and his men ahead of us should have turned back by now! Why have we heard nothing from them?" Saying which, I gave her shoulder a squeeze, and she blushed.

So it was decided that we would follow my advice and walk a little farther. By now our group had swelled to about four hundred people, because the Eleventh Army which was behind us [in the retreat from Jieyang] had by now caught up with us. With the slim hope that the news was false and that we might still find food and drink in Chaozhou, we walked on, determined.

About five or six *li* farther on, our hopes were completely dashed. The escort of the second-in-command [who had been ahead of us] had retraced his steps and met up with us. It is true, he said, both Chaozhou and Shantou have been taken by the Guangxi warlord Huang Xuchu, and our second-in-command himself has fled to who knows where. Or he might have been taken by Huang Xuchu, whose scouts were four or five *li* ahead.

At this news, we four hundred were dumbstruck.

"Lost! All is lost!" Hong wailed.

"What shall we do?" was on everyone's lips.

"Don't worry. It's the hazard of war. Our retreat is a strategic move.

But for now, since we cannot go forward, the only thing we can do is to march back. But," I added, "since the enemy in Chaozhou is only twenty *li* from where we are, we must be prepared in case they pursue us." After some consultation, it was decided that comrades from the Eleventh Army would form up to protect our retreat, while we also armed ourselves.

We retraced our steps, expecting to meet up with Headquarters, which had been behind us according to the formation [of the retreat after crossing the river in Jieyang].

After walking about ten *li* back the way we came, hoping to run into Headquarters, we were in for a new shock. It turned out that after crossing the river, Headquarters had not marched in our wake as planned. The fact was, they had barely started out before they ran into the remnants of the Third Division after the latter's defeat in Chaozhou. Thus the members of the Revolutionary Committee and the remnants of the routed Third Army were all gathered [outside] Jieyang.

Headquarters decided then and there, we now learned, first to regroup in Paotai, and from there to head off for Hai-Lu-Feng. But our group had already left by then, and General Headquarters had sent a staff member to catch up with us to give us the latest decision, with orders for us to join General Headquarters in Paotai. Now this messenger had finally caught up with us.

"How far is it to Paotai?" Hong asked.

"Eighty *li* by the main road, but under the circumstances, we must take the back road, which is about a hundred *li*," the staff member answered.

"Oh no, another hundred *li*!" someone muttered dejectedly.

By now the enemy, which had taken Chaozhou, was barely twenty *li* away, while Jieyang at the other end was occupied by the enemy, which was also about twenty *li* away, according to a staff member. After three days and three nights basically without food or sleep, we were now hemmed in by the enemy in front and behind.

"Comrades, come on, let's make it to Paotai as soon as possible!" a soldier from the Eleventh Army burst out.

Our local guide knew the way to Paotai, so instead of being led to Chaozhou, we now changed course and followed him on the back road to Paotai.

By the time we were ready to go, it was almost two in the afternoon. The weather was fine, and we followed our guide along the back road, not daring to stop for food or drink. It was only after we had covered over ten *li* that we felt safe enough to stop for some porridge in a village. Hong managed to cajole a peasant household into giving her two [boiled] eggs and gave me one. I never liked eggs, but now I took a bite and thought it delicious.

"What day is it today?" Hong suddenly asked me.

"October third," I told her.

"It is my birthday, today I turn eighteen."

"Then let me give you this egg for your birthday," saying which, I stuffed my unfinished egg into her mouth; she did not object but just smiled at me. "Thank you," she said in a low voice, as we shook hands firmly.

We still had around ninety *li* to go, and could not afford to linger.

We walked nonstop that whole night, and reached Paotai at dawn.

We met up with Headquarters, and hoped for a chance to catch our breath.

But it was not to be. Headquarters was just starting off for Guanfu. We had no choice but to follow. Luckily for us, Guanfu was just forty *li* away.

Headquarters had hired a steamship, and I was invited to join them. There was only space for one; the rest of my team at the Political Department could not be accommodated. The idea of getting some rest was appealing, especially as I was half-dead after four days on the march. But what about my staff at the Political Department? My boss Liao Qianwu was not around, I was in charge. I could not leave my men for the sake of my own comfort.

I thanked Headquarters and said I would rather stay with my men, but suggested that Miss Hong, who was really suffering, be allowed to get on the steamship instead. Headquarters gladly agreed. But Miss Hong did not gratefully accept as I had expected.

"Are you getting on the boat?" she asked.

"No, I am not, but you're exhausted. Do get on the boat."

"If you are not getting on the boat, then neither am I. Let us stay together," she said firmly. I was indescribably happy; I really did not want us to be separated.

Thus Hong and I continued to walk together. I must confess that I never had any designs on Miss Hong, though our comradely affection was more than ordinary friendship. I knew that back when she was still at the Wuhan campus she stood out among her peers. But since we started out from Nanchang on this march, I got to know her better. Being thrown together with Hong during this retreat, I could not help being affected. Women do have a special power, and I felt myself strangely drawn [to her]. Though I treasure the memory of my young lady in Canton, I couldn't bear to be away from Miss Hong. We walked together, we rested together, and we chatted together. Our intimacy was noticed by our comrades, and they assumed that we had come to an understanding. But Miss Hong and I, we were very candid about our relationship. Miss Hong knew about my young lady in Canton. Hong and I talked about everything: our backgrounds, our views of the situation, what we read; we talked about everything under the sun with the single exception of love. Whenever our conversation verged on the topic of love, we would skirt around it.

We had started out for Guanfu on the morning of October 5 and arrived at about two in the afternoon. When we found our way to our base, I lay down and slept like the dead. Refreshed from a good night's sleep, I was ready for the new march. But my spirits were dashed by the absence of Hong; she was assigned to work at the Revolutionary Committee. I walked alone dejectedly, feeling the pain of her absence.

We covered sixty *li* that same day.

I reviewed in my mind all that had transpired during this campaign:

We had been defeated at Tangkeng [our first destination] and had lost one-third of our forces.

Then, the defeat of the Third Division in Chaozhou, an additional loss.

Added to that, we had lost touch with the Twenty-fifth Division stationed at Sanheba.

As a result, we had four Divisions in name (the First, the Second, the Third, the Twenty-fifth), but only two Divisions in reality. Obviously, it would be impossible to take Canton with this meager force.

We were now heading for Hai-Lu-Feng [Hifeng-Lufeng area] where we held a solid base. There, we could garner popular support and wait for another opportunity to march on Canton.

We set out on the morning of October 6; our first stop would be Yunluo, where we planned to camp for the night.

At two in the afternoon, we arrived at Liusha, which was very close—only a dozen *li* or so to Yunluo. The locals of Liusha made porridge, and members of the Revolutionary Committee and General Headquarters rested in the quarters of the Peasants' Association. It was uplifting to see the flag of the Peasants' Association, adorned with the sign of the sickle, looking down on us from on high—the first time we had seen this flag since entering Guangdong territory.

[Zhou] Enlai was sick; he could not even swallow porridge.

At about three in the afternoon, after resting for an hour or so, we made ready to resume our march.

Just then, the sound of shots rang out. The enemy was on our right, positioned on a small hill in front of us. Headquarters decided to stay put in Liusha to direct the battle. After that defeat in Tangkeng, my heart always sank at the sound of gunfire.

As the battle was being engaged on the hillock to the right, shots rang out from the left. Ye Ting led his Twenty-fourth Division and held the enemy on the right, while He Jinzhai's First Division engaged the enemy on the left. After an hour or so of exchanging fire, our side began to falter. We pulled out all our forces, including the rifle brigade of General Staff led by Li Mingke himself. But the outlook was not good.

At about half past four in the afternoon, after more than an hour's fighting, Headquarters ordered the forces from both left and right to make a concerted dash through the center, hoping to make it to Yunluo, and to plan our next move once safely there.

But it was not to be. We were hardly two *li* on our way before we were surprised by more enemy forces *in front* of us.

At the sound of shots, our ranks broke in disarray, our gear cast off, everyone racing toward the rear in an unstoppable wave.

Unlike that defeat outside of Tangkeng when we had conducted a planned retreat, this time we were like a breaking wave. We ran for our lives as the enemy pursued us from right, left and behind. Bullets whistled past our ears. As I ran, I was aware of people falling down around me. Both my orderlies were close at my side, and then the older one dropped to the ground. I could do nothing for him, and kept running. My legs had been so heavy through the march of the last couple of days that I could hardly lift them. But now I ran like the wind.

As I ran along with the fleeing mass, I was conscious of being with Tan Pingshan, Ye Ting, Zhou Enlai, Yun Daiying, Guo Moruo and others, except that I could not locate He Long, the commander-in-chief, and my boss, Liao Qianwu, and I wondered about their absence. But I kept running, sticking with the crowd. Bullets flew everywhere to the sounds of the enemy's wolf-like howling: *Sha! Sha! Sha!* [Kill! Kill! Kill!]

Suddenly I was aware of a young woman in front of me being hit. She dropped down like a slaughtered lamb, and lay unmoving.

"Is it Hong?!" Heedless of everything around me, I ran to where the body lay, unmoving. My God! She had been shot in the head. She had stopped breathing.

For a moment, I lost consciousness and fell at her feet.

As if in a dream, I felt something hit me in the leg and I regained consciousness to see my leg soaked in blood. I had been shot. Blood was seeping from a hole in my trousers, but it was not a deep wound. The group that I was fleeing with had now disappeared into the distance, and I was alone. All around me were people lying on the ground, dead. Hong lay quietly by my side. "My dear comrade, . . ." I murmured as

I embraced her, smeared with her blood. Hong's body lay softly in my embrace.

I sat holding her, and could not control my tears. I rarely ever cried. "Blood, not tears!" had been my motto, but now I cried helplessly.

"I am not killed!" I said defiantly as I stood up, my heart bursting with rage.

The enemy had disappeared in pursuit of our fleeing forces, and I took Hong up in my arms. What was I to do with her body? There was a deserted cottage down the road and I brought Hong's body over, placing it in an empty room. What was I to do? I could not stay and keep a wake for her. More enemy were coming and I would be asking for death at their hands. A meaningless sacrifice, not what Hong would have wanted for me. I found a scrap of paper, took out a fountain pen from my pocket and wrote: "These are the remains of Miss Hong XX. Please give her a burial. You have my heartfelt gratitude!"

I kissed Hong's stone-cold forehead and walked out of the cottage. But I could not bear to leave, I went back for another look, tears streaming down my face. "Goodbye, Hong!" I said firmly and walked away.

The sound of gunfire had quieted down. I ran eastward, trying to catch up with my comrades. Under these circumstances, it was a matter of life and death to stay with a group.

I was able to walk despite the wound in my leg, and fortunately I caught up with my group—Tan Pingshan, Zhou Enlai, Zhang Guotao, Guo Moruo, Wu Yuzhang, Ye Ting, Yun Daiying—they were all there among the crowd.

It was getting dark. We sat down on a knoll to catch our breath. What next? We had no idea.

An artillary shell exploded on the knoll where we were sitting. Some people in the crowd dropped dead. I rolled down the knoll and fell into a gully, clambered up and ran for my life, forgetting everything—Hong's death, the wound in my leg, my very life. I just ran. Bullets whistled by. People were running all around me.

We kept running off and on for more than two hours, finally shaking off the pursuing enemy. It was night and I sat down on a knoll to catch my breath. The stars looked down silently on the hilly countryside around me, and I thought of Hong. Dead!

To most people, Hong's death would be considered a tragedy: so young, so bright, so attractive, to die at the tender age of eighteen, thousands of *li* away from home, with no one to see to her burial. But to us revolutionaries, such a death was a fitting end to a revolutionary life. It was not a tragedy, but a glorious death. Hong had fulfilled her ultimate commitment to the Revolution!

As I sat there musing, I became aware of the pain in my leg. More serious, I discovered that my pistol was gone. The gun that I had acquired in Huapo County, Henan Province from the hands of that rascally police chief Feng Guobi! I had treasured it—it was my weapon:

> Open a path
> With sword and gun!

I loved that song. But now I did not know who was holding my gun!

That day—October 6, 1927—will remain one of the most memorable days of my life—the conference in Liusha,[6] the military defeat, the rout of the Revolutionary Committee, the death of my beloved Comrade Hong, the loss of my weapon. My life has become a leaf in the wind—who knows where the winds of fate would fling me? Whatever it is, let it come!

Now that my group had rested, we decided to move on.

As I walked in the darkness, I was suddenly gripped by dread—I had lost touch with the people that I knew—Pingshan, Daiying, Moruo, Yuzhang, Enlai! I could not find them among the people that I was now walking with. They were all strangers, the people that I was walking with right then! And it is dangerous to be among strangers when you were fleeing for your life.

I put my hand over my pocket. My gun was gone, but I still had a lot

6. The conference at Liusha—presumably Zhu Qihua was present.

of cash on me. There was a sum worth twenty to thirty thousand *yuan* belonging to the Political Department, composed mostly of foreign currency: 2,000 dollars in U.S. currency, 100 pounds in banknotes, and 10,000 *yuan* in the unconvertible Wuhan government-issued currency. It had been in the keeping of the cashier and borne by the hired porters with our other baggage. When we were setting out from Guanfu, I had worried about its safety and took it out. I gave the 10,000 in Wuhan currency to a staffer by the name of Zhou, and kept the rest on my own person. Now, after the debacle of Liusha, the personnel of the Political Department were scattered.

With the foreign cash on my person, I felt more or less reassured. Not that I had any designs on public funds. It meant that I could not only save myself, but also had the means to save other comrades in trouble.

For a moment, I thought I could go back and give Hong a proper burial, and even return in the future to hold memorials for her on the day of her death. But I immediately realized that it was a fantasy: it was out of the question for me to go back to the village, much less to hold a memorial for her. Besides, such a fantasy was totally meaningless: even if I had been able to bury her and hold a memorial, Hong herself would not have allowed it. To a true revolutionary like Hong, there is nothing after death. An emperor's funeral is no different from a beggar dying of exposure. Hong did not need a meaningless show for her memory to live on. I would march on in the trail of her blood!

After crossing several more hills during the night, it was daylight by the time we reached a village. Now it was perfectly clear to me that I had lost touch with my friends and associates; I had been cast among complete strangers. They were mostly soldiers from the Twenty-fourth Division, led by Commander [Gu],[7] who was not a personal acquaintance of mine. There were two others who had been with the Workers and Peasants' Committee whom I had run into in the course

7. Gu, the only officer that is not mentioned by given name, although he is referred to at least four times in the text (see pages 218, 255, 280, 281)—a clue that Zhu Qihua may have deleted Gu's given name, owing to the uncomplimentary remarks he made about the man.

of work, but I didn't know their names and we had never spoken. I did not like them; they had the look of the stock villain in traditional drama. As for Gu of the Twenty-fourth Division, I knew that he had served under Ye Ting and was not a CCP member, and I knew for a fact that he was a knave. To be in the company of two villains and one knave! In any case, they ignored me with contempt.

Having walked since the afternoon of the day before, I was now hungry. I followed this new group into a village, where the locals prepared some porridge. Commander Gu's orderly, however, secured two chickens and made soup for his master. The two villains joined him, fawning all the while, but they ignored me. Without so much as a "by your leave," I sat down and helped myself to the chicken, picking out the choicest cuts. Commander Gu didn't seem to mind, but the two villains gave me ugly looks, which I totally ignored. "Fawning dogs!" I cursed them under my breath. *If villains like these are not purged, there will be no hope for the CCP,* I thought to myself.

There was no point in fleeing with the likes of these; with about thirty rifles between us, what could we hope to accomplish, not to mention the fact that they had cold-shouldered me all the while. I decided to take off on my own. But it was easier said than done. I had cash on me, true, but stuck in my military uniform, how could I make my way around the Guangdong countryside? Especially for someone like me, who would be listed as a "fugitive officer of the renegade army."

Just as I was weighing the pros and cons, a small group appeared down the road in the distance, three men and three women, six altogether. My wish had come true: some of them were familiar faces. Wu Ming was an old acquaintance. Then there was Li Renyu, political instructor of the Seventieth Regiment, and Qin Guangyuan, commander of the Second Division, all acquaintances of mine. I did not know the three women, but I was sure that they had been classmates of Hong, and the thought saddened me. If Hong had been among them, what a joy that would have been! How we would have clasped our hands tightly together and never let go. But no, it was not Hong, it will never be Hong, except in my dreams.

Wu Ming and I shook hands as we gazed at each other wordlessly. We had not been close in the past, but I felt that Wu Ming was dependable, and I was glad to join up with him. If not for thoughts of Hong, which weighed heavily on me, I would have shouted for joy.

The rascally Gu had left with his men, and I stayed behind and joined Wu Ming's group. We were now four men and three women.

As the new arrivals stopped for a meal, Wu Ming and I talked over our situation. Our forces had been completely routed. We were now left each to his own devices. Wu Ming and I decided to head for Shantou—from Shantou we could easily reach either Shanghai or Hong Kong. Before my new companions had finished their meal, more stragglers approached in the distance, this time around forty soldiers. We decided to avoid them. We scrambled up a knoll and lay close to the ground among the bushes, not daring to sit up. I did not move even when huge spider-like creatures crawled over me. My thoughts flew to Hong, wondering if such creatures had violated her remains; I could not bear to think of it. We lay low for a full two hours before the soldiers disappeared. Only then did our little group of seven continue our march.

We had no idea where Shantou was located, but we figured that we could not go wrong if we kept heading south. That same night we stayed with a peasant household. Wu Ming had silver coins in his keeping, so we were able to buy two chickens for our meal.

We needed to change into civilian clothes to enter Shantou, and use Shantou as a steppingstone to Shanghai or Hong Kong. But in the backwoods we were passing through, all we could manage to buy was the simplest kind of peasant clothing. In a short yellow peasant jacket and dark blue wide pants all made of coarse homespun, I still sported a pair of expensive spectacles and a stylish haircut, though I did not wave my hair or use gel. This outfit matched with a pair of straw sandals on my feet completed the very picture of oddity. I could not help laughing at myself. But it was better than appearing in military uniform

I took care to secure the cash on my person. The foreign banknotes I wrapped up and tied inside my trousers; the Hong Kong currency I packed separately and kept ready to hand.

The next morning, October 8, we were able to find a local guide who had been with the Peasants' Association and was sympathetic to us.

The man advised against going to Shantou—it was too far away and the place was teaming with spies. He told us that there was a little port nearby called Jiazi Harbor, where we could board a vessel straight for Hong Kong. We agreed and arrived at Jiazi Harbor the next day, October 9. It was a lively little place with a market, and we were able to sit down to a solid meal.

Despite our precautions, the seven of us made a strange impression in that small place in rural Guangdong, especially the three young women, who immediately attracted a crowd of curious spectators. It would not be a big deal in the villages—the peasants could gawk all they liked—but here it was dangerous. If we ran into the local defense regiment, we would be in serious trouble. Our guide was aware of the situation; he told us that there was no vessel for Hong Kong that day, and that it was dangerous to spend the night in this place. If we hired a sailboat, he said, we could set sail right away, though the price would be steep. Money was not a problem. Wu Ming, Qin Guangyuan, and Li Renyu all had cash on their persons, and of course so did I. For the price of 800 *yuan*, we hired a private boat.

It was a large sailboat which was anchored offshore, and we had to reach it by a little skiff. We had expected to set sail the minute we got on the boat. But in fact we had to wait for the tide. But once on the boat, we felt safe. Overcome by the extreme fatigue of the last few days, we promptly fell asleep. We were shaken out of a deep sleep by our guide. In great alarm, he whispered "Run for your lives." He did not stop to explain but made us follow him. The moon looked down coldly from behind thick clouds. In the dim light, we saw a boat in the distance heading our way.

Our guide got us into a small rowboat and kept urging on the oarsman. The seven of us dared not make a sound. We had no clue as to what was going on, leaving everything to fate. By the light of the new moon, we could make out cliffs in the distance, and the gleam of the moon reflected in the water. The rowboat was skimming swiftly over the water as we seven kept our heads down, being taken we knew not where, escaping from we knew not what. It would be a poetic scene, except that we were not in a poetic mood.

Our little rowboat was definitely swifter than the boat in pursuit. Soon we were out of their line of vision and after two hours in the rowboat we went ashore, not in Jiazi Harbor of course, but somewhere farther down the coast.

We had abandoned the sailboat in such haste that I had forgotten my shoes. I was not aware of the problem when fleeing in the rowboat, but how my feet hurt once we went ashore! I tottered along in excruciating pain as we continued our flight over a dirt road. Our pursuers having lost us at sea now resumed their pursuit on land, and we had to keep running for our lives.

Halfway through our flight, Qin Guangyuan, commander of the Second Division stopped in his tracks and howled in dismay. It turned out that he had had on his person a large sum—possibly something like 10,000 *yuan*—and he had left it behind on the sailboat! He actually started crying, but what good was that?! A division commander no less, crying over money! What a good-for-nothing fool!

After about two hours onshore, we shook off our pursuers and reached a deserted village where we rested in a hut. Heavens, my feet were a bloody mess of cuts and bruises! The hut belonged to a relative of our faithful guide, and here we could rest safely.

"Where are we?" I asked our guide.

"The east gate of Huilai."

"Goodness, we have actually made it as far as Huilai!"

Now rested, we put our heads together to make new plans. Wu Ming, pointing out that the seven of us men and women traveling together attracted too much attention, suggested that we separate. After some discussion, it was decided that the three young women would stay with our faithful guide for a while and he would see them safely to Hong Kong when the situation quieted down. We four men also divided into two groups, Wu Ming with Li Renyu while I partnered with Qin Guangyuan.

Qin and I decided to go to Shantou since from Huilai, where we had now ended up, it was only a two-day trip to Shantou. For starters, I spent one *yuan* on a pair of cloth-sewn shoes.

It was October 10 when Qin and I set off for Shantou. The locals had hired two covered sedan chairs for us; we pulled down the curtains as we passed through the little town of Huilai, thus avoiding any attention. As night descended, we stopped at a little roadside inn which charged fifteen *fen* per night, excluding food.

The morning of October 11, Qin Guangyuan and I walked to a little unnamed township nearby and headed for Chaoyang, the first stop. Chaoyang and Shantou, where we were heading, faced each other across a bay, actually a narrow strip of water. There was an hourly electric-powered boat which ferried passengers back and forth across the bay between the two townships.

Once we arrived in Chaoyang, we made a beeline for the ferry to Shantou. On the ferry, we were happy, our spirits buoyed by the prospect of soon being in Hong Kong. Unfortunately, just as I was daydreaming, disaster struck. A troupe of armed "inspectors" boarded the ferry. My ill-fitting outfit caught their attention. These self-appointed inspectors, bandits actually, surrounded me. My cash was discovered. I was bound and dragged onshore. "You wretch, you fallen general, you are going to be a target!" meaning they would shoot me. One fellow gave me a shove in the back with his Mauser.

"By what right are you arresting me?" All I got for my protests were curses. I was taken to a detached room near the ticket office of the electric-powered ferry.

Their chief was sitting inside: "Aha! A fallen general!" the fellow hooted when he saw the cash.

"Can we use him for target practice?" one of the underlings appealed to the chief. The chief nodded and his men started to haul me out.

My God, am I going to end my life in this place! For a moment, the world turned dark and I seemed to have lost consciousness. Then I forced myself to regain control.

"Just a moment, I have something to say." Desperate to grasp at life, the words tumbled out in spite of myself, although I had no idea what I was going to say.

The bandit chief signaled to his underlings, and I was dragged back. My fate now took a new turn. I said "Chief, we are both men of adventure. You know there is the saying: 'at home rely on family, out in the world rely on friends.' Killing me profits you nothing. I am giving you all that money. Let me go, and we will be friends—we may meet again . . ."

The fellow deliberated for a moment: "Are you a regimental commander?" he asked.

"No, I am a secretary."

"Impossible. You are not a secretary. You might even be a commander . . ."

"Out in the world, rely on friends. We are both men of adventure . . . Just give a helping hand . . ."

". . . . ."

He was undecided, but finally said: "All right, you may go!"

Within three minutes, I had snatched my life back from the jaws of death. I could not believe what was happening. Was I dreaming?

I was free, but without a cent. How was I to get to Hong Kong? I had to make a further request.

"Thank you! But can you help me with some travel money?'

He picked up my wad of cash and asked: "How much is there in this pile?"

"The equivalent of about thirty thousand *yuan* . . ."

He took out three ten-*yuan* notes from the Hong Kong Charter Bank. "Here, take this," he said, "I don't want to be cruel . . ."

I took the money, turned around, got myself to the ticket office nearby, and bought a ferry ticket for Shantou, where I arrived that same afternoon.

In Shantou, I met up with other comrades, among them Mei Dianlong and Liu Mingxia.

On the boat to Hong Kong, we were joined by He Chang, Huang Rikui, and a couple of others whom I did not know personally, though I knew that they were our people.

October 11 I set foot in Hong Kong.

CHAPTER NINE

Hong Kong and Shanghai

I reached Hong Kong on the afternoon of October 11.

I had only been away from Hong Kong for thirteen months; the water in the bay was the same deadly green as it always was, but Hong Kong itself had changed greatly since I was there the previous September. By now the great strike was long over and the city had returned to business.

In contrast, how things had changed on the mainland! The past thirteen months had witnessed such upheavals in domestic politics, and now they were just a memory. The same moon is looking down on an entirely different country.

After we checked into a hotel, I went off to look up old friends. I borrowed some cash and got myself a new suit. I went and stood in front of the huge mirror at the Wing On department store and scrutinized myself: Yes, I could pass muster as a young man-about-town, with no trace of the fugitive running for his life.

I had dinner at a gourmet restaurant, and recalled one moonlit night the previous September[1] when I was dining and drinking in this same

1. In September 1926, Zhu Qihua had been to Hong Kong and had met this young lady from Canton. See Translator's Note.

restaurant with the young lady from Canton.[2] The poet Zhao Jia's poem expressed my sentiments completely:

> Alone in the pavilion,
> Moonlight like water, water like sky,
> Where is she who had been with me as we enjoyed the moonlight,
> The scenery is unchanged from last year.

From the young lady in Canton, my thoughts turned to Hong, who had died for the Revolution. I am afraid that by now even her corpse had rotted away. So many young men had been infatuated with her, I wonder how many of them still remember. In addition to Hong, who had died before my eyes, I am afraid that many of the young female comrades at the Wuhan campus had shared Hong's tragic fate. Revolution, Revolution, is this your bequest? I wonder what their families' reaction would be had they known how their loved ones had died. I should consider myself lucky, a solitary drinker sitting in a posh restaurant in Hong Kong. Had I died in Liusha, I would have been a feast for wild dogs. Now if Hong and I had changed places and I had died in her arms, I wonder how she would have reacted. Perhaps she would have been even more stricken than I am now?

I stayed for one night at the hotel and moved in with an old friend the next morning. As soon as I was settled, I lay down in the bed and slept through three days and three nights.

I had initially planned to move on to Canton as soon as possible, but the new situation convinced me that it was not advisable. After all, by now I must be considered a fugitive. Isn't it true that "the victor is hailed as a king while the defeated is condemned as a bandit"? In the current situation, it is obvious that we were the "bandits." As much as I wanted to, I realized that I could not risk going to see the young lady in Canton. I wrote to her asking her to see me in Hong Kong.

Hong Kong is such a small place, you meet up with acquaintances every time you walk out of the house. Since the debacle at Liusha,

2. Apparently this episode was among the cuts made by the author.

when I had fortunately escaped with my life, I could not stop wondering what had happened to the rest of us: I was especially worried about my boss, the sick and elderly Liao Qianwu, and Enlai, who had fallen ill at the time. I dreaded that perhaps some of them had shared Hong's fate.

Fortunately, four days after my arrival in Hong Kong, I got news that all the leaders were safe. Yun Daiying was in Hong Kong; I actually ran into him at Causeway Bay. He told me that he had also been taken from the ferry by bandits as I had been, but that he had managed to escape. Enlai and Moruo had left for Shanghai straight from Shantou. Tan Pingshan, He Long, and my boss Liao Qianwu had ordered a boat as we had done, but were stopped at the port of entry and had to pay a bribe of 3,000 *yuan* before they were allowed to pass through. Pingshan had left for Shanghai the moment he arrived in Hong Kong and it was the same with Li Lisan. As for Lin Yuhan and Zhang Guotao, it was said that they had made straight for Shanghai without the detour through Hong Kong. Ye Ting, I was told, was also in Hong Kong. In a word, not one among the leaders had lost their lives in the recent debacle, meaning no one above section head in administration, and no one above regimental commander in the military. That was unexpectedly fortunate.

Mei Dianlong, who had arrived with me in Hong Kong, had stayed barely two days before he left for Shanghai.

I stayed with my friend at his place in Weijing Street and did not get into touch with those new arrivals. I was incredibly lonely. I decided to settle down and write something in memory of An Ticheng and Hong, both of whom had died for the Revolution.

The young lady in Canton sent a warm reply to my letter. She had been so worried at the news of our defeat, she wrote, and had wanted to come and join me in Guangdong, but had been stopped by her parents. Now that I was in Hong Kong, she wanted to see me but could not travel due to illness. She enclosed 100 *yuan* in case I was short.

Indeed, I was short of cash and was grateful to her for her warm letter and her solicitude. I had considered going to Canton to see her, but in her letter, she had advised against it. There was nothing furtive about my plan, but in the current situation in Canton with random executions being carried out right and left, one needed to be cautious. I knew for a fact that people were being shot every day at the Huanghuagang[3] and the Eastern drilling ground. I was lucky to have escaped, and should not risk going to Canton.

Speaking of the Huanghuagang, I remember that when I was working at the Propaganda Department of the GMD CEC back in the old days in Canton, my office had been right across from the Huanghuagang, facing the four stone tablets dedicated to the martyrs. At the time, the road which wound its way below my office window was already part of the suburbs of Canton. It led past the Huanghuagang to other famous sites, White Cloud Mountain and Yan Pond, and was always busy with traffic. Hundreds of one-wheel barrows passed by daily under my window, the noises of their squeaky wheels penetrating right into our offices, especially during the spring when the windows were open.

Speaking of spring, especially spring in the southern regions, when willows are budding and peach trees are in bloom, young people my age would be particularly restless. At the time, the many young women passing in and out of the office would each leave her own particular scent lingering in her wake. Laughing and chatting they would pass by, exaggeratedly oblivious of my presence, and it would drive me to distraction.

My co-workers were carrying on affairs right under my nose. At the time there had been the three of us in the office: Xiao Chunv,[4] Ge Jiying, and myself. Ge was the wife of Yun Daiying's younger

3. The Huanghuagang was a site in Canton dedicated to the martyrs of the failed Huang Xing Uprising of 1911. Following the collapse of the march to Canton ending in October 1927, Qu Qiubai called for an urban uprising in Canton for December of the same year, on orders from the Comintern. The short-lived "Canton Commune" was crushed with much bloodshed, Huanghuagang being the place of execution. The scattered members of the debacle in Liusha were also being pursued, as the author feared, as part of a massive anti-CCP suppression.

4. This is the standard pinyin rule for the sound "yu" in certain combinations, 女, 吕, 绿 etc., but not for玉, 去, 句, though the words rhyme. This sound is often rendered with an umlaut as "Ü" in pinyin.

brother, a woman in her late twenties, her best days already behind her. But to the bachelor Xiao Chunv, already in his thirties, she was prime game, and he pursued her relentlessly. Ge Jiying, on her part, was put off by Xiao's unprepossessing looks, but Xiao was nimble with his pen and could write her reports for her, not to mention the fact that his infatuation tickled her vanity. At the time, I was so upset by their behavior that I moved my desk to the window overlooking the Huanghuagang, showing them my back. My window looked down on the suburbs; apart from the squeaky one-wheel barrows, young couples walked by in droves, kissing and hugging. That inflamed me all the more, without offering any release for my own frustration.

At one time, I was sharing an upstairs space with Kong Lingjun on Dadong Street. Downstairs was a small socks-making workshop with two beautiful young female workers whom Kong and I had tried to attract with no success. Later, I discovered that the daughter of our landlord was a stunning beauty, so I shifted my attention to her. Our landlord lived behind our street, and I tried to approach this beauty under the pretext of paying rent. Once I actually stuffed a note into her hand, asking her to meet me at the Huanghuagang at a certain day and hour. I waited a long time, but of course she never showed up.

To think that this had happened barely a year ago when I was last in Canton, and the Huanghuagang that I had tried to use as a trysting place was now converted into a killing field! I wonder where the beauty has ended up by now. At the time, we had been so cocky, so full of ourselves, as if the world belonged to us. And now, I am a fugitive on the run. Such are the ways of the world. As to the young lady, the daughter of my landlord, I wish you happiness. Who knows, we may meet again in this wide world. Please forgive my rashness in asking you to meet me at the Huanghuagang. If possible, please go and take a look at the place. Remember that once upon a time, a young man who was enamored of you had asked you to meet him there. Go and see how many people are being killed on that spot right now. The stone tablets of the Huanghuagang originally gray, are probably crimson by now, stained with the blood of the dead. Ah, the lovely but now terrible Huanghuagang!

Hong Kong and Shanghai

Liao Qianwu used to say that women are hard to figure out, and now I am beginning to see his point. Women indeed seem to cast a spell wherever they are. In the past when I was immersed in work, I had been more or less impervious to their charms. Now on the loose in Hong Kong with time on my hands, I felt the need for female companionship. The young lady living on the other side of the fourth floor in Weijing Street where I was now staying was very pretty and I was attracted to her. We'd often run into each other, both being on the same floor. There was no elevator in the building and we had to climb up three floors to reach our rooms. Once as I returned from outside and had my foot on the stairs, it happened that the young lady was also going up. We climbed the stairs together and got into a conversation. Since then we often chatted, and sometimes I asked her into my room. Her father was rarely home, her mother busy on household errands, so the young lady was often left alone. She was obviously interested in me. The opportunity was there, I could easily have taken advantage of her, but I was held back by my own squeamishness and thoughts of the young lady in Canton.

One day as she was chatting with me in my room, I happened to ask her what her father did, being, as he was, so often away from home.

"He is a detective," she answered casually.

"A detective?"

"Yes, he is a police detective of the Guangdong Provincial Security, now posted in Hong Kong. There are a lot of reactionary elements flocking to Hong Kong from Shantou, you know, so my father is busy making arrests . . ."

It gave me a real shock. Although I was keeping a low profile, there was no guarantee that I would not be arrested and dragged to the Huanghuagang, especially as the girl knew that I had arrived from Shantou. Supposing she happened to mention me to her father; wouldn't the detective be alerted? Thinking thus, I decided to leave Hong Kong for Shanghai. The reason that I was stopping in Hong Kong was purely for the sake of the young lady in Canton. She was ill, and would have come to see me as soon as she could. Under the circumstances, I decided not to wait any longer. I could not run the risk of being dragged to the Huanghuagang.

October 19. I boarded a vessel and we left port at midnight. I was traveling with my friend Yang. On this precipitate trip to Shanghai, I was a penniless wanderer. Shanghai had been my home. When I had first left Shanghai for Canton in the fall of 1925, I had cherished such high hopes. Later, as I set out from Canton, I had been bursting with confidence, expecting to return to Shanghai in the wake of the victorious Revolutionary Army. And now, all my hopes have turned to ashes.

I had already spent the 100 *yuan* sent by the young lady in Canton. For this trip to Shanghai, a friend had paid my fare. In those days, my friends were also hard up, the difference between us being poor and poorer. So there was little they could do for me. My traveling companion, Yang, was in the same predicament as I was. After paying for two cheap third-class tickets, we had four *yuan* left between us.

Being dumped in the third class bunk was painful to the likes of us who had been used to living it up. More infuriating was the insolence of the stewards, who fawned on the first-class bunk travelers and treated the rest of us as so much trash. Deeply depressed, we felt gambling could be an outlet for our frayed nerves, but we could not afford to risk our last four *yuan*. Yang, not longer able to resist, sat down at one of the tables. He was wiped out in a twinkling, and still owed a few *fen*.

Actually there were few expenses on the boat, except for the stewards' tips which was usually sixty *fen* for third class passengers, or one *yuan* minimum for two traveling together. But Yang and I did not have a *fen* between us. We were approaching port and had to find a way out of this dilemma. Desperate, we resorted to rabble-rousing, proclaiming to the third-class passengers that we have been insulted and should not give the stewards' tips. Surprisingly, the ploy worked. When the vessel docked, all third-class passengers—over a hundred—stood together and refused to tip the stewards, who, caught off guard, had to take it lying down.

Our boat docked in Pudong which was unfortunate as we did not even have the few *fen* to pay for the ferry to Shanghai proper, where we were heading. Fortunately, there were hotel vehicles parked around the harbor, waiting to pick up guests. We decided to take a chance. Yang and I handed over our luggage and got into one of the shuttles and were driven to the Heping Hotel. It was the usual practice at local hotels that so long as you had luggage you could stay and eat on credit and pay every five days. I had a worthless cotton blanket in a string bag, and Yang had several pieces of luggage, so we checked into the Heping Hotel and took a room on the third floor, Room 68.

It had been two years since I had last been in Shanghai, and the city was greatly changed. I had last been there in the aftermath of the May Thirtieth Movement, when the warlord Xing Shilia[5] was in power and had massacred revolutionary figures. Now Xing was gone, and so was Sun Chuanfang, another warlord. Gone too, were the five-barred flags of the old days.

After I settled in, I immediately went to look up old friends. But they had all moved. I had more than a dozen friends in Shanghai, and I could not locate a single one. This was a blow indeed. The fact was, I had been totally unprepared for this trip to Shanghai, hoping that my friends would do something for me on my arrival. And now I had no one to turn to. I had always regarded Shanghai as my "native place," after Hangzhou, where I was born. But now it was clear that after the past two years of political turmoil, things had changed.

The hotel provided food, so we did not have to worry about meals for the first couple of days. But as we went around to look up people, we could not do without cash. I had nothing valuable except my Western suit, which I had recently ordered in Hong Kong, the only outfit I had to my name, and a fountain pen. I decided to exchange the fountain pen for some cash. I made the rounds of the pawnshops, but my fountain pen, which had cost eighteen *yuan*, was now worth nothing. I finally managed to exchange my fountain pen for three-and-

5. Xing Shilian, warlord of the Northeastern faction, security chief for Shanghai during the May Thirtieth Massacre of striking workers in 1925.

a-half *yuan* in a used clothing store specializing in used Western suits. I gave one *yuan* to Yang and the remaining two-and-a-half *yuan* I used for transportation during the few days when I rushed around town looking up friends. Now, after running around fruitlessly for four days, we were about to face the fifth day's reckoning at the hotel. The bill for the last four days' room and meals would probably add up to about twenty *yuan*, no big deal in the old days, but now totally beyond our means. On the third night, Yang actually lay in bed and cried. I rarely shed tears and have contempt for men who cry, but Yang's predicament was pitiful indeed. I could easily walk out and not return, but Yang had to hang on to his luggage or he would be unable to return to his native Hunan. The next day was the fourth day—if we did not come up with something, we would not be able to walk out the gate.

In desperation I came up with a temporary solution, which would at least defer the final reckoning. The fact was, Yang had managed to locate someone from his native place who was currently a low-ranking army officer. The man offered Yang accommodation but no cash. According to my scheme, the officer would drop by on the evening of our fourth day in the hotel. He would take Yang away with him with all his valuables and leave an empty trunk to throw dust in the eyes of the hotel staff.

Everything went according to plan: the officer came, and proceeded to leave with Yang.

"Sir," said a sharp-eyed steward, "please pay your bill before you leave."

Yang blushed and stood rooted to the spot, tongue-tied. Calmly I went to the rescue. "What's the rush? I'm here. I will settle the bill tomorrow. Just make sure you wake me up, I need to leave first thing in the morning."

I had only twenty *fen* on me, but my spruce Western suit, not to mention the royal dishes that I had ordered at every meal, was enough to convince the stewards that I was some well-heeled man-about-town, no less that my bedroll and Yang's trunk were also on display for their benefit.

With Yang gone, I felt relieved of a responsibility, but I still had to figure out where to find the twenty-some yuan for the next morning's hotel bill and the stewards' tips. All I had in the room was an empty trunk and a worthless bedroll. There was a steward stationed at the staircase landing, making sure that guests didn't leave without settling their bills.

Laying on the bed trying to come up with a way to get out of the fix, I heard the stewards whispering outside my door.

"What! Has Number 68 left?"

"One left, the other is still here. They haven't settled the bill yet, but the luggage is still here. Keep your eyes peeled tomorrow, don't let this one go until he's paid up."

The stewards were sitting right outside Room 68, and I could hear them clearly. It was obvious that I was under their surveillance. *Damn it,* I thought to myself, *the worst that can happen is to be locked up for a couple of days.* Thinking which, I fell asleep.

As I was drifting off, sounds of lascivious laughter and struggling drifted in from the next room, and got me all fired up. I sat up and tried to peer through the crack in the thin board separating the two rooms, but all I could make out through the crack was the abandoned rocking of the bed under the mosquito netting.

The saying goes that a well-fed body hankers after sex, but I was tempted, even in my current deprived state. I now regretted this rash move to Shanghai. The detective's daughter, wasn't she ready for me? Why did I not take her then and there? I was a fool; I want to slap myself for being such a fool.

The obscene sounds continued to drift in from the other room, while the stewards outside my door continued talking.

Women, detectives, sex, hotel bills, tips, tomorrow—with these concerns drifting in and out of my consciousness, I barely slept a wink all night.

The next morning, I ordered a bowl of chicken noodles and asked for the bill. I had only twenty *fen* in my pocket, but I behaved as if my wallet was bursting with money.

The steward showed me the bill: twenty-four *yuan,* eighty-four *fen!* Expecting a big tip, the steward was very respectful as he handed me the bill. I put my hand in my pocket, then stopped. It was empty anyway. "Is the barber shop open? I really need a haircut before I go." I knew there was a barber shop on the second floor, one floor down. "Yes, sir, it is open," said the steward respectfully.

"Shut the door, I'll get a haircut before I go," I said. To quell his suspicions, I threw my hat back into the room, and walked down the stairs. The wily steward had been fooled.

Once out the door, I hopped on a rickshaw and signaled him to get a move on; the man picked up the shafts and ran. Being morning rush hour, there was lots of traffic. Still, I directed the rickshaw puller to make several turns to avoid pursuit.

"Sir, where shall I take you?" Yes indeed, where?

"Go straight ahead." I needed time to decide where to go. Then I remembered that I only had twenty *fen,* eleven cents in my pocket and could not afford to keep going on and on. "The French Park," I ordered.

I got off at the Park, paid the rickshawman twenty *fen,* leaving eleven cents in my pocket. At the time, the French Park did not require tickets for entry; anyone respectfully dressed could walk in. Although I only had eleven cents in my pocket, I strode into the Park with my head held high, solely on the strength of my Western suit.

After walking around the Park, I came out and walked down Avenue Joffre. I thought of the expression "with four bare walls for a home" to describe extreme poverty, but I did not even have four bare walls! In the vastness of Shanghai, I now did not have a place to put down my head. I spent eight cents on a copy of the *Shenbao Daily,* and had three cents left. It was early winter, people walked about with hats on their heads and I looked out of place without a hat. Well, I just had to pass muster with my Western suit, even if I only had three cents in my pocket. It was laughable.

The bowl of chicken noodles had long since been digested, and my stomach now started to rumble. There was a little Chinese pancake stand in an alley off Avenue Joffre, and as I passed the stand, the mouth-watering whiff of thin pancake drew me over. I took out my last three cents, but the stall keeper was so flustered at the sight of a gentleman buying a pancake that he gave me two instead of one. It was fortunate, as one would not have filled my belly, but I could only afford one with my last three cents.

It was out of the question for a "gentleman" like me to eat a pancake while walking down the street. Besides, I was tired of walking and needed to sit down. Where should I sit? In the Park, of course. So I wrapped my pancake in the newspaper and walked back to the French Park. I found a quiet corner, unwrapped the pancake, and ate it while reading the paper. I ate every crumb, not missing a single sesame seed. But I was still hungry.

While I was an officer, I had dined in restaurants every day, but now even a pancake was beyond my means. My fortunes had sunk so low.

How I congratulated myself on extricating myself from the hotel, but now I began to have second thoughts. If I had not made off in the morning, I would probably be sitting in a police station by now and would spend a peaceful night there. But now, where was I to lay my head? Not in the Park certainly. Today I had had two pancakes, but what about tomorrow? I racked my brains, thinking of ways to keep afloat, letting my thoughts run wild.

I remember reading in a newspaper that in Harbin some Russian refugees would pee in public places. The police would take them in and they would say that they did it for a free meal at the police station! Similar things had also happened in Shanghai. A White Russian had smashed a laundry store's glass window. He was dragged to the police station and enjoyed a few free meals, just as he had expected. Right now, I probably would have to sink to the same level.

I had not slept properly the night before, and having walked around the whole morning, I now felt drowsy. There was no one about, I lay back on a bench and dozed off.

I woke up with a start. It was about three or four in the afternoon. I opened my eyes and saw a beautifully made up young woman sitting on the bench across the path, looking at me.

"Is it Mr. Zhu? We have not seen you for a long time!"

"Oh, it is Mrs. X!" I suddenly remembered. It was before I left for Canton. We had played mahjong at a friend's house a couple of times. She knew my name, but I only knew her as Mrs. X, the second wife of Mr. X. Slightly older than I was, the beautiful Mrs. X had a reputation for being romantic and had shown a decided interest in me. Being an eighteen-year-old raw youth at the time, I had been smitten but was too timid to pick up the hints. After leaving Shanghai for Canton, I had completely forgotten about her.

"Have you been in Shanghai all this time?" she asked.

"No, I was studying in Peking."

Under the circumstances, it was lovely to meet an old acquaintance, and I moved over and sat down beside her. I had been very disturbed by sounds from the neighboring room of the hotel the night before, and could not stop daydreaming about the detective's daughter back in Hong Kong. Now with this young woman sitting next to me, I could not bear to squander this opportunity thrown my way.

We now met like old friends and chatted amicably together. I used my charms on her, and I could see that she was letting down her defenses. The two pancakes have long since been digested, and I was hungry. I asked her to dinner.

Together we walked out of the park, she leaning against my shoulder. Once out of the park, we ordered a car and went to an expensive Western restaurant. I had made do on two pancakes that morning, and now was a guest at a posh hotel.

We both drank wine; emboldened by the wine, I dragged her to the Asia Hotel and ordered a room.

I must confess that I was completely shameless. I satisfied myself and pleasured her. She gave me eighty *yuan*, and then we parted. I felt like a gigolo. But did God not make gigolos just as He made everything else? Can you not forgive me?

Shanghai is a strange city where anything is possible. We had spent a night together, and I still knew nothing about her, not even her address. But I told her what I had gone through in Canton, Wuhan, Henan, and Jiangxi. As I recounted the narrative, I felt that it sounded unreal—only someone who had lived through it all could believe it. What a memorable night—October 27, 1927, Room 604 at the Asia Hotel, Nanking Road, Shanghai!

Thanks to the eighty *yuan*, I was able to rent a room and buy another hat to replace the one that I had left in the Heping Hotel. Once installed in my new quarters, I ran into Luo Bojun. He had been with the Organization Department in Wuhan. When the Wuhan Government collapsed, he had quit and moved to Shanghai. He had been in love with Zeng Hua, a colleague at the Organization Department, and their romance had ended happily in Shanghai. The couple was living close by, which explained how we met in the street.

I had now become a fatalist. If I had known that Luo was living here, I would not have gone to the French Park after my escape from the Heping Hotel, and thus would not have met Mrs. X, and the night in Room 604 at the Asia Hotel would not have happened.

If God existed, I would give Him thanks. I had successfully disengaged myself from danger and now lived peacefully in Shanghai. My room was clean and bright, conducive to reading and writing.

Looking back at the last several years of my life, I am convinced of my own lack of learning. I am a failure. I am determined to mend my deficiencies. Where there's a will, there's a way. Our country is so lacking in talent: we study hard to prepare ourselves and answer the call when it comes. I made a plan, first to study a foreign language, second to read economics and philosophy, and third to write a memoir of what I had lived through.

I ran into my former boss Liao Qianwu when I was shopping in a department store, and we stopped for a moment at his place in Taigu Road. He left shortly thereafter for the north, and gave me 100 *yuan*. It was very helpful, as the eighty *yuan* from Mrs. X had been exhausted.

The young lady from Canton wrote, sending me another 100 *yuan*. She told me that she had gone to Hong Kong, notwithstanding her illness, and had found her way to the building in Weijing Street. There she met the daughter of the detective, from whom she learned that I had left.

"I was very touched. Sick, she had dragged herself to Hong Kong to see me, only to be disappointed. What can I say to console her, my young lady from Canton!"

I was cursed with this failing: the moment I had cash on my hands I would fret until I found a use for it. Money left lying around gave me insomnia—no, I was not afraid of being robbed. My problem was that I would be dogged by questions of where to go shopping. What to buy? I want to get started on the memoir, but with money to burn, I could not bear to be shut up in a room. I did not enjoy dancing or watching movies, nor did I visit the entertainment districts. What I liked was shopping at the department stores.

After returning to Shanghai I had kept to myself and had cut off ties with former political friends. I dropped them all, and pursued a policy of escape. I only kept up with people who had no interest in politics.

I heard my friend Luo Bojun mention that Zheng Junsheng was in Shanghai, living in a wretched garret in Xicheng Alley on Malang Road. Zheng had cut off all political affiliations and had changed his name to Zheng Rongzi. I went to call on him. We shook hands firmly without saying anything. It was just a separation of a few months, but so much has changed!

We had been colleagues at the Military Department, as well as housemates in No. 2 Dongxing Lane on Dadong Road in Canton. When we headed for Nanchang, he was with us. He was a cadre at the Whampoa Alumni Association and had moved to Nanchang along with the Whampoa Alumni Association.

I remembered one cold winter evening in Nanchang when we had gathered in Mao Du's room at No. 1 Three-Hole-Well Street: Zheng Junsheng, Duan Zizhong, Zhang Shengchuan, Tian Ruqin, Mao Du, and me. We six sat around a charcoal fire, chatting about this and that, with the snow falling outside. We talked about personal problems, and then our conversation turned to the frustration of politics, a feeling which we all shared. Zheng Junsheng and Duan Zizhong initiated the idea of forming a secret leftist club to be called "Forging Ahead," with the six of us as cadres, At the time, I was not supportive of the idea, because my own views did not entirely coincide with theirs. But because I could not extricate myself, I was elected a member of the "standing committee" and head of propaganda. We spent the whole night drafting programs and articles of faith, talking up a blue streak, but it had all come to nothing. Looking back it was really quite ridiculous.[6]

Zheng Junsheng, now Zheng Rongzi, living humbly in a garret, had managed to secure the woman of his heart's desire despite the ups and downs of a wandering life. He had met his beloved Jianxia in Nanchang. More than one of my friends had found love in Nanchang: both Zheng Junsheng and Mao Du had found their mates among the students of the Baoling Girls' School.

November 6. It was a month since Hong's death in Liusha.

I got up early in the morning, bought a length of black cotton cloth and pinned it to my left sleeve. I was devastated by Hong's death, not only for our friendship, but also because she was the most talented among the young women activists, and her death was a deep loss to the Revolution.

The 100 *yuan* from the young lady in Canton and the other 100 *yuan* from Qianwu were all gone. I wrote to Shao Lizi, asking him for a loan of fifty *yuan*. He wrote back, inviting me to call on him, making no mention of money.

Shao still lived in the old place in Sanyi Lane at Taiping Bridge. The entrance to the alley was as dirty as it ever was. It was the time for waste disposal, and the stink nearly knocked me over. I entered through the back door into the living room. It was but a year since we last met, but Shao had aged a lot. People age so quickly, even thinking about it is depressing!

6. This bit of reminiscence could be a veiled attempt to explain away the label of "Trotskyist" which had been cast on Zhu Qihua—that he was one of eleven Trotskyists, though he was named twice in this same group by mistake due to his many pseudonyms.

We talked over many things that had transpired since our last parting. The year before, he had attended a meeting of the Third International as a representative of the GMD, and we talked about the meeting. He told me something that had hurt his feelings at the time:

"After the meeting, I wanted to leave in [Tan] Pingshan's company; he agreed and said he would let me know when he was ready. So I waited and waited. After two weeks, I went to his place to look him up. It turned out that he had left long ago! If he didn't want my company he could have said so! Why keep me waiting like that? As if I could betray him . . ."

All the years that I had known Mr. Shao, this was the first time I heard him complain. And his complaints were not limited to the above. "When I returned to Shanghai," he continued, "the April Twelfth Massacre had taken place, the Nanjing government was set up, the rift was open between the CCP in Wuhan and the GMD in Nanjing. I was in a dilemma: should I go to Wuhan? I disapproved of the way the CCP was running things. Besides, considering my personal relations with Chiang Kai-shek, it would be a betrayal. I decided against going to Wuhan. Should I go to Nanjing? Then I would be betraying my CCP friends in Wuhan. So I decided to join neither. But I had to make a brief trip to Nanjing. I was not looking for a position. The fact is, at the time, if one did not make a nod in the direction of Nanjing, it would be hard to survive in Shanghai. Besides, Chiang had entrusted me with some private business for this trip to the USSR. So I decided to make a personal visit to Nanjing. In Nanjing, Chiang offered me the job of general secretary of the Party, I declined. He asked me to be director of the General Political Department, I declined. He offered me money, I refused. I stayed for two days and left for Shanghai. But guess what? My son wrote to me from Moscow, accusing me of being an anticommunist and declaring an end to our relationship . . ."

I felt Mr. Shao's pain. "Now in Shanghai, all I do is watch opera, or play mahjong . . . I rarely pick up a book," he said sadly.

I looked around his sitting room, which I had frequented in the past, and noticed a change. Previously there had been a calligraphic dedication to him, "Guide to Youth," written by Sun Hongyin,[7] which had now been taken down. Moreover, there had also been a set of four hanging scrolls by Tan Yan, which had also disappeared. In their place, there were now two matching scrolls by Yu Youren.

The disappearance of Sun Hongyin's calligraphic dedication had made me wonder. During the heyday of the *Republican Daily*, a paper which had played a role in arousing youth, Shao had prided himself on being a "guide to youth." He had happily accepted the title and proudly displayed the "Guide to Youth" calligraphic scroll in his living room. Why was it taken down? Did it mean that Shao has stopped being a guide to youth?

Speaking of the CCP, Shao had a lot of complaints: "The CCP really made a mistake in opposing Chiang Kai-shek, especially in setting up Tang XX to oppose Chiang; that was really bad judgment. Besides, some of their positions do not make sense at all. I was in Moscow when news arrived that Shanghai had been taken. The CCP immediately celebrated, claiming that the workers had taken Shanghai. I made a speech at the meeting, saying that the workers had helped the Revolutionary Army take Shanghai, and they objected, saying that I had stopped being a revolutionary . . .

"Then what is the reason for the CCP's defeat, according to you?"

"The fundamental problem is that their organization is too tightly controlled . . ."

"How can tight organization lead to defeat?" It did not make sense at all.

"The CCP's defeat is due to overly tight organization. This sounds contradictory, but it's true. Within the various levels of the CCP leadership, the top is excessively demanding, so in their reports their staff at the lower level would exaggerate their achievements. Take the

7. Sun Hongyin (1870–1936) was a native of Tianjin. Sun formed the Democratic Party in Shanghai following the overthrow of the Qing dynasty. He then joined the Progressive Party and played an active role in promoting democracy and in drafting China's first constitution. Sun had served briefly as head of education for the early Republican Government, later resigned and turned his efforts to upholding the constitution and opposing the warlord Duan Qirei. In 1920 he served briefly as adviser to the Revolutionary Government in Canton.

workers' movement, for instance. Say there are only thirty activists within a CCP cell at a certain plant. But their work report to the district would increase the numbers to forty or fifty. Now the district report to the county level would further exaggerate that figure, and the successive figures would grow at every level. By the time they actually have ten thousand activists at the national level, the figure would be fifty or even eighty thousand by the time it reached the International. When the International makes its plans, it does not start out from reality. Moreover, the CCP has this discipline of absolutely sticking to orders whatever they are. Thus, the CCP cannot avoid being led down the wrong path. Each level of leadership has to exaggerate their achievements because their direct superiors are too demanding. This goes on in a vicious cycle level after level, inevitably leading to catastrophe . . ."[8]

We chatted for about two hours before I left. As he saw me out, he stuffed three ten-*yuan* notes into my hands.

December 28, 1927. Today is my twentieth birthday.

This day last year, I had arrived in Nanchang.

Now I am a drifter in the Shanghai concession.

The young lady in Canton sent a letter, congratulating me on my birthday, but I am full of guilt.

Twenty years of my life have passed, and what achievements do I have to show for those years? I am buried in shame.

I changed one word in an old poem and used it to commemorate my own twentieth birthday, replacing the word "one quarter" with "one-fifth," and sent it to the young lady in Canton:

> One fifth of a century has passed me by,
> My future is vague and unknowable,
> Fortunately my head is still on my shoulders,
> I am ready to meet you with my valor intact.

---

8. This eerily foreshadows what was to happen thirty years later during the 1958 Great Leap Forward when crop yields were increasingly exaggerated up the chain of command to meet the targets the leadership was demanding, leading to massive starvation. See Yang Jingsheng, Tombstone: *The Great Chinese Famine 1958-1962* (New York: Farrar, Straus and Giroux, 2012).

TRANSLATOR'S NOTE

Discrepancies in the narrative regarding "the young lady from Canton"

Zhu Qihua states that he was interested in a "young lady in Canton" starting in September 1926 while he was living in the Dongshan area of that city, that they never spoke, and that when he left Canton, they parted never to meet again, and he "never knew her name." (Chapter One) Then, at the end of the memoir when he arrives in Hong Kong in October 1927, he reminisces about a dinner he had with "the young lady from Canton" in that same restaurant "last September, " "thirteen months ago," meaning September 1926, *when they would have just met, by his initial account.*

The translator's conjecture is that in deleting the story of his first year in Canton (September 1925–December 1926) for this publication, Zhu Qihua changed the date, or made a mistake by writing September 1926, instead of September 1925, as the date of his first interest in the young woman, which is to say as soon as he arrived Canton. It would make sense if they had met in September 1925 and were intimate enough a year later to travel together to Hong Kong. (Chapter 9)

After Zhu Qihua left Canton in the retinue of the Revolutionary Government, they reconnected by mail during Zhu's two months in

Nanchang from late December 1926 to end of February 1927. Zhu confides, "I had started a correspondence with a young lady in Canton, sending her love letters regularly." (Chapter Two, Section 4)

Since then he had kept in touch with the young lady in Canton, even sending her letters during his Henan expedition. (Chapter Four, Section 7) The young lady had also sent him letters, asking him to return to Canton. (Chapter Four, Section 12)

By Zhu Qihua's own account, the young lady had followed the course of their ragtag army's itinerary through Guangdong Province, offering to go and see him against her family's wishes. During his stop in Hong Kong, the young lady supported him financially and had gone to see him. Zhu wrote: "Sick, she had dragged herself to Hong Kong to see me, only to be disappointed. What can I say to console her, my young lady from Canton!" (Chapter Nine)

By the end of the Memoir, the young lady, by sending a letter, was the only person who was with Zhu Qihua in spirit, when he celebrated his twentieth birthday and sent her a letter in return.

The claim in Chapter One that they parted for good might have been inserted to protect the young lady's name, when Zhu had initially decided to delete the episode from publication. Later, he might have changed his mind, or in the rush of publication, he might have failed to follow through with the deletions consistently.

In any case, following the clues sprinkled through the chapters, "the young lady" interlude, along with the Miss Hong interlude, casts a tender light over the figure of CCH, highlighting his affectionate nature and the vulnerability of his youth, and calls for our sympathy.

Zhu Hong

INDEX

*Page numbers in **bolded italics** indicate illustrations*

Index

Index

Index

Index

Index

About the Translator

Zhu Hong, former member of the Chinese Academy of Social Sciences, was a visiting professor at Boston University from 1992 to 2005.

Her translations from the Chinese include the following:

The Chinese Western: Stories of Contemporary China (Ballantine Books, 1991)

The Serentity of Whiteness: Stories by and about Chinese Women (Ballantine Books, 1992)

A Higher Kind of Loyalty: Autobiography of Liu Binyuan (Pantheon, 1990)

The Stubborn Porridge and Other Stories by Wang Meng (George Braziller, 1994)

Will the Boat Sink the Water? The Life of China's Peasants, by Chen Guidi and Wu Chuntao (Public Affairs, 2005)

About the Editor

Doug Merwin is the publisher of MerwinAsia. He was the founding editor of the East Gate Books imprint at M.E. Sharpe.